# Scotland's Castles

*Also by Hubert Fenwick*

ARCHITECT ROYAL
THE AULD ALLIANCE
SCOTLAND'S HISTORIC BUILDINGS
THE CHÂTEAUX OF FRANCE

HUBERT FENWICK

# SCOTLAND'S CASTLES

PHOTOGRAPHS BY THE AUTHOR

ROBERT HALE · LONDON

ISBN 0 7091 5731 2

*Robert Hale Limited*
*Clerkenwell House*
*London EC1R 0HT*

Printed in Great Britain by
Lowe & Brydone (Printers) Ltd, Thetford
and bound by Weatherby Woolnough, Northants

# Contents

# Acknowledgements

Plans and sections have been taken from MacGibbon and Ross, and prints from Slezer's *Theatrum Scotiae*. The Picture Staircase at Blair Castle appears by courtesy of the Duke of Atholl. Richard Waitt's portrait of the Clan Grant piper is reproduced by permission of the late Countess of Seafield. The interiors of Brodick, Craigievar, Crathes and Culzean, and the coats of arms of the baronets of Nova Scotia at Menstrie were supplied by the National Trust for Scotland. All the exteriors are the author's.

# Illustrations

# Plans, elevations and line drawings

# Glossary

ASHLAR: Dressed stone.
ASTRAGAL: Supporting bar between window panes.
AUMBRY: Wall cupboard.

BAILEY: Castle courtyard.
BARMKIN: Outer defence wall.
BARREL-VAULT: Semicircular roof of stone or timber.
BARTISAN: Battlemented sentry post.
BEE-BOLE: Opening in garden wall for bee-skep or hives.
BILLET-AND-CABLE: Stone corbelling imitating logs and rope.
BOSS: Covering at junction of vaulting.
BRETÈCHE: Look-out over entrance of castle with space for dropping deterrents on besiegers.

CAP-HOUSE: Small building at top of stairs opening onto roof.
CAPONIER: Low-level tunnel defending fosse or ditch.
CARYATID: Support in form of human effigy.
CORBEL, CORBELLING: Projection in stone or timber to support walls or beams, several courses of projections used either structurally or decoratively.
CROWSTEPS: Stepped gable ends.
CRENELLATION: Indentation on battlements.
CURTAIN WALL: Link between defences.

DONJON: Keep of Norman castle.
DOOCOT: Dovecote or pigeonloft, circular or rectangular, and when domed known as 'beehive'.
DYKE: Stone wall.

EMPARKMENT: Enclosing parkland by a stone or brick wall.
ENCEINTE: Enclosing wall of medieval castle.

FESSE-CHEQUEY: Horizontal band across armorial shield with chequerboard pattern of alternate squares.
FORESTAIRS: External stairs of wood or stone.

FOSSE: Ditch or moat, dry or wet.
FREESTONE: Soft, easily quarried stone.

GARDEROBE: Medieval closet or lavatory.
GROIN: Junction in vaulting without ribs.
GUILLOCH, GUILLOT: Continuous entwined cable pattern.

HARLING: Sand, lime and ballast rendering to rough masonry.

JAMB: Ingo or side support to doorway or window.

LABEL MOULD: Drip stone above window, also used decoratively
in corbelling.
LAICH: Low or lower.
LANCET: Narrow window with pointed arch.
LUCARNE: Dormer or roof window, usually of stone.

MACHICOLATIONS: Openings between corbelled supports of
parapet.
MOTTE: Mound, often artificial, upon which timber fort was built.

NEWEL: Central support for spiral staircase.

OGEE: Shape in which convex and concave curves combine.
ORIEL: Projecting window.
OVERSAILING: Single pitched roof replacing conical cap to tower or
turret.

PELE: Wooden palisade, later tower of stone.
PEND: Vaulted passage.
POTENCE: Movable ladder in circular dovecote.

QUOIN: Corner stone: BUCKLE-QUOIN: In shape of buckle.

RAVELIN: Triangular forework.
RIB VAULT: Arched roof with ribs at groins.
ROMANESQUE: Buildings derived from Roman and characterized
by the use of rounded arches.

SCALE-AND-PLATT: Straight stair with landings.
SHOT-HOLE: Hole for use of firearms against unwanted visitors.
SHUT-HOLE: Literally hole that can be opened or shut, usually near
the door for ventilation.

SHUTTER-BOARD WINDOW: Window with fixed upper lights and opening shutters below.

SOLAR: The lord's or upper hall in medieval castle or manor.

SQUINCH: Arched support for angle turret that does not reach the ground.

STUDY: Small room in turret.

SWEPT-DORMER: Dormer window with swept-up roof.

TROMPE: Similar to squinch but more ornamental.

TURNPIKE STAIR: Spiral or corkscrew staircase.

YETT: Iron grill or gate.

# Introduction

In *Scotland's Historic Buildings* I dealt almost wholly with the
vernacular in Scottish architecture, avoiding archaeology,
ruins and conjecture and concentrating on roofed structures,
or buildings that could be re-roofed and used without much
difficulty. In particular I refrained from lengthy comment on
romantic abbeys and castles and instead chose those aspects
of Scottish building that distinguish it from building elsewhere, giving it what the late Dr Douglas Simpson called a
'National Style'. This I did in no spirit of chauvinistic pride
but rather because I believe that unless we do something
about it soon we may lose our cultural heritage altogether as
a living force, museums and frozen folklore being no substi-
tute for the real thing. Nowadays information and interests
largely depend on easily identifiable images, whether in
words or pictures, and thus Scotland has acquired a com-
posite, readily recognizable face in which tartan and bagpipes, haggis and heather, not to mention the Edinburgh
Castle Tattoo, predominate; which brings me to castles and
the subject of this book. Of all the quick architectural pictures of Scotland, none is quicker and more acceptable than
that of the traditional Scottish castle, or what purports to be.
These castles, ruined or entire, nineteenth-century baronial
or genuinely ancient, attract because they are part and
parcel of a small nation's own peculiar history, one interestingly if tragically threaded with lost causes and bitter-sweet
memories of the sort a romance-starved twentieth century
cannot resist.

For the most part Scottish castles belong to the sixteenth
and seventeenth centuries; I refer now to the specifically
native castle, not to the hoary remains of Norman penetration nor to later medieval structures that differ little between
England, France and Scotland. The historic Scottish castle

was built for defence not so much against foreign invaders as against predatory neighbours, which accounts for one peculiarity they exhibit to a remarkable degree—namely their extraordinary height. When enemies or even rude creditors appeared on the scenes the inmates made for the topmost storey of their eyries, whence they hurled abuse, and if necessary more material dissuasions upon the disturbers of their privacy; and such activities were still common when James VI of Scots became James I of Great Britain. He tried very hard to bring Scotland into line with the rest of his united kingdom. In England they had long before given up living in uncomfortable old castles and taken to pleasant half-timbered or brick manor houses and handsome stone halls, their castles, if left standing, being usually thoroughly modernized.

If one were to list Scotland's castles in groups they would fall roughly into four significant periods. The first covers the thirteenth to fifteenth centuries, when war with England if not actually in progress was intermittent, and of these not a single complete example remains inhabited. The architecture of the period is, of course, European, not specifically Scottish, and it need not concern us here, except as a preparation for what follows. It has been well described by both Douglas Simpson and Stewart Cruden, Inspector of Ancient Monuments in Scotland in succession to the late Dr James Richardson. Mr Cruden, in his *Scottish Castles*, provides an excellent background to the subject, while Dr Simpson, in his *Ancient Stones of Scotland*, goes into greater detail on individual buildings, introducing the reader to the second, more important period of Scottish castles in the sixteenth and seventeenth centuries. These constitute the northern kingdom's unique contribution to world architecture, half-defensive, half-domestic castles and tower houses which have no exact equals elsewhere and which provide the bulk of the reading matter and illustrations in the present volume. They are recognizably Scottish and native and can hold their own in any company. The third period comes rather surprisingly at the end of the eighteenth century in the wake of the romantic movement, itself the child of a Scottish cult that revolved round the misfortunes of the Royal House of Stuart, and notably the last scions of that race, 'Bonnie Prince Charlie' and his brother, exiled in Rome. Robert Adam was the principal agent in this new style, which, relying on Scottish history and scenery for much of its being, betrayed a strong Italian flavour. It needed Adam's genius for success, a fact clearly seen in the lesser works in the genre which appeared after his death. With Culzean, his masterpiece in Italian-castellated barely finished, the fashion was left to others less gifted, less travelled and less in tune with the true European ethos to try their hands at a fourth period, in the nineteenth century, 'Scotch Baronial'. This still relied on the Caledonian legend and landscape for its effect, and is best remembered by Abbotsford and Balmoral, though the comparison is odious since the first was the loving creation of a collector and antiquarian, a romantic, literary figure of international repute, while the second represents a cold exercise in Scottish castle building by a pedantic German prince whose unfortunate example was copied far beyond Deeside, on the Continent and all over the world.

Geographically speaking the majority of the Jacobean castles are in the north-east of the country, where strife with England was negligible compared to the south, and fratricidal strife less destructive of property. Aberdeenshire was prosperous and reasonably well-integrated by the sixteenth century and many of its finest buildings were commissioned by merchants and magnates with no great aristocratic pretensions. Craigievar, the home of an importer of timber, is the most obvious case in point, being really more of a 'château' than a castle, a castellated country house that never saw war and was never intended to. It was completed in the first year of the reign of Charles I, and has to be compared with the smaller Jacobean mansions of England to be seen in perspective. In this respect, as in some others, Scotland more resembles France than her nearest neighbour, where similarly fantastic displays of late-gothic and early Renaissance art in the form of playful gargoyles, elaborate dormers, richly carved corbels and amusing turrets are few and far between. Much has been said and written about the

French connection, which historically is of ancient lineage, some art historians belittling its cultural influence, others exaggerating it. R. W. Billings in his inimitable *Baronial and Ecclesiastical Antiquities of Scotland* and MacGibbon and Ross in their later *Domestic and Castellated Architecture of Scotland*, take opposing sides; but whatever one's opinion the fact remains that French influence was direct and considerable on some Scottish buildings, notably in royal palaces and castles built by families with strong Continental links.

There are several explanations for the remarkable flowering of Scottish castellated architecture in the late sixteenth and early seventeenth centuries. One which I have not seen offered by anyone previously concerns the dual make-up of the Scots themselves, for most Scots are both Celt and Saxon, both mystic and hard-headed go-getters. The pure Celt rarely makes a good architect, there is too much mathematics involved, but he often excels as a sculptor. Hence, surely, the splendid carving in so many Scottish castles, themselves the creations of lowland thrift. One suspects that this dual make-up was partly responsible for the genius of Robert Adam, who, although designing his largest and finest neo-classical houses in England, chose Scotland for his most original works, his Italianate castles. Naturally there are other factors, the climate and materials available, the backwardness of much of the country and the thrawnness of folk who preferred to live in tall, awkward towers when most of the rest of Europe enjoyed less ostentatiously uncomfortable homes. Yet there is an irresistible attraction in these bijou castles, these miniature *châteaux*, that exists nowhere else to the same degree, certainly not in Britain, and perhaps only matched in the Auvergne, that mountainous core of Gallic France where they still play the bagpipes and the gentry are mostly native.

The visitor coming from England will not at first meet so many castles in Scotland as 'pele towers', a species of defence found on both sides of the Border, which evolved from a simple redoubt behind a wooden palisade into a stone 'keep' in the fifteenth century. There are castles in the Borders, mostly decorative ones or enlarged 'peles', or castles turned into follies in the gardens of eighteenth-century mansions and large farmhouses. Further north, closer to Edinburgh, is Borthwick, the completest medieval pile in the country, and Crichton, Scott's favourite, and, of course, the royal castles of Edinburgh and Stirling. In the South-west is the great castle of Caerlaverock, the subject of a famous medieval poem, *Le Siège de Karlaverock*. This predates the wars of independence and was besieged by Edward I, the 'Hammer of the Scots', in 1300. It bears comparison with Edward's mighty fortresses in Wales and boasts one of the earliest and most distinguished Renaissance courtyards in Scotland. Still in the west is the last Scottish castle to be built in the old tradition, Drumlanrig, seat of the Duke of Buccleuch. It was begun in the reign of Charles I and not finished by the time his second son, James VII and II, had gone into exile. It is big and baroque, with baronial attachments, and serves as a memorial to the building mania of contemporary Scottish magnates, being erected almost at the same time as Glamis was rebuilt by the third Earl of Strathmore and Kinghorne.

Culzean is in Ayrshire, and is the Carrick shore's principal monument, while Craignethan, which Sir Walter Scott called 'Tillietudlem' and once thought of adapting instead of building Abbotsford, still rises evocatively from amidst the orchards of the Clyde valley. Moving into central Scotland the famous names come thick and fast, Loch Leven, Kellie and Blair, but it is when one arrives in the North-east that the true galaxy appears, headed by Craigievar and Crathes, Midmar and Fraser, but also including Huntly, Glamis and Dunnottar. The Highlands proper are not 'castellated' to the same extent, the islands and far North even less so. This is partly because they have been less developed and are more sparsely populated, partly because lawlessness and uncertainty reigned there until comparatively modern times, and partly because the Celts were not noted builders in stone and what rude forts they made have mostly disappeared. Dunvegan stands on an old site and contains valuable records of the history of Clan MacLeod, but its battlements are nineteenth century, while Kisimul, most romantic of island fortalices, does not date from before the fifteenth century, when the ancestors of the present MacNeill of Barra first went there. A large number of Scotland's castles are open to the public, the majority ruined and the responsibility of the Secretary of State for Scotland, acting through the Department of the Environment, a list of which appears at the end of this book. Of the inhabited castles, some of the best, indeed four of the best (Glamis being the odd one out and remaining the property of the Earl of Strathmore) are in the care of the National Trust for Scotland: Craigievar, Crathes, Kellie and Culzean. Others open on special occasions, or only in summer. One can travel to practically any region, not excluding Orkney and Shetland, and discover a castle worth visiting, though it is more in the Aberdeenshire valleys of the Don and the Dee that the concentration rivals in its own way that of the *châteaux* of the Loire.

# I

# *The Borderland*

IT IS curious to recall that before the end of the thirteenth
century, and the disputes over who should inherit the crown
of Scotland following the death in Norway of the heiress to
Alexander III, the borderland between England and
Scotland was generally peaceful and prosperous. There were
as yet no so-called 'pele towers' or other private defensive
structures of note, only a few feudal castles held in fief by
baronial lords for the king. The feudal system, in which
monarch, church and barons joined to keep the peace and
maintain order, was established in Scotland, as in England,
in all but the remoter areas of the Highlands, and in Orkney
and Shetland, where the Danish Udal Law prevailed. Consequently, there was no need for that multitude of small
towers and castles that later appeared all over southern and
eastern Scotland and on both sides of the Border. It was in
pursuance of his role as supreme overlord that Edward I of
England, to whom Scottish kings paid homage and owed
suzerainty for much property in England, was asked to
mediate in the Scottish dynastic dispute and who, quite
rightly, chose John Balliol to succeed the 'Maid of Norway'.
It is unfortunate that Balliol was a weak and unsatisfactory
person, but his claim, as Gordon Donaldson, Professor of
Scottish History at Edinburgh, has pointed out, was certainly
the best, and indeed the equivalent in its day and age of the
superior claim of James Francis Edward Stuart over George
I in his. We tend to forget this when denigrating the
character of John Balliol, but the crown was undoubtedly his
by the law of primogeniture, and given the circumstances the
English king really had no option but to nominate him as
King of Scots over the claims of Robert Bruce. I mention this
here because unless it is appreciated one can scarcely understand the changes that took place afterwards in Scotland

as a whole and particularly in the Borderland. For English wrath at their nominee's subsequent turning against them and making a pact with the King of France was the principal cause of the 'Hammer of the Scots' arriving on the scene once more, not as neutral arbitrator but laying waste the land from the Borders to the Moray Firth and re-garrisoning every strong point he thought necessary to restore his authority. Edward died before the complete subjugation of Scotland was accomplished and before he was able to build a ring of magnificent feudal fortresses such as he had done in Wales. Instead, existing Anglo-Norman redoubts were captured and strengthened, but not for long, as on his death the Scots took heart again and under Bruce threw many of these castles down, so that few rose again in anything like their old form. Of these Dirleton, in East Lothian, a seat of the De Vaux family, Kildrummie, in Aberdeenshire, built by Gilbert de Moravia, Bishop of Caithness, and Caerlaverock, in Dumfriesshire, the siege of which is fully described in a celebrated medieval poem, are perhaps the best known.

Dumfriesshire is one of the three Scottish counties bordering directly on England, the others are Roxburghshire and Berwickshire; Selkirkshire, Peeblesshire and parts of the Lothians being permitted honorary Borderland status by the non-pedantic. At the Dumfriesshire end stands Carlisle, a wholly English city, and at the other Berwick, a town that has changed hands many times in its long and turbulent history and until comparatively recent years was considered neither in England nor Scotland, but enjoyed extra-territorial rights. My father's grandfather was Mayor of Berwick on several occasions, at which period it still enjoyed 'free-town' status, and actually declared war on Russia on its own account in 1854. Of the thirteenth-century castle in whose Great Hall Edward I made his choice of John Balliol as 'subject' King of Scots little remains, its site being largely covered by the present railway station—a fact that did not pass unnoticed by Robert Stephenson, who commemorated his completion of the Royal Border Bridge over the Tweed in 1856, and the erection of the new railway station, by placing over the entrance to the latter an inscription bearing the words, 'The final act of union'. What Berwick does still have are its unique sixteenth-century fortifications, unique in Britain and amongst the finest examples in Europe. The walls and ditches, sea gates and bastions were designed by Italian military engineers, possibly by some of those who in the first half of the century strengthened the defences of Leith and Inchkeith, in the Firth of Forth, and are designed on the same principle as the walls of Lucca and other contemporary Italian cities. In the eighteenth century the great French military engineer, Vauban, covered western Europe with star-shaped forts based on the same idea of bastions projecting from the main line of the walls so as attackers could be raked with fire from behind. There was even some suggestion that a star-shaped 'forework' should be added to Edinburgh Castle in the seventeenth century, and although this was not done the Vauban system was later employed at Fort George, near Inverness, after the Forty-five rebellion, with William Adam and his sons supervising. So far as Berwick is concerned some indication of the burgh's unusual status may be gauged from the fact that the 'Italian' walls, ostensibly defending a Northumbrian town, are listed by the Ministry of Public Works and Buildings in their *Illustrated Guide to Ancient Monuments in Scotland*.

The tiny county and burgh of Berwick-upon-Tweed stretched a few miles north of the Tweed to Lamberton Toll, on the slopes of Halidon Hill as it falls by rocky cliffs straight into the German Ocean. My great-grandmother was born in what was then the first house in Scotland, on a site which witnessed the battle of 1333 when the English took their revenge for Bannockburn. Beyond this now peaceful spot, almost in the suburbs of Berwick, road and rail pass close to the edge of the cliffs, with exciting views of the coast, of fishing boats dipping up and down, of tiny fishing harbours such as Burnmouth, and away to the north the outline of the coast of Fife. Suddenly as one turns inland the whole scene changes, one enters the green and wooded valley of the Ay, or Eye, to be greeted with the perfect vision of a Scotch Baronial pile as it might have been conjured up in a film set or an operatic back-cloth. I refer to Ayton Castle, which although mainly fake and not medieval at all, having been designed by James Gillespie Graham in the early nineteenth century, does epitomize in a not entirely unsatisfactory way what the average person imagines as a true Scottish castle. Graham, who was only Gillespie until he married an heiress and added her name to his, was one of the abler participants in the initial stages of the so-called 'Battle of the Styles', in which the supporters of neo-classicism and revivalist gothic fought for supremacy. Thus, in contrast to this evocatively baronial red-sandstone edifice, replete with central turreted border tower and mock-medieval outbuildings, the same architect designed some of the plainest and heaviest 'Greek' terraces and crescents in the New Town of Edinburgh. He was much better in the 'Gothyke' mode, having had some tuition from Pugin, and undoubtedly Ayton Castle, a seat of the Hay, or De Haya family, who came here as part of the Norman penetration, is successful in its object provided one does not go too near and simply enjoys it as a first glimpse of the Scottish castellated style after crossing the Border.

Perhaps the majority of visitors to Scotland arrive via the east coast route and will have Ayton Castle as their first happy experience of native baronial, but long before the days of rail and the motor car the Romans made a more central approach, avoiding the dangers of the narrow sea-cliff pass and running straight on beyond Corstopitum, the modern Corbridge, along Dere Street to Carter Bar and so over the Cheviots into the heart of the Borderland. It is still the quickest way. Coming from the south one reaches the Tyne valley and a stupendous panorama over the hills, sweeping down past Dilston Castle, ruined seat of the tragic Earl of Derwentwater, a grandson of Charles II by the actress Moll Davis, who made common cause with the Scottish Jacobites at Kelso in 1715, and afterwards lost his head for his pains. Across the Tyne one climbs rapidly towards the line of the Roman wall, stone from which was used to build the Saxon church at Corbridge, possibly also the Vicar's 'Pele' there, and certainly Halton Tower, which is a true Border fortalice, replete with simple battlements and bartisans, or open corner turrets supported on corbels that served as lookouts. Within sight of this is Aydon Hall, which is quite a different type of building, but like Halton gives a foretaste of things to come. Halton looks older, and was in existence in 1415, but Aydon, which is that rare thing in England, and rarer still in the North, a fortified manor house, dates from the late thirteenth century, and was wholly complete by the early fourteenth. Its interest here lies in the fact that it has an exact contemporary in Hailes Castle, on the Scottish Tyne, between Haddington and Dunbar, which was built, as Aydon probably also was, by a member of the Northumbrian family of Gourlay. Unfortunately Hailes, having survived the Wars of Independence without scaith, became a bone of contention between the Douglases and the Hepburns once its southern owners had been displaced. It was fought over and had to be rebuilt and extended in parts until the days of Cromwell, who finally put paid to it in 1650. Today this romantic ruin, where James Hepburn, Earl of Bothwell, entertained Mary, Queen of Scots, is all that remains of the only fortified manor of its period north of the Border, while its near twin, Aydon, still served as a farmhouse until 1968, when it was taken over for conservation by the Ministry of Public Buildings and Works.

Hadrian's Wall is soon reached after this; the road along it from Newcastle to Carlisle was restored and widened by General, later Field-Marshal, Wade, who 'pacified' the Highlands in the eighteenth century and rather fancied himself and his forces as the heirs to Caesar and the Imperial legions. The road north leads on through increasingly desolate country, up and down the hills in proper Roman fashion, passing close to Otterburn, scene in 1388 of the battle of that name, known to Englishmen as Chevy Chase, in which the Earl of Douglas, having defeated Harry Hotspur, returned to pick up his pennant, which he had lost, and was himself killed in the event. The North Tyne Valley, which one crosses en route to Carter Bar, was the more usual way used by Border reivers, or cattle thieves, as it gave them more shelter, and it was by this same route that the men of Galloway descended upon the ancient town of Hexham, laid waste to it and killed all the boys in the Grammar School in the thirteenth century, a fate that had already befallen them four hundred years earlier, when the Danes arrived in this outpost of northern Christianity. Hexham was an important staging post in the spread of Augustinian religion north of the Border and its eventual supplanting of that emanating from Iona and the Irish Mission of St Columba. Hexham at one time was a bishopric, one of its best-known and loved bishops being St Cuthbert, a shepherd boy from Melrose whose 'chair' is still shown to visitors. The former cathedral, later priory, was dedicated to St Augustine's favourite saint, Andrew, whose cult was brought across the Border when the abbeys of Jedburgh, Kelso, Dryburgh, and Melrose were founded, and eventually arrived at St Andrews itself, when St Columba was supplanted as Scotland's patron.

Jedburgh is the first sizeable town on the Scottish side of the Cheviots and is noteworthy for the house known as 'Queen Mary's', which was a minor seat of the Ker family, the 'Ker-handed' clan who carried their swords in their left hands and whose staircases correspondingly spiralled to the left. The one in 'Queen Mary's House' does anyway. The building was adapted as a bastel, or communal shelter for the townsfolk during times of war or a raid. Similar edifices can be seen on the English side. One at Melkridge, between Hexham and Haltwhistle, retains its firebucket, a feature more common on the Scottish side and in Dumfriesshire, as we shall see. The firebucket took the form of an enlarged chimney-stack, or what looks like one, in which a warning beacon was lit when a raid was imminent or in progress. This was done on the orders of the Warden of the Marches, an office which alternated between a Scottish and an English Borderer, the rules of the game being more or less accepted whenever the martial strength of the Warden was sufficient to enforce them.

The Kers were for many years Wardens of the Middle and Eastern Marches and near Jedburgh will be seen their castle of Ferniehirst, the first in Scotland to greet the visitor which is neither a reconstruction nor a restoration, unless one counts a late sixteenth-century rebuilding as such. Ferniehirst is a typical L-shaped fortalice, with one arm, the newer,

*Ferniehirst Castle, a Ker seat: general view; the turrets*

much longer than the other, the older containing the stair turret and original entrance. It is not a 'pele', in fact that term is scarcely applicable anywhere, since it really refers to the timber stockade, or palisade, which enclosed and protected the hall or tower of a border laird, and not a stone erection at all. The latter first appeared about the beginning of the fifteenth century, Halton in Northumberland being one of the earliest, but it was not the tower that was the 'pele' but its outer defence. The old castle of Ferniehirst was occupied in 1547 by the troops of Henry VIII of England, who were, however, dislodged by Sir John Ker leading a mixed force composed of his own clansmen and French auxiliaries, when the building was undermined. What we see today is a late sixteenth-century stair tower attached to an elongated seventeenth-century wing, the stair being contained in a splendid spiral corbelled out in the angle, the corbels reaching to within a few feet of the ground; a typical example of the thrawnness of Scots masons, for it could just as easily have risen from the ground directly without any corbelling. It is well supplied with shot- and shut-holes, the difference is usually detected by the form, since a shot-hole must give a wide enough angle for the use of a musket and is usually a longitudinal or latitudinal slit or loop, while the shut-hole, made merely to provide air and most commonly found in staircases and near the front door, is almost always round, and not splayed, and can be closed inside with a wooden panel. There is a nice complement of conically-capped corner turrets at Ferniehirst, not to be confused with bartisans, which they imitate as a decorative feature but are not. The whole purpose of a bartisan is external and for defence, and they are very rarely roofed over, while the corner turrets which are such a feature of Scottish Jacobean castles are properly known as 'studies'; they are internal in function, opening from the upper rooms to which they are attached. There is a certain amount of Renaissance detail around the doors and windows at Ferniehirst and the castle courtyard is entered through a handsome classically inspired archway. The building is now a Youth Hostel.

At the western end of the Border there are no significant

hills to form a natural boundary between England and
Scotland and no broad river like the Tweed. The Esk has
never played the same role, and even today the Border runs
north and west of it, coming towards it via a long artificial
ditch, the Scots Dyke. There is not a lot to choose between
Longtown, in England, and Langholm, in Scotland, both on
the banks of the Esk, and no great difference in scenery and
general effect as one passes from 'south Britain' to 'north
Britain'. Indeed, one is reminded of Professor Esmond
Wright's reply to some nationalistic outburst by Hugh
MacDiarmid, the Scottish poet, that he could not see the
difference between being born a few miles south of an
imaginary line in Cumberland and a few miles to the north
in Dumfriesshire. The whole area was known as the Debatable Land and administered by the jointly appointed Wardens and their posses. One has only to think of the North
American 'Wild West' to get an idea of what conditions were
like along this part of the Border in the days immediately
preceding the Union of the Crowns in 1603. James V of
Scots, father of Queen Mary, made an effort to stamp out
lawlessness, making an example of Johnny Armstrong, the
cruellest and most ruthless of all Border reivers. Legend has
turned this ruffian, a gangster of the worst possible type, who
stole from poor and rich, showing mercy to no-one and
killing off those who stood in his way, as a sort of Scottish
'Robin Hood', which is completely false, having not the
slightest existence in historical fact. James strung him up,
but was not thanked for his trouble, in fact the Borderers
never forgave him for interfering in what they considered
their own private quarrels; and when he sent an army to
fight the English his men deserted him on the battlefield,
offering themselves as prisoners to anyone they could find
willing to accept their swords, even knocking at the doors of
cottages and giving themselves up to the wives of their
enemies. The news of this, plus the birth of a daughter when
he wanted a son, broke the King's heart; and he died soon
after learning in such a bitter way that Borderers are Borderers first and Scots or English second.

As one approaches the Scots Dyke one passes close to

Kirkandrews, with its delightful Caroline church and old tower of the Grahams, the latter dating from the fifteenth century, but restored. Within sight of it, on the eastern bank of the Esk, lies Netherby, another Graham redoubt now turned into a comfortable country house. It stands on the site of a Roman station and was the scene of young Lochinvar's daring abduction of his bride. The Grahams incurred the wrath of James VI of Scots, I of England, whose more serious attempts to curb lawlessness in the Debatable Land, especially after he had ascended the throne of Great Britain, included the driving of the Grahams from their home and confiscating their property, a more thorough way of eradicating them than any amount of hanging of ringleaders, which, in any case, no more deterred the Border reivers than the beating of selected badly behaved schoolboys does. Once across the river one arrives at Gilnockie, where the tower of the Armstrongs, rivals in crime of the Grahams, has completely disappeared except in name, though a little further on Hollows Tower still stands, an identical type, rectangular, gable-ended and with one chimney made in the form of a large stone firebucket. The tower is roofless and empty, but retains scraps of its ornate corbelling supporting ancient lookouts. It is a gaunt reminder in its dark vacancy of life in the Debatable Lands as late as the beginning of the seventeenth century.

Much of the eastern half of Dumfriesshire was included in this jointly administered area, which in truth did have almost as many links with England as with Scotland. It must be remembered that Edinburgh and Glasgow are as remote from Galloway and Dumfries as they are from Aberdeenshire and the north-east of the country; they are still three hours away even in a car, and the considerable hills that have to be crossed are often snowbound in winter, and must have been decidedly treacherous in the old days. It is curious too how one of the great legendary battles between the Scots and Saxons took place near the Solway Firth at Brunanburgh in 937, when Athelstan King of Northumbria defeated and humbled Constantine of Scots. The whole event was 'miraculously' transplanted in later years to the village of

Athelstaneford, in East Lothian, and defeat turned into a magnificent victory. What a pity mythology could not have done something similar for poor James V! More positively the Diocese of Galloway in which Dumfries also is, formed part of the Province of York almost until the Reformation, the only Scottish diocese not controlled by the Scottish Church except Orkney and Shetland, which went in with Trondheim until the end of the fifteenth century. The important Norman families of de Balliol and de Bruis, or Bruce, settled in Dumfriesshire when they moved by stages from County Durham and Yorkshire into Scotland in the twelfth and thirteenth centuries. Balliol College Oxford was founded by Dervorguilla of Galloway, mother of Edward I's nominee, on behalf of her husband; while the Bruces had their seat at Lochmaben, slightly to the north-east of Dumfries town. Lochmaben Castle was levelled to the ground by James VI and I as an example to others, and the entire area is dotted with the remains of small or larger fortalices, some serving as follies in the gardens of more modern mansions, others partly restored and attached to the modern mansion.

Amisfield and Elshieshields are good examples of Border towers that have survived more or less intact, the first standing erect and alone beside its Georgian supplanter, the second joined and merged with it. Before saying any more about these two, however, one must make a comment about Caerlaverock, which is in the same vicinity only nearer the Solway Firth and which, although a ruin, was the seat of the principal family hereabouts for many centuries, the Maxwells. This book is not about ruins but no account of Scottish castles could ignore Caerlaverock, its most interesting shape and history and influence upon castle building elsewhere in the country. It already existed before the siege by Edward I, and was the second fortress to be built on or near the same site. An earlier castle stood closer to the sea and was probably of timber, erected on an artificial mound, or motte, made in the boggy ground and surrounded by a moat, or fosse which when filled with water could be used as a small port. In the thirteenth century a new site was chosen and a new castle arose on a tiny rocky outcrop in the marsh, again

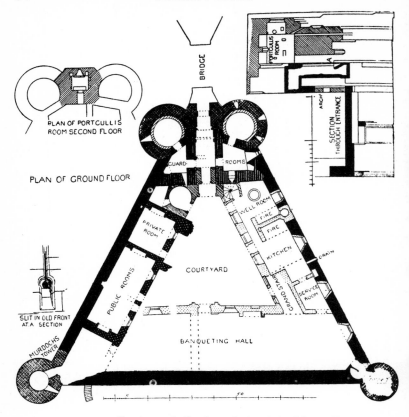

PLAN OF PORTCULLIS
ROOM SECOND FLOOR

PLAN OF GROUND FLOOR

SLIT IN OLD FRONT
AT A SECTION

*Caerlaverock Castle, redoubt of the Maxwells:*
*plan of ground floor*

with moat and water, but this time planned like a shield, a
fact noted by the chronicler of *Le Siège*. It is unlikely that
much of the present edifice belongs to that period, though
the plan is the same, with two immense round towers commanding the entrance and two smaller ones at the far corners
of the 'shield'. Gun loops and other later features tell their
own story of rebuilding, the remains of a cluster of turrets
with unnecessarily elaborate corbelling cannot date from
before the fifteenth century. Alan Sorrel, whose splendid
re-creations of ruined castles appear in a number of official

*Caerlaverock Castle: general view; view in courtyard, looking south-west; courtyard, showing pedimented openings*

guide books and are sold as postcards at the relevant buildings, has now made his own book of reconstructions in which
Caerlaverock appears as it might have been. I am sure he is
right when he says that the upper parts of the castle were
built more for dramatic effect than for solid defence: in other
words represent decorative military architecture rather than
strictly functional, and suggest the sort of picture represented
in late-medieval Hour Books, citing the well-known *Livre
d'Heures* of the Duc de Berry, now at Chantilly. It is this
romantic vision, of course, that one sees recreated at Ayton,
and throughout the rash of later baronial edifices erected in
Scotland both in the Jacobean and Victorian periods. What
makes Caerlaverock particularly interesting, and relevant in
the present context, is the design of the inner courtyard,
behind the 'shield', which was rebuilt and refaced in the first
half of the seventeenth century by the Earl of Nithsdale, and
displays one of the earliest and most sophisticated essays in
Renaissance detail of that age. It predates the Civil War. Its
pedimented openings, with their classical illusions carved in
the tympana, were the creation of a philosopher-earl of the
Maxwell family of which he was the head, the most powerful
clan in the South-west and one that remained Roman
Catholic throughout the difficult days of the Covenant and
after. Maxwell protection of the Abbot of Doulce Coeur, or
Sweetheart Abbey, founded by Dervorguilla in the thirteenth
century as a shrine for her husband's heart, features in
Scott's novel *The Abbot*; Gilbert Brown, who held on to his
benefice after the Reformation and well into the seventeenth
century, defied all comers to remove him. It was also to
Maxwell territory that the fleeing Mary, Queen of Scots
came in her extremity before being rowed over the Solway to
become Elizabeth Tudor's hostage.

    In the Covenanting Wars of the latter part of the reign of
Charles I Caerlaverock and its philosopher-earl were besieged
by the Protestant legions, who took three months to reduce
the household to surrender, compared to the two days taken
by Edward I's siege machines three hundred years earlier. It
would appear from this that cannon was less effective against
strong walls than big stone-hurling catapults, battering rams,

and landing stages from which the besieged could be attacked on their stone battlements. There was also the question of supplies, many castles could probably have held out
longer, even medieval ones under extreme pressure from
giant siege engines, had they been assured of plenty of food
and drinking water, which of course Caerlaverock was not, in
its isolated position in the middle of a coastal swamp. Lord
Nithsdale made a precise list of all his possessions before
handing the castle over, detailing every object right down to
the last sheet and blanket, and afterwards he claimed
recompense for any items missing. The Maxwells then made
their principal seat at Terregles, on the west side of Dumfries,
but eventually moved to Traquair, in Peeblesshire, whose
present laird, the twentieth, is Peter Maxwell Stuart and a
lineal successor. At Traquair they have the bed in which
Mary, Queen of Scots is said to have slept at Terregles,
together with an amusing Jacobean door, carved with the
device of the lion fighting the unicorn. A similar door, but
showing Samson slaying the lion, was at Amisfield, but is
now in the Museum of Antiquities in Edinburgh. The Earls
of Nithsdale died out with the sixth of their number in 1773.
He was the son of that Jacobite earl who escaped from the
Tower of London in 1715, with the assistance of his wife who
lent him her clothes for the purpose.

Amisfield is simply marvellous, superior in its way to the
castles of Aberdeenshire since it is all of a piece, unrestored
and unaltered except for the introduction of sash windows,
and displays almost every Jacobean baronial conceit in a
single complete rectangular tower. Its date is 1600, which
means that lawlessness was not quite ended, though nearly so
in the Borders, and its masonry has a finesse unusual both for
its period and place. It is not by accident that the lower
storeys are built of random rubble, with worked quoins, or
corners, and that smooth stonework, or ashlar, is reserved for
the window and door surrounds and the upper floors,
including a maze of turrets, semicircular and rectangular
projections, ending in a double cap-house. The stone is a
warm red, which matches the more varied hues of the lower
masonry rather well, and makes one doubt the theory that

the tower would look better harled or roughcast. What colour would one have it, for instance, and why should it be harled when it has survived without harm or significant wear all these years? It is odd this mania for harling, the idea that every bit of stone which is not smooth ashlar should be coated with road chippings and cement, a sort of masonic porridge. Sir George Bruce's little Flemish 'palas', his town house, at Culross, which I described in *Scotland's Historic Buildings*, is the latest victim of this process, the 'porridge' actually spreading right over the top of the crowsteps onto the inside of the gable ends, covering up the chimneystacks and obliterating door and window openings so as not to leave a chink of stone visible in the structure that would show its age or erstwhile appearance. Fortunately Amisfield, despite suggestions that it should be given 'the treatment', has not yet been touched, and while the present proprietors are there I doubt if it will be.

Amisfield is one of a trio of perfectly preserved, or nearly so, Scottish towers of defence, the other two being Scotstarvit, in Fife, and Coxton, in Moray. They are all different. Coxton, which dates from 1640, though one can hardly believe it, is partly harled to reveal on the upper storey a simple bartisan and short sentry walk reached from a circular stair turret with conical roof, all in stone and of surpassing delight. It is not certain whether it was ever meant to be lived in and was not built as a folly in the first instance; it may never have been lived in permanently by anyone, the last, and only known occupant having been a gardener in the last century. Scotstarvit is faced entirely in ashlar, has no turrets or bartisans, but it does have a run of open parapet and an amusing miniature doocot opening near the top of the stair tower. Unlike the others it is not square, but boasts a tiny nib where the stairs come, thus making it the more traditional L shape on plan. Amisfield is the tallest of the three, with seven levels in all, the more interesting being the top three. Indeed nothing very much happens in the way of bulges and break-outs until the fourth floor is reached, when a circle of conically capped corner turrets, dormer windows and small rooms projecting on corbels begin the process of making the uppermost storeys the most impressive part of the tower. The ground floor is vaulted and was used as a store, above was the kitchen, and above that the laird's hall, with bedrooms above that, and then three more floors each contained within tiny box-like rooms, diminishing in size to the top one, which was probably more a means of reaching the fire-bucket or beacon, a watching place, or cap-house, rather than a habitable chamber. Its size is a mere six feet by five. Amisfield was only marginally meant for defence, its shot-holes being all in the high up turrets and stairwheels, and none down by the door which was the more usual place.

There are a number of features about Amisfield which are worth describing for themselves as they represent many of the same features one finds miles away in the north of Scotland, even in the west, which are here used in true Scots style: that is making use of what were once medieval defensive features as a form of decoration and display. There are no battlements and no bartisans; instead, there are double-storeyed corner turrets such as one finds almost uniquely elsewhere at Craigievar, but Amisfield was finished two decades before Craigievar, and the workmanship is greatly superior. The corbelling is interesting as we see here for the first time over the Border the billet-and-cable device so beloved of northern stonemasons, in which billets, or stylized logs are used to break up the cable pattern in the corbelling. The way the dormers are treated is also interesting, since at Amisfield, and incidentally at Crathes, on Deeside, the old French form of *bretèche*, twin supports for a centrally placed projection, with gap between for dropping boiling oil, are made to support projecting dormers. Other features that have medieval echoes are the dog-tooth motif, which surrounds some of the windows at Amisfield and the armorial panels, as it does in far-away Dunderave, ancient seat of the MacNaughtons on Loch Fyne, and the continuously entwined cable pattern, known variously by its French name of *guillot*, or Scots guilloch, which seem to have Celtic connotations. The tower was built by the Charteris family whose coat of arms is one of two appearing above the door. Today they are represented by the Earl of Wemyss and

March, the intricacies of whose descent are too complicated to go into here.

Elshieshields is a little later than Amisfield, which is surprising when one considers the first king of Great Britain's efforts to pacify the Borders and his apparent success; but perhaps this particular tower was never the subject of a raid and the enormous firebucket at the highest point of its watchtower never contained a warning beacon. Unlike Amisfield, Elshieshields is not rectangular but L-shaped, the tower being wholly reserved for defensive purposes, with a shot-hole commanding the door and narrow slits for windows. It is built of random rubble and harled, and looks as if it had always been, lacking notable décorative features, dressed stone being reserved for the firebucket and chimney-stacks. It has corner turrets with conical caps, crowsteps and a spiral staircase, but no battlements, only a tiny cap-house, reached by an extra spiral the course of which can be made out by a bulge near the top supported by simple corbelling. The old tower is not inhabited, but remains intact beside the modern house to which it is joined, it is not built of the same stone as Amisfield and its harling, which used to be an attractive creamy-grey, can probably be dated to the seven-teeth century, which is rare. One is always looking for a Scottish castle which can be proved to have been harled before, say, the end of the sixteenth century, or the beginning of the seventeenth, and this may be one. The late Sir John Stirling Maxwell, a pro-harler, could find no evidence of any building being harled before the fifteenth century but he does not mention any examples. I think, however, one can safely say that some of the Aberdeenshire castles, such as Craigievar, which was completed in 1626, and Crathes, which is some thirty years younger, were harled originally, and wear their old coats quite well. It is only unfortunate that modern harling, even where it is necessary to cover up new or unsympathetic work, or for the protection of decayed masonry, is not composed of the traditional river bed ballast, which, mixed with sand and lime, worked by hand or float in a circular motion, has an appeal all its own, and is as different in texture and effect from the chippings and cement

(above left) *Amisfield Tower.* *Elshieshields Tower:* (above right) *side view (note the firebucket);* (below) *general view*

more commonly used as, for instance, vegetable dyed tartan is from the chemically dyed variety.

Langholm stands at the junction of the Esk valley and Liddesdale, up which, until the Beeching cuts, one of the most scenic of Scottish railway lines ran. Indeed, I well recall Sir John Betjeman when he came to address the Cockburn Association used most of his lecture to enthuse over what he saw between Carlisle and Edinburgh on this route. One thing he did not see, but missed by a mere quarter of a mile or so, was Hermitage Castle, the grimmest and largest of the semi-ruined Border fortalices, which is sited a little apart from the main valley by the Hermitage Burn, so named after a hermit's cell, the remains of which can still be made out, which stood near the present castle. Hermitage is now vacant, its walls open to the skies, though it was restored to some extent in the nineteenth century by the Duke of Buccleuch whose family owned it. The plan and development is unusual, for here we have neither an L shape nor a Z shape, nor any of the normal plans, but a central oblong tower, the original Border redoubt, which has been literally turned inside out, that is to say, its roof was removed in the fifteenth century so that its gutted interior could become a courtyard for new, surrounding additions, and its windows adapted accordingly. Such utilitarian methods seem unusual and the result is visible to this day. In the following century further additions were made in the form of two end towers, a pair at either end of the castle, these being linked at battlement level by highly placed arches to make a single outer wall, thus creating an H plan. This is not all, however—in the course of the continual modernization of this strong but isolated fortress wooden galleries, or hoardings, the French *hourds*, were placed immediately below the battlements on the outside and the corbelled supports for these have survived *in situ*.

Not only has Hermitage Castle an unusual and long history of gradual but complete change, its owners have also been many and notable. It is said originally to have been built by Walter Comyn, of the family Bruce antagonized by stabbing John Comyn, a rival for the crown, in the Kirk of

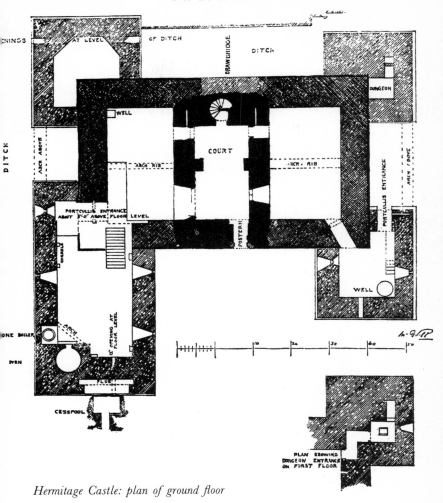

*Hermitage Castle: plan of ground floor*

the Greyfriars in Dumfries in 1306, by which date Hermitage
had already passed to Nicolas de Soulis, a baron who was
himself replaced as local overlord for taking the side of
Edward I in the Wars of Independence, when the Anglo-
Norman ascendancy in Scotland was broken. Officially de
Soulis died in prison in Dumbarton Castle, but Border

*Hermitage Castle*

legend will have it, and backs up its story with a poem commemorating it, that the wicked seducer of fair maids and extortioner of the poor was abducted by the people themselves and boiled in lead. The fate of the builder of the central tower of Hermitage is not the only grisly tale told about the place, for the next lord was none other than Sir William Douglas, who, though he rejoiced under the twin titles of 'Flower of Chivalry' and 'Fair Knight of Liddesdale', presumably because he was the friend of Bruce, imprisoned a rival for power in the castle and starved him to death, the victim's life being prolonged, it is said, by his pit prison, or dungeon, being near the granary from which trickled minute quantities of grain, so that he gnawed at these miserable crumbs for seventeen days. Still later, Hermitage witnessed one of the more romantic events in the life of Mary, Queen of Scots, when her lover, James Hepburn, Earl of Bothwell, lay wounded there after a scrap with Border reivers. She was at Jedburgh, presiding over the Courts of Justice and granting the burgh a Royal Charter, and staying in the little

Bastel House I mentioned earlier, hence its present naming. The building is really a small castle, L-shaped on plan, with stair turret in the angle, and was thatched but now tiled. From it she rode over to Hermitage, a distance of at least twenty miles, to see Bothwell, and made herself so ill that on her return the same day she was given up for dead. What was actually wrong with her no-one at the time seems to have known, but twentieth-century research suggests she suffered from periodical attacks of what has been called 'Royal Purple'; her urine was tinted and during these attacks she endured great agony; thus she seemed 'close to death'. The same authorities say her father and son were similarly afflicted and that the same unpleasant disease came down to George III, hence his many lucid moments alternating with 'madness'. Whatever the truth of this, when Mary, Queen of Scots went to her execution at Fotheringhay, at the age of forty-four, she was already an old woman in physical terms, prematurely so even for the period in question.

R. W. Billings, in his pioneer volumes on *The Antiquities of Scotland* published in the mid-nineteenth century before the bulk of the baronial reconstruction and rebuilding of Scottish castles took place, frequently alludes to the Scottish penchant for legend, and where legend occasionally gives place to historical fact the association is nearly always with Wallace or Bruce, understandably. That was more than a hundred years ago, today one would say that Mary, Queen of Scots and Bonnie Prince Charlie have probably outstripped those national heroes in popularity, though neither of them was given much of a chance when they were alive. Yet if either Queen Mary or Charles Edward so much as paid a call, far less stayed a night anywhere, or was thought to have done, that house, castle or cottage will by now have acquired a mystical halo of romance that defies credulity. Wallace and Bruce are too distant in time for this sort of thing, too impersonal and sturdy, they were not magnificent failures either; although Sir William Wallace was captured by Edward I and hung, drawn and quartered, he did beat the English beforehand and died proudly and defiantly. The old Bastel House at Jedburgh, built by the Kers with a left-handed staircase, is now named after Mary, Queen of Scots with scores of others all over the country, and her strenuous ride from there to Hermitage Castle and back enshrined in the national memory for ever; while the fact that her great-great-great grandson, Prince Charles Edward, spent a night in another house in the same town is thought of sufficient importance to be recorded for posterity in the official guide.

Liddesdale gives way to Teviotdale beyond Hermitage, and the valley of the Tweed is reached at Kelso. Before this lies the grey factory town of Hawick and a final narrow pass guarded by four souvenirs of a wild and less industrious past. The ancient Scott redoubt of Branxholm styles itself a castle, its place in history assured by being included in *The Lay of the Last Minstrel* as the scene where twenty-nine knights hung up their shields—a bit of a crush if they tried to do it now, as the tower has shrunk in the course of the centuries, having been rebuilt more than once and reduced to a modest manor beside the main road, where its banner can often be seen flying from the topmost turret. Harden, another Scott re-treat, also survives, at the head of a rather secretive glen up

*Branxholm Tower, a Scott seat*

*The Hirsel, Coldstream*

which stolen cattle used to be driven in the bad old days, whenever the mistress of the household laid a stirrup on the table. Opposite Branxholm the nucleus of Fenwick Tower is contained within the walls of a later farmhouse, while above this, on a high spur commanding the entrance to the valley, stands Goldielands, impressive as a silhouette. Teviotdale and Tweeddale taken together might be called the Scottish Dukeries, the respective seats of the Dukes of Buccleuch, Roxburghe and Sutherland being in the area, the first at Bowhill, over the Border in Selkirkshire, the second, Floors, or Fleurs, a Vanbrugh and William Adam castle greatly enlarged and 'Tudorized' by William Playfair, on the outskirts of Kelso, and Mertoun, a Queen Anne house near St Boswells designed by Sir William Bruce and recently restored. There are earls and marquises about here too: Lord Haig, for example, lives at Bemersyde, a seat enshrining a more ancient tower, and Monteviot is the newly reconstituted country home of the Marquis of Lothian. Lord Home, as he is again after a spell as Sir Alec Douglas Home, has his

Border home at Coldstream, the old L-shaped tower of his ancestors being tacked onto one end of the big Georgian and Victorian mansion erected by his more immediate ancestors. It is called 'The Hirsel', which denotes more peaceful proclivities for the Homes than some of them actually displayed, a hirsel being in origin a sheepfold. At least it makes a break from cattle reiving, which would in any case have been a difficult exercise as Coldstream lies right on the Tweed, with England on the other side and no shelter.

Of real castles in the neighbourhood there are few, the largest and most important, Roxburgh, no longer exists. James II of Scots, of 'The Fiery Face', was killed at its siege in 1460, by the exploding of one of his new-fangled cannon. The castle surrendered two days later, when the main aim of its attacker, re-possession of the town of Berwick-upon-Tweed, was posthumously achieved. His son, James III, still only a child, was crowned almost at once in the Abbey at Kelso. Of this huge fortress not one stone remains upon another, only the mound by the Tweed where it once stood, and the name of a county, a minute hamlet and a grand dukedom remaining to remind us of it. In place of castles *per se* there are a number of free-standing Border towers to be seen, notably at Smailholm, which was Sir Walter Scott's favourite as a boy, his grandparents living in the adjacent farm; Darnick, which he coveted so much that he became known to intimates as the 'Duke of Darnick'; and Hume, which is a folly erected on the site of an older edifice. Hume and Smailholm overlook a vast expanse of valley and hill stretching southwards to the Cheviots and having complete oversight of the Eastern and Middle Marches, while Darnick sits prettily down by the river near Melrose. It is inhabited and may be visited. Its date is the second half of the sixteenth century, not very old, having in common with many other Border towers, had to be rebuilt after the English invasions earlier in the same century. It is faced in dark volcanic stone with attractive purply tinges, the quoins and smoother masonry being red. If one cannot entirely believe in the crenellations now marking the battlements, and the surrounding garden scarcely points to any terrible events such as occurred there in 1526, when the laird was killed in a fight between Scotts and Elliots, and the sacking by the Earl of Hertford in 1547 seems a long way away, the tower does breath a little of those ruder days in its crowsteps, shot-holes and sturdy stone-slate roof. Its shape is made more interesting by the projection of a small rectangular stair tower, with cap-house and miniscule doocot in the gable. There is no harling.

Smailholm Tower cannot be so easily dated as Darnick, indeed, as it stands today it is mostly of the seventeenth century, or the eighteenth if the date 1707 mentioned in some records is correct, but it probably stands on much older foundations. The site is extraordinarily barren and deserted and somehow separated from the lush valley of the Tweed below, the farmlands and comfortable towns and villages. No wonder Scott remembered it all his life and returned to it with the painter J. M. W. Turner in the year he died to reminisce. Almost as extraordinary is the rocky, unwelcoming sight of the building itself, uncompromisingly rectangular and bare, roofed but empty, once having four storeys now reduced to the vaulted basement and upper floor, it yet

*Darnick Tower, Melrose*

*Smailholm Tower*

contains a handsome chimneypiece and stone window seats in what was once its hall. Perhaps it is the overall setting, on a bumpy terrace of whin and volcanic outcrops from which the whole countryside can be seen at a glance, and the contrast between this and the nearby "land flowing with milk and honey", that makes Smailholm so appealing and so enthralled Scott. The latter, incidentally, suggested it might have been built in pursuance of James V's pacification of the Borders programme, though there seems some doubt as to whether this was any more successful here than in the south-western parts of the country. A tower must certainly have been in existence in the sixteenth century, but whether it was the present little one cannot be vouchsafed; probably not and it may have been rebuilt by the Scotts of Harden who arrived in the seventeenth century; one of them being the third Earl of Marchmont, who rebuilt Hume Castle in the form of a folly in the eighteenth. More commandingly placed even than Smailholm, this splendid fake castle, slightly further to the east, is an empty shell of tall crenel-

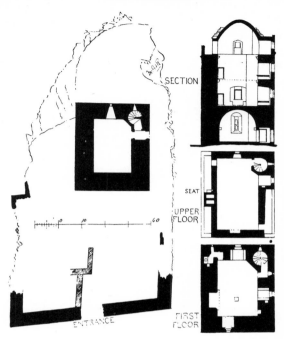

*Smailholm Tower: plans and section*

lated walls erected on the site of an older fortalice that stood there until 1650, when Colonel Fenwick, Cromwellian Governor of Berwick, had it demolished. What the original Hume Castle looked like we do not know, but it would undoubtedly have been provided with some sort of lookout and a firebucket for the lighting of a warning beacon in times of trouble, as was actually done in 1804, when Napoleon's invasion of Britain was falsely heralded.

A more authentic Border tower of defence is at Gordon, a small village between Hume and Smailholm consisting of a few houses at a crossroads, and Greenknowe Tower, as it is called, on account of the grassy mound upon which it stands. It is roofless but hale as to its main walls and complete with iron yett, or grilled gate, at the entrance, which in Scotland took a particularly strong form in that the arrangement of

the iron bars was reversed in each quarter. Greenknowe is
L-shaped, has the remains of bartisans supported on corbels
at the corners, crowstepped gables and an extra large chimney, obviously a firebucket, at one end. It dates from 1581
and belonged in the seventeenth century to the Pringle
family, previous owners of Smailholm. There is also a castle
at Duns, formerly spelt Dunse and still correctly pronounced
as such, but this is another sham, one of Gillespie Graham's
'Gothycke' conceits, much more of one than Ayton and not
Scotch Baronial at all. The site is, as usual, older and the
family who live there are a branch of the Hays, which in the
eighteenth century was strongly Jacobite and provided a
secretary for James Francis Edward, the 'Old Pretender',
who made the holder 'Earl of Inverness'. The result of this
connection could have been seen, until the sale in 1966, in
the form of four presentation portraits by Louis Gabriel
Blanchet of the 'Old Pretender's Queen', Clementina
Sobieska, himself, and his two sons, Charles Edward and
Henry Benedict. These and other items were sold at Christies
when, through the perspicacity of the then Duke of Hamilton, the two Stuart princes were bought on behalf of Her
Majesty the Queen and now hang in Holyroodhouse, of
which Royal Palace the Dukes of Hamilton are hereditary
keepers. Near Duns is Manderston, which is an Edwardian
re-creation of the style of Robert Adam at Kedleston but
which I mention here since its outbuildings represent,
perhaps, the finest group of modern recreative Scots architecture that exists. The architect was John Kinross, who had
previously undertaken the restoration of Falkland Palace, in
Fife, for the third Marquis of Bute, and begun that of
Pluscarden Priory, in Moray, works that influenced in their
turns Sir Robert Lorimer and the late Ian Lindsay and may
be said to have set standards of restoration and understanding of historic buildings that have not since been surpassed. Amongst Kinross's successes at Manderston must be
named the Border tower which today does service as a
folly-dairy and tea-room. It is a perfect recreation of its kind,
enhanced by the addition of steps and ornament taken from
the old Quadrangle of Glasgow University, which was

(left) *Greenknowe Tower, Gordon: detail of entrance with yett.* (right) *Manderston: tea room and dairy*

demolished in the nineteenth century. It is part-harled, but
with the proper mixture.

Between Darnick and Bowhill lies Abbotsford, Scott's
'clarty-hole', where he built a new house intead of buying
Darnick. It does not concern us here except *en passant*, being
less of a castle than a museum of archaeology and historic
mementos. One is bound to say in defence of it, however,
that compared to many of the later effusions that passed for
Scotch baronial Abbotsford is almost dull and certainly
cannot be taken as the inspiration for the numerous Bal-
morals that were erected on our soil in the second half of the
Victorian era. The head of the Scott clan was and is the
Duke of Buccleuch whose principal Scottish seats are
Dalkeith Palace in Midlothian, Drumlanrig Castle in
Dumfriesshire and Bowhill, a Georgian house near Selkirk
with some interesting things inside. In the early eighteenth
century Anne, Duchess of Buccleuch in her own right, and
Duchess of Monmouth after her marriage to the illegitimate
son of Charles II by Lucy Walters, lived at Newark Castle in
the grounds of the present mansion. Following the beheading
of her unfortunate husband for his part in the revolt against
James VII and II in 1685, the Duchess returned to Scotland
bringing north with her many perquisites from Whitehall,
including marble chimneypieces and carved items by
Grinling Gibbon, court stools and her own canopy and chair
of estate. At first she took them to Dalkeith, where she had
a palace built to the designs of James Smith, successor to Sir
William Bruce as Surveyor Royal in Scotland, who encased
the ancient family tower within his new creation, completely
hiding it. Since then, almost everything worth keeping has
been removed either to Drumlanrig or Bowhill, and Dalkeith
stands roofed but empty, despoiled of its contents.

Newark Castle is a maintained ruin, standing on a mound
which must originally have served as the motte of an earlier
structure, possibly a wooden pele house with stockade, but
not necessarily, as in the case it was a royal hunting lodge,
with first the Douglases and then the Scotts of Buccleuch
appointed as captains and keepers of the surrounding Ettrick
Forest. The royal arms appear on the existing castle, a

'newark', or new work of the mid-fifteenth century, when the Douglases, in feud with the king, were replaced by the Scotts as Royal Captains. It was made the scene for the reciting of *The Lay of the Last Minstrel* by the Bard of Abbotsford, and retains, besides the main tower, parts of its outer defences, its *enceinte* or barmkin wall, through a gap in which the drive to Bowhill passes. The castle is very simple in shape, rectangular with end gables and small cap-house. Here in 1645, after the terrible Battle of Philiphaugh, in which a small force of six hundred royalists under Montrose was decimated by six thousand Covenanters under David Leslie, wounded prisoners were massacred in the courtyard, the ministers of the Kirk being able to persuade their general to show no mercy to opponents who did not share the same religion. In all a mere handful of royalists escaped, including Montrose, who had wished to end his life with the others and who, when he knocked at the door of Traquair House for shelter, was turned away by King Charles's former Lord High Treasurer, the first Earl of Traquair, who pretended he was not at home. More than three hundred women and children, stable boys, cooks and other menials were ruthlessly murdered by the victorious Covenanters, besides straggling, exhausted soldiers who were pursued over the moors until everyone had been shot, piked, or axed, or thrown into the river to drown. As a contemporary Scottish historian has remarked, the event makes Cromwell's excesses in Ireland pale by comparison and is not one that any self-respecting Scot would wish to remember, though he must when considering the ultimate revenge which the royalists took on their enemies at the Restoration. The Covenanters richly deserved their fate. They were neither martyrs nor Christians, but blood-thirsty bigots who asked for and gave no quarter.

Traquair is not a castle, though it is based on an old tower which has been added to down the ages and is said to be the oldest continuously inhabited house in Scotland. Like Newark it was a royal hunting lodge, and can rival Abbotsford for souvenirs and memorials of the past, including many of Mary, Queen of Scots and the family that, after the

*Traquair: the Bear Gates*

trimming first Earl had died of penury, begging in the streets
of Edinburgh, distinguished itself by its loyalty to the ill-
fated royal house and to the Roman Catholic faith. The
famous Bear Gates are associated with a legend that after a
visit to Traquair by Bonnie Prince Charlie the laird swore
they would never again be opened until a Stuart sat on the
throne once more. They have certainly not been opened, but
for what reason no one really knows, or even if the Prince
actually did visit the house. In fact, the gates are probably a
folly, old prints showing the area around them as grazing
ground, with no drive, the latter being where it is now, to
one side. Still, they are very handsome gates indeed, amongst
the finest examples of Scottish wrought-ironwork, as almost
everything else about Traquair is unique and wonderful and
deserves to have lasting legends told about it. There is, on the
other hand, one myth that we might just as well dispose of,
especially as the laird himself, Peter Maxwell Stuart, has
disposed of it, and that concerns Montrose's coming to the
door and knocking for sanctuary from the unhelpful, weak-

kneed first Earl. There is a beautiful doorknocker on the door, and it was this that Sir Walter Scott said Montrose knocked by. Unfortunately, that knocker was not made until many years after the event.

A few miles to the west of Traquair, beyond Peebles, and still on the Tweed, is Neidpath, well known both to fishermen, who have it in their view all day, and tourists, who come here in their thousands to visit and photograph one of the most evocative sights in the Borders. It is an old castle, parts probably dating from as early as the late thirteenth century, when it belonged to Sir Simon Fraser of Lovat, who displayed the same coat-changing habits as his notorious descendant in 1745, both chancing their luck once too often and both being executed for it. The first had the honour of having his head placed on a spike next to that of William Wallace on London Bridge, which was unkind to the memory of the latter, who was killed for a crime he did not commit, never having owed any allegiance to Edward I or the English. Bruce changed sides more than once, and would certainly have been condemned to death on a tenable charge had he been captured. It was a tricky business knowing just

*Traquair: ogee-roofed pavilion*

when to make the move and the hero of Bannockburn seems to have been adept at it. Sir Simon Fraser of Lovat, who was not, is interesting though, because he was one of the knights-banneret who took part in *Le Siège de Karlaverock*, having his armorial *fraises*, or strawberries, depicted on the manuscript. His pay was meagre by our standards, four shillings per day, and that of his esquire half that, but at least he was restored to his lands at Neidpath for turning coat on this occasion and later made Keeper of the Royal Demesne at Traquair. Unhappily for him he was subsequently taken prisoner fighting on the Scottish side, and not forgiven this time.

Neidpath has been considerably altered since the days of Sir Simon Fraser, whose daughter and heir married Gilbert de Haya of Yester, yet another of the numerous Hay clan whose origins were Norman and who probably acquired their name from the *haies*, or tall hedges of the Cotentin peninsula where they came from. The Hays remained lairds until the end of the seventeenth century when the first Marquis of Tweeddale sold the castle and lands to the Duke of Queensberry. The fourth duke in that line died a bachelor in his eighties in 1810, having cut down all the woods on his estates and generally ruined the property, when the dukedom went to the Scotts of Buccleuch, and Neidpath to the then Earl of Wemyss and March, who claimed descent in the female line. Neidpath is still a Wemyss property and provides a subsidiary title for the second sons in the family. The bulk of the alterations to the castle were actually undertaken by the first Marquis of Tweeddale after 1650, when Cromwell knocked the building about a bit, removing much of the top storey. The Marquis was a great horticulturalist and planted a fine avenue of yews leading up to the castle, one side of which survived the fourth Duke of Queensberry's axe; it protects the partly walled garden which can still just be made out beyond it, The steps leading from the drive up to the garden are interesting because they are bowtell steps, that is to say, the nosings running along the edge are returned down the sides, a typical seventeenth-century Scotticism, which proves their date and origin. Lord Tweeddale

*Neidpath Castle: view from the Tweed; the entrance*

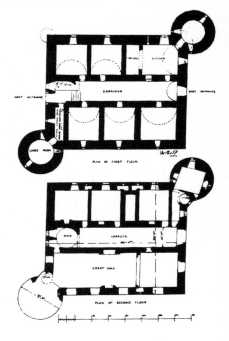

(above) *Neidpath Castle: section*

(right) *Drochil Castle: plans*

was also responsible for the existing half-ruined outbuildings and the amusing Renaissance arched gateway, rusticated with Fraser strawberries, a small bunch of which hang below the keystone under the Hay family crest, a goatshead. It would appear from this that the Tweeddales were quite proud of their Fraser descent and wished to perpetuate it.

Neidpath is still roofed but empty, its upper storey having been restored and raised by the Hays, when the lookouts at the corners were roofed over and the old sentry walk made into a balustraded balcony. There are not many windows but two of them retain their original iron bar protection, which here unusually repeat the form of yetts, that is to say, the pattern of the bars changes diagonally at each quarter. The building has no right angles on plan and although technically L-shaped does not look it, the rounded corners giving it more the appearance of a proverbial 'keep'. Indeed, MacGibbon and Ross remark on its similarities to Drum

Castle, in Aberdeenshire, whose late thirteenth-century tower also has rounded corners. Genuine 'keeps' in the widely accepted sense are few and far between in Scotland, most in ruins and strangely represented by a group of remote and ancient West Highland castles with clear Norman precedents. There are, however, no 'keeps', ruined or otherwise, on the model of, say, Newcastle, or the Tower of London, our Norman castles normally taking either the form of halls attached to an *enceinte*, or wooden redoubts atop a motte, with strong defensive gateways. In other words motte-and-bailey castles. Bothwell, on the Clyde, has a stone 'keep' of sorts, a round one, but it is not in the centre nor does it crown the summit of a mound, being attached to the outer walls and serving as the living quarters of the lord, not the final refuge romantic literature of the nineteenth century would have us believe. Neidpath has two vaulted rooms, the basement and the hall, which is divided by a wooden floor; it is a severe, gaunt building, very tall and forbidding, its walls are in places ten feet thick and it rises warningly upon a rocky eminence high above a particularly picturesque bend in the river. Yet despite its appearance, and apart from the deviations of its first, Fraser, lord, and Cromwell's siege, there is no stirring history connected with it.

The Tweed valley continues westwards and south, having near its extremity Drochil Castle and Broughton Place. The former is an enigmatic ruin beside a farm, half hidden by trees, and thought to have been built by the Regent Morton in the second half of the sixteenth century to retire to once all his murders and treachery were completed, and his pockets well lined. In the event, and deservedly, he was found out and executed for at least one of his known crimes, participation in the murder of Henry, Lord Darnley, and Drochil, whose defences included cleverly contrived, concentrically angled shot-holes that could repel shot arriving as well as facilitate the dispatch of shot from within, was never finished or inhabited by him. The plan is unusual, but has counterparts in far-away Orkney and Shetland, where at Noltland and Scalloway rectangular keep-like buildings have been made Z-shaped by the addition of angle towers, round

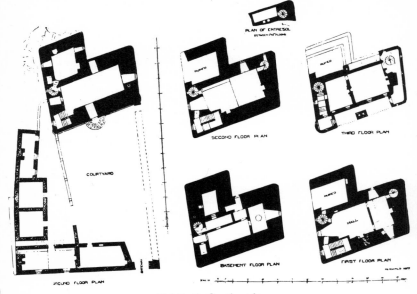

PLAN OF ENTRESOL
BETWEEN FLR FLOORS

SECOND FLOOR PLAN

THIRD FLOOR PLAN

BASEMENT FLOOR PLAN

FIRST FLOOR PLAN

COURTYARD

GROUND FLOOR PLAN

*Neidpath Castle: plans*

and square; at Drochil they are both round. More than this, however: it had a central corridor from which the various rooms could be reached, a refinement familiar to us but almost unheard of then; and this can be seen still in the vaulted central passage that survives at ground level; the upper floors have fallen in. There is some good corbelling with rich detail and a Renaissance armorial panel over the original main entrance with simplified pilasters and a pediment, but lacking the Douglas heart and crown which the boastful Morton had already put up above the royal arms on the portcullis entrance to Edinburgh Castle. This little pedimented and pilastered feature undoubtedly derives from the larger, more grandiose version in Edinburgh, and has another brother at Aberdour Castle, in Fife, ancestral seat of the Earls of Morton.

Broughton Place is not by definition a castle, though it is what is called 'castellated'. In fact it is instructive to notice how the terminology has varied down the ages, depending as much on fashion as anything else. For instance, few today would deny castle status to Glamis, yet in the seventeenth century it was known as Glamis House, and at the wish of its laird, the Earl of Strathmore; while Aldie Castle, in Kinross-shire, has been renamed The House of Aldie since the last war. This is rather against the present trend, which is to call anything with a turret a castle, whether it is entitled to it or not, as seems to have been the case in Jacobean Scotland, a land of *nouveaux riches* and the newly ennobled. Anyway, there Broughton Place stands, a model .tower of defence, white harled and tall, inviting in its fine setting in the rolling countryside of the upper Tweed. It was the home of Lady Elliot, widow of the late Walter Elliot, M.P., but is of more interest here as having been that in the eighteenth century of Sir John Murray, secretary to Prince Charles Edward, and a most unsatisfactory one too. In order to promote his own ends and those of his friends he did not hesitate to denigrate others, including Lord George Murray, whom he managed to put the Prince against; and finally he saved his own skin by betraying even his friends, excusing his behaviour by saying that only one of them was executed as a result. Not a nice person or nice story for so nice a house, 'castellated' yet not a castle, but typical of the home of a bonnet, or minor laird in the seventeenth and eighteenth centuries: converted to comfortable living from what must have been a place of great discomfort; with everyone living on top of each other in small cubicles, with little light or warmth, smelling to high heaven and terrified of being caught off guard by rivals or enemies. No wonder when the chance came they eventually broke out from these multi-storeyed midden-prisons and built projecting crow's-nests or eyries, on top, which was safer, lighter and healthier; finally making additions at ground-floor level, either directly at-tached to the old tower or nearby.

The biggest and most sumptuous of all Border castles worth the name, and ancient in origin, is Thirlestane, seat of the Earls of Lauderdale, and in his day of John Maitland, the one and only duke, the L in the 'cabal' that ruled Britain during the reign of Charles II. No more than a Border tower

*Thirlestane Castle: the main façade*

like the others until the seventeenth century, Thirlestane was transformed by the Duke of Lauderdale and his second wife, Bessie Dysart, reputedly Cromwell's mistress, who saved her future husband from the gallows when he was prisoner at the Battle of Worcester by using her influence with the Lord Protector. It was some twenty years later that she actually married the earl, as he then was, six weeks after the demise of the first Lady Lauderdale; and in the same year the dukedom came from a grateful Charles. Through her new husband, who was the King's 'viceroy' in the North, the Duchess, a rapacious and ruthless woman of immense ambition, controlled the affairs of Scotland, and to some extent those of England, enjoyed the *entrée* to Whitehall and did more or less as she liked. She also changed the Duke's character quite rapidly; he seems to have lost his native common sense and tact and henceforth did as she told him even when he knew it was unwise. Indeed, Bessie was his and her own undoing, but not before they had together made a pretty good showing, and for more than a decade had their way almost without serious opposition. The Duchess was a Bruce on her mother's side, and it was through this connection that William Bruce, the young Scots architect, rose in the world, satisfactorily completing a commission for his cousin at Ham, near Richmond, to be rewarded with the task of reconstructing and enlarging Thirlestane, and after that the Palace of Holyroodhouse itself. It is not perhaps true that Bruce became a baronet and Architect Royal entirely through the efforts of the Lauderdales to promote his career, as he himself had played an important part in furthering the restoration of the monarchy, acting as intermediary between Monk, Governor of Scotland under the Commonwealth, and the King in exile, in Holland; and it was on these trips to the Continent that he first became acquainted with Renaissance architecture, an acquaintance he used to tremendous effect at home, in the end creating for himself the finest Palladian mansion north of the Border, and one of the most civilized and perfect Renaissance buildings in Britain, Kinross House.

At Thirlestane the King's architect and surveyor had a particularly difficult task, one not made easier by the pedantry and frequent changes ordered by his patron and patroness, the correspondence, which survives *in toto*, being little short of voluminous and covering more than three years. Every minute detail was examined and approved, or not, by Lauderdale and his spouse, and Bruce found himself already at work at Holyrood before Thirlestane was finished. In fact, he himself was busy on his own account at Balcaskie, in Fife, and elsewhere. Sir William Bruce was that rare person amongst Renaissance and Palladian architects who did not despise the architecture of the past, nor native traditions in building and decoration. Instead of pulling down an old, shabby, unfashionable and certainly uncomfortable castle, as here, he retained the shell of it, made a repeat to produce symmetry and linked the old and the new by a simple but remarkably successful expedient, namely by making two balustraded balconies, one immediately above the new, central front door, another much higher up near the eaves level, and bringing the whole thing together under a generously proportioned central tower crowned with a

*Thirlestane Castle: seventeenth-century print by John Slezer*

magnificent ogee roof. This is the first example in Scotland of recreative Scotch Baronial as opposed to the original variety and so inspired Sir David Bryce when he came to Thirlestane to make additions in the nineteenth century that he not only tampered with the building much less than might otherwise have been the case, but repeated Bruce's ideas when he re-baronialized Blair for the Duke of Atholl. Bryce threw out oriels from Bruce's side pavilions, put slim astragals in the windows and made much more pointed roofs to the turrets than had pertained before, but otherwise the castle remains recognizable for the one drawn by John Slezer in the second half of the seventeenth century, when Bruce redesigned the old Border seat.

John Slezer was an artillery captain who used his time whilst stationed in the North to make sketches of the principal castles and seats, churches and towns in Scotland, dedicating them to the appropriate noble lord, magnate or provost, presumably in the hopes of selling copies of them either separately or in a book he was preparing. Some of the plates are incorrectly labelled, Dunnottar, for instance, is really Wemyss Castle, in Fife; Inveraro (Inveraray) is really Castle Gordon in Moray; Glammis House (Glamis Castle) he depicts before the Earl of Strathmore recast it; and in the case of Thirlestane he produced two views, one labelled correctly the other as 'Lauder Castle', This is understandable, and interesting because it shows a side elevation with all those peculiar little towers at the back which Bruce tried to tidy up and make acceptable in the age of symmetry by linking with a continuous balcony at parapet level on the model of the grander arrangement on the front. It is difficult to see from Slezer's drawing or a modern photograph exactly what the architect did, how much is the original Border seat of the Maitlands, how much late additions and how much his own clever covering up. The plan would seem to have been a rectangle with round towers at the corners, and Bruce was intending to repeat and modify these to make a cohesive whole. In the event the Lauderdales ran out of money, or were unable to divert as much from public funds as they wished, and what we see today came into being instead. The central tower with the ogee roof was not in the first scheme, but is a *tour de force* nevertheless; and it is perhaps worth adding that Thirlestane, Bruce's masterpiece in recreative Scotch Baronial, only just survived being completely altered and turned into one of Robert Adam's 'Italian' castles

*Thirlestane Castle: the south side*

towards the end of the eighteenth century. This was a fate it did not deserve and fortunately escaped, for Adam, genius though he was, or possibly because he was, had little regard for the Scottish past, quite unlike Bruce, or Bryce, who could be fairly ruthless on occasion but did respect the work of the first and in some ways the greatest Scottish architect.

Many of the craftsman employed by Bruce at Thirlestane were sent up from England by the Lauderdales, who were at the same time embellishing Ham House, and these included 'Germanes' who did much of the elaborate joinerwork in the castle, giving the interior a quaintly central European look. Others who came at the time were George Dunsterfield and John Halbert, Charles II's favourite plasterers, or rather 'Gentlemen Modellers', to give them their proper designation. They played a significant part in the spread of the art of plasterwork in Scotland in the seventeenth century, following the earlier excursions north of the Border of English Jacobean plasterers; and this being so it is odd how a number of Scottish art historians have claimed that most of our finest plasterwork was either by Italians, if too good to be locally done, or by native Scots apprentices, and ignore English influence. Chauvinism can go no further, especially since the names of these two experts, and indeed of Joseph Fenton in the earlier period, are well known and documented. So far as Dunsterfield and Halbert are concerned the actual bills of payment are extant, with details of where they worked and how. They were responsible for the ceilings in the State Apartments at Windsor Castle, got ready for the arrival of Catherine of Braganza, and went on to Thirlestane, whence they repaired to the State Apartments in Holyroodhouse. Bruce subsequently employed them on his own account at Balcaskie and Kinross, and there can be little doubt that they, with their assistants, walked across the fields to neighbouring Kellie Castle to assist in the making of one of the finest plaster ceilings of the period outside Holyrood, the celebrated Vine Room at Kellie, of which more anon.

Charles II's gentlemen modellers were masters of their art, very superior beings who were allowed to wear their swords at work, though one imagines they took them off whilst actually busy on a commission. The method was uncomfortable and intuitive, the modellers having to lie on their backs, like Michelangelo, on boards, and work hard and quickly, calling for the various tobacco leaves, roses and thistles, crowns, pea-pods, hops and vines as they were needed and apply them at once to an already laid out ground. Assistants stood by with buckets of flowers and leaves to add to the pattern as the modellers felt the urge or a gap had to be filled, they using twigs or pieces of lead or iron, anything that was available, to place and fix the still half-wet items, even to re-shape them where necessary. This explains why in different ceilings the same items appear in slightly varied forms and positions, and how the Vine Room at Kellie, for example, is not quite the same as a similar but less imaginatively conceived room at Fyvie, in Aberdeenshire, which also has a vine and hop pattern. This was probably as far north as the plasterers went, and the Fyvie 'Vine Room' may have been done by gifted assistants and not the 'masters' themselves. At Thirlestane and Balcaskie the effects are more daring and spectacular than elsewhere, particularly at the latter where such items as a bunch of grapes seem literally to hang suspended from the centre of a plaster ring of fruit and vegetables, having been 'thrown' there, as the term goes. At both Balcaskie and Kellie the Dutch painter de Wet, likewise employed at Holyrood with the King's plasterers, was responsible for inset panels in the ceiling, but not, curiously enough, at Thirlestane, where the ballroom is the *pièce de résistance,* rich and vulgar and in keeping with the tastes of wealthy, newly 'arrived' patrons. The Lauderdale eagle is well represented at each corner by remarkably realistic birds, wings outstretched and in extraordinarily deep relief. One cannot help admiring the skill of the modellers here, and if the result is a little overpowering, it is certainly ingenious; and the elaborate plasterwork less ostentatious looking than it must originally have appeared when all picked out in colour.

Besides Thirlestane Sir William Bruce was engaged by the Lauderdales on other of their properties in Scotland, notably Brunstane House, near Edinburgh, a 'villa' by the sea, where

he did on a small scale what he and already done at
Thirlestane, Holyrood and Balcaskie, namely, repeated
existing features and joined them with a central entrance,
creating in this case a double 'L' out of a modest laird's
tower of traditional form. Brunstane is really out of this
chapter, but it is interesting as having the first sash windows
ever hung in Scotland, the work of joiners from Thirlestane
and Ham. Lennoxlove, the older Lauderdale seat Bruce was
asked to modernize, is also not a Border house, but in East
Lothian, near Haddington, and the King's architect did very
little there. It was so named after Frances Stewart, the lady
who ran away from 'The Merry Monarch' and married the
Duke of Richmond and Lennox; but in Lauderdales's day it
was still called Lethington, being the principal seat of the
Maitlands and the erstwhile home of Mary, Queen of Scots'
Secretary and Ambassador to England, William Maitland of
Lethington. There it remains, north of the Lammermuirs yet
in essence a Border tower, with unindented battlements,
sentry walk and bartisans, cap-house, iron yett and vaulted
lower rooms. The newer portions dating mostly from the
eighteenth and nineteenth centuries. I shall have more to say
about Lennoxlove later; suffice to say here that so much
money was spent on other ploys by the Duke of Lauderdale
that Bruce was ordered to hold his hand there, and all we
can trace to him are some modest outhouses at the foot of the
tower. I mention it specifically, however, because it has a
strong family resemblance to the one John Kinross designed
as the dairy and tea room at Manderston, which, as already
hinted, is almost nearer to an orvinal Border redoubt than
many genuine old ones that have been irretrievably altered
down the ages.

# II

# *The Lothians, Edinburgh and Fife*

THE ROAD over the Lammermuirs runs north from Lauder
via Soutra and used rarely to be crossed by travellers
between November and April, indeed, one has friends in the
Borders who still follow this rule. Another world lies on the
other side, the broad champaign of the Lothians and the gap
through the middle of Scotland broken only by the Pentland,
formerly Pictland, Hills; a volcanic range with a silhouette
curiously reminiscent of the Malverns, looking quite mountainous but not reaching two thousand feet. Where the
Lammermuirs sweep down and round to the coast, effectively cutting off the Borders from the Lothians, are a
number of small tower houses and two splendid and famous
castles, recalling that even here, many miles from England
and the 'auld enemy', raids were not unknown. The actual
boundary between Berwickshire and Midlothian occurs at
the top of the pass, whence a wide panorama northwards
reveals much of central Scotland, as far as the Highlands in
the west, and across the Firth of Forth to Fife in the east.
Unseen, but lurking in a fold of the hills just below one is
Cakemuir Castle, really a border tower transplanted, lying
hidden from the main routes along a side road, under the
bield of the bare moors yet itself set in a sheltered vale,
peaceful and almost deserted. When I went to take photographs I felt as if I was back in New Zealand, in a world of
animals and open fields, no hedges, few trees and widely
dispersed farms. Of course Cakemuir is not a wooden bungalow with a corrugated iron roof, but the feel was there, it
alone being tree shrouded and long settled.

In origin Cakemuir Castle was probably a fortified hospice
for pilgrims going to Melrose and the other Border abbeys

*Cakemuir Castle: the old tower*

*Borthwick Castle*

from Edinburgh and the north of the country, hence its strategically snug position. Hence too its remarkable similarities with an ancient Border tower. Today the old fortalice-cum-retreat has been added to and is not the principal part of the house, which means that it has retained many of its more interesting features and especially two sentry walks on the battlements and two covered sentry boxes. I know of only one other such survival, at Elcho, near Perth. The day I went to Cakemuir happened to be the anniversary of the flight there of Mary, Queen of Scots on 11th June 1567, on her way to rejoin Bothwell at Dunbar. I had no idea of this at the time until I noticed a panel with an armorial device and the information upon it in the building. She may have spent a night at Cakemuir, perhaps not even that, only a brief halt to take breath, for she and her seducer were making their separate ways from nearby Borthwick in order to avoid detection, she dressed as a man. Another stop was made at Hailes, to the east of Haddington, where they met up again for a while before heading for the coast. Their flight to Borthwick and beyond is one of the only two historic events of note associated with that enormous and celebrated castle. The other was when Cromwell sent a polite note to its owner, a noted royalist, asking him to vacate, or else! Lord Borthwick paid no attention, so Oliver brought up his guns and knocked off a piece of parapet, causing the laird to change his mind and depart before any more damage could be done. That small run of parapet is the only scathe Borthwick Castle has suffered since its building in 1430, apart, that is, from some slight decay in the outer defence walls, or *enceinte*, with which it was later surrounded. One knows it was later because the pill-box edifice by the entrance, with its twelve-foot thick walls protecting an eleven-foot across interior, could have no other purpose than defence against and with guns, and gunpowder was not in use until the second half of the fifteenth century.

The main castle has neither gun-loops nor shot-holes, nor any provision for defence against cannon, but is a tall, double L-shaped tower, strong and fierce, immaculate and quite unlike anything else in Britain. Being wholly medieval

*Borthwick Castle:* (right) *plan of first floor:* (below) *plan of basement and* enceinte

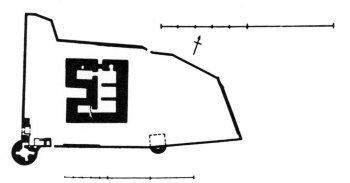

it lacks those amusing and often purely decorative touches that are such a feature of many Scottish castles and which find their apotheosis in Craigievar, which is, however, only a castle in imagination, dressed like a warrior in fancy armour long after the days when knights were bold. Craigievar does share with Borthwick itself the apotheosis of the pre-gunfire age, a concentration on height, Borthwick reaching one hundred feet from the ground; but what a difference in other respects. The beautiful smooth ashlar has no counterpart, nor the immaculateness of its sparsely fenestrated walls, its complete lack of turrets or elaborate corbelling, only the handsome machicolations supporting uncrenellated battlements break the plainness of its outline. There is a slight projection at the corners to provide low, rounded bartisans, and the roof is composed of stone slabs. The entire castle is of stone, floors, ceilings, roof and walls, and would seem almost indestructible. Why such a building was ever erected here, so near Edinburgh and by a comparatively minor knight, Sir William Borthwick, cup-bearer to the Earl of Rosslyn, remains one of the mysteries of life, the chance by which we acquired this splendid and unique specimen of late-medieval architecture, standing unharmed, or virtually so, inspiring rather than grim, beside a tumbling burn in the pleasant Midlothian countryside. Sir Walter Scott said it made him feel old looking at it, he being changed between visits, Borthwick unchanging. The castle has been lightly restored, just enough to make it habitable in summer, and then not for long, its walls are nearly fifteen feet thick and not much sunlight penetrates the narrow windows to make the huge vaulted chambers warm; but to be habitable at all after more than five hundred years, and no appreciable improvements in comfort, is remarkable enough.

Scott's own favourite castle in the neighbourhood was actually Crichton, which rises much more gauntly and grimly than Borthwick, though it is not tall and not menacing so much as sinister. This may or may not result from the characters of its builder or its last occupant, the first being Chancellor Crichton, who engineered the so-called 'Black Dinner' in Edinburgh Castle, when the Earl of Douglas and his brother, invited to keep the young James II company, were murdered, the second being Francis Stewart, Earl Bothwell, 'natural' grandson of James V and a constant thorn in the side of James VI, who was plagued by royal bastards and their descendants, not to mention activist members of his father's family, the Lennoxes. Francis Stewart was a wizard and on one occasion chased the king round Holyrood in his nightshirt, until, overcome by the exercise and James's cringing attitude, he craved forgiveness and ran away. On another occasion he was caught sticking pins into an effigy of King James, and for this and other annoyances he was banished. He lived in Italy for many years improving his 'art', and returned to Crichton to embellish the courtyard of the castle in imitation of the Palazzo dei Diamante in Ferrara, so that a quaintly exotic atmosphere pertains there to this day, the whole of one side being decorated with diamond-cut masonry. The same arcaded wall, incidentally, bears the cypher and anchor device of his predecessor in command, Queen Mary's lover, who was Lord High Admiral of Scotland. Crichton is a ruin, and has been for centuries, but it is worth visiting for its 'Italian' courtyard if nothing else, for its curiously deserted site and the fortified kirk which Chancellor William Crichton built nearby.

Crichton has an extraordinary remoteness belied by the facts of geography, which shows how well they chose the site for a castle in the old days, to be seen but not until one was near enough to be apprehended. It stands almost at the head of the Scottish River Tyne, which flows eastwards through Haddington to the sea between North Berwick and Dunbar. The landscape becomes increasingly green and attractive, and castles tend to be replaced by Jacobean or Caroline manor houses, or fake fortalices and much restored towers. Close to Crichton itself is the house of the same name, a whitewashed L-shaped building, with a polygonal stair tower in the entrant angle and not a single defensive or martial feature. Then a mere mile or two beyond, at Pathhead, are no less than two castles and a large country mansion of southern English proportions, replete with walled garden, informal plantings, folly and aristocratic lodge-gates. The castles are Ford, which contains the nucleus of a small tower much enlarged and added to in the Edwardian era, and Oxenfoord, which is an Adam 'Italian' castle completed by Tudorist William Burn, the adjacent styles demonstrating most forcibly the difference between Gothic Revival, in which Burns was a practitioner, and Robert Adam's adaptation of Italian military architecture for the Caledonian scene. I might say something more about that difference here, as although Culzean, Adam's largest example, is far away in Ayrshire, and Airthrey, his next, is in Stirlingshire, Seton, his masterpiece in the *genre,* is here on the coast near Edinburgh.

A reviewer of my *Scotland's Historic Buildings* made the comment that Robert Adam's castles are "by no means all in Scotland", and it is true that his name has been associated with two in Northumberland: Ford, where, however, any work he may have done was covered up by Sir William

Playfair in the nineteenth century, and Alnwick, where Adam was certainly responsible for a face-lift undertaken for the first Duke of Northumberland. In that case too a subsequent restoration removed practically everything he had done, except the odd 'gothycke' chimneypiece. More pertinent still is the fact that whatever he did do out of Scotland was in the Gothic Revival style, which is entirely another thing from his 'Italian' castellated. One has only to look at the fenestration of any revivalist gothic castle: Inveraray, for example, which was designed some thirty years before Culzean and is wholly gothic in its windows; but you will not see a single gothic window, revivalist or otherwise, at Culzean, Airthrey or Seton, or in the Adam part of Oxenfoord, all is 'Italian' and Renaissance, the only concession being in the battlements, uncrenellated at Airthrey and Seton, and the occasional mock arrow-slit. In other words, far from heralding the Gothic Revival these buildings mark the end of the Renaissance; and it is in this respect, and the fact that they needed a Caledonian background for their transplantation from the Roman *Campagna,* that their particular qualities derive.

Oxenfoord is now a girls' school but is open once a year under Scotland's Gardens Scheme. Seton I will come to in a moment. Meantime one must follow the Scottish Tyne through a region which is sometimes called 'The Garden of Scotland', a title which is also claimed, with at least as much justification, for the Laich o'Moray, the lowland area around Elgin. Still, East Lothian is a desirable part of the world where, although folk have seen the passage of armies down the centuries, war has not been taken too seriously and what castles there are are mostly hoary ruins of the days of the Normans, and were already ruined before the great castle-building period of the sixteenth and seventeenth centuries. In this fruitful countryside are some of Scotland's most delightful small laird's residences, the majority dating from the post-Jacobean era, but they are not our special concern here, their relationship to any castle is purely circumstantial, scarcely architectural. One, Fountainhall, may be considered partly defensive though it lacks shot-holes, battlements or

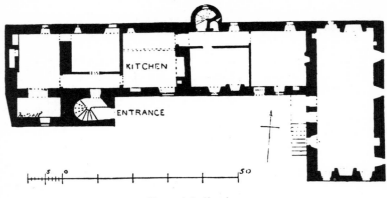

*Fountainhall: plan*

bartisans, and relies for safety on a few iron bars on the
downstairs windows, a front door protected by being in the
angle of a short projection, and thick walls. Fountainhall is
more in the manner of, say, Traquair: an old house that has
grown in successive stages to become rambling and
pleasantly worn: by this I mean displaying its undoubted age
in a wonderful patina of half-stone, half-mortar and part
creeper that is unusual in Scotland, causing one of our
better-known architectural historians to compare it to a
Cotswold manor. It is not, of course: the reference is purely
atmospheric; Fountainhall's corbelled stair turret could be
nowhere else but here; its sundial attached to the corner of
the house and its twin lean-to, doocots, one fake, the other
functional, for symmetry, are all in the Scottish vernacular
manner. It was the home of Lord Fountainhall in the second
half of the seventeeth century, a legal luminary whose
professional utterances and comments on contemporary
events were freely made and have been written down for
posterity. He is said to have administered rough justice for
minor felonies in the hall of the last addition to the house,
felonies which in more ancient times might have fallen
within the right of 'pit and gallows', granted by the king to
certain nobles in the Middle Ages under the title of *Fossa et
Furca*, which provided for the drowning of women miscreants
in the moat and the hanging of men on a fork-like gibbet. It

*Fountainhall: entrance,
seventeenth-century wing*

is a lovely Caroline addition this, almost separated from the main building, with a pend· through to the formal garden, and ballroom upstairs in the roof, which is lit by dormer windows, each decorated with the crests and monograms of the builders. This wing has close affinities with the home of another judge, Lord Magdalens, erected in Prestonpans in place of his ancestral 'skyscraper' in the same village; but 'Magdalens' is entirely a 'town-house'.

Haddington is the county town of East Lothian and of the former county of the same name, and it would be odd if it had no great house or castle at its gates. The one that most interests us here is Lennoxlove, the original building of which was and still is L-shaped, with plain battlements, sentry-walk and cap-house, and probably dates in its lower portions from the mid-fourteenth century when the Maitlands of Thirlestane first came here. It has been considerably altered and added to in the course of time, and notably in the nineteenth century when a credible essay in recreative medievalism, not dissimilar from the old tower of Affleck, in Angus, replaced the crow-steps and simpler forms of the existing southern end of the house. Lennoxlove was named by 'La Belle Stewart', the pretty lady who ran away from Charles II and married the Duke of Richmond and Lennox. She was the model for Britannia on the first pennies, and said she would only accede to the king's wishes if he married her. So infatuated does the 'Merry Monarch' seem to have been that for a time he did entertain the idea of divorcing the barren Catherine of Braganza. He gave Frances Stewart a magnificent silver-mounted toilet service of French manufacture which went to Lennoxlove and having been lost, or forgotten for about three centuries, suddenly re-appeared in an attic and is now in the Royal Scottish Museum in Edinburgh.

Lethington was the former name of this old Haddingtonshire redoubt, which enters general history in the reign of Mary, Queen of Scots, when it was the country seat of her Secretary of State and devoted follower, William Maitland of Lethington, who only escaped execution himself by dying in captivity shortly before the day appointed. The notorious Duke of Lauderdale was a slightly later successor who did

*Lennoxlove, tower of the Maitlands of Lethington*

little more at Lethington than keep it weather- and water-tight, and make it adequate for the occasional visit of his Duchess, though he and she had to make improvements when the king's brother, James, Duke of Albany and York, and his consort, Mary of Modena, arrived in 1679. It was then that the emparkment of the property is said to have taken place, after a taunt by the king's royal viceroy that few estates in Scotland seemed to have a park wall. In fact the wall was built five years before all this, as the documents aver, and at the same time as the house was being modernized according to seventeenth-century standards. The Lauderdales had no male heir, and Lethington eventually came to Lord Blantyre, largely through the munificence of 'La Belle Stewart', a relative, who sent him the money for the purchase of the property with the proviso that it should be called 'Lennoxlove', which it has remained ever since.

Lord Blantyre's ultimate descendants, the Bairds, sold Lennoxlove in 1947 to the Duke of Hamilton, whose seat it is, the contents now somewhat outstripping the building in interest, for the splendid furniture and pictures from the Hamilton Collection are here, in a more modest and restricted setting than they enjoyed previously. Sir Robert Lorimer did some restoration work at Lennoxlove including the clearing out of the old Great Hall, revealing its stone vaulting and two holes therein which acted as flues for a central fire. The dungeons survive and may be visited, also guardchambers, and there are two iron yetts, even the death-mask of Mary, Queen of Scots, to see. In the newer part of the building is the patent granted to the eleventh Duke of Hamilton by Napoleon III creating him Duc de Châtelherault and giving him and his family precedence next to that of the Bonapartes at Court. The Emperor did this because the Duchess was his second cousin and a former 'flame'. *Burke's Peerage* uses the phrase "claims the Dukedom of Châtelherault" in respect of the Duke of Hamilton, and rightly, as the Duke of Abercorn is the actual holder of the title, his ancestor having been the Earl of Arran, who received it from Henry II of France in order to obtain his approval of the marriage of Mary, Queen of Scots to the

Dauphin; and his nineteenth-century descendant had the title upheld in the appropriate court. Two cabinets owned by Frances Stewart are on view at Lennoxlove, also a double portrait of the Earl, as he then was, of Lauderdale, and the second Duke of Hamilton, painted during the Civil War. Prophetic, perhaps, that this should come here three hundred years after it was painted, and Lauderdale should have escaped the gallows through the friendship of his future Duchesss with Cromwell, while the second Duke of Hamilton died of wounds received at Worcester the same battle in which Lauderdale was taken prisoner.

From Lennoxlove to Hailes is but a short run, but whereas the former sits proudly amidst woods, well preserved and homely, the latter lies broken and 'tummeldoun' beside the Tyne, bereft of life and shelter, a sorry sight from what it must have been when Mary, Queen of Scots came here to rejoin her third husband, or even until Cromwell's guns reduced it to its present shambles. It is difficult to imagine the old place as a comfortable manor house, with gardens by the river and happy secluded life, for it is right at the bottom of the valley, overlooked by neighbouring hills, which proves it was never meant for offensive purposes. Today the Department of the Environment maintains the castle with its usual care, every remaining fragment pointed and repaired in exactly the way Ruskin deplored, with "green shaven lawn, and our piece of ruin emergent from it, a mere *specimen* of the Middle Ages put on a bit of velvet carpet, to be shown, and which, but for its size might as well be on a museum shelf at once, under cover". This was written before the setting up of government agencies such as the one that now takes responsibility for our major ruins, in the days when it was still fashionable to have a ruin in the garden, on the lawn, as an ornament. The author of *Frondes Agrestes* would probably have disliked Dunbar Castle less, for what scanty ruins that survive of that are so indistinguishable from their surroundings, the rocks and harbour pier they once protected, that no-one could call them a sham, or ornament, or even say they were 'on show'. They were not thrown down by Cromwell, like Hailes and other buildings in southern

Scotland, but by the confederate lords after they had defeated Queen Mary at Carberry Hill, imprisoned her in Loch Leven Castle, and Bothwell had fled to Denmark, where he died in obscurity.

More impressive, by its extent and size rather than in wholeness, is the great rugged mass of Tantallon, which is ministerially maintained, enormous and unmistakable for man-made masonry, yet worn enough by the sea and cannon fire almost to rival the works of nature, certainly not to be subservient to them or ornamental. At a distance cliffs and curtain wall merge with Turneresque effect, and it is not so much a castle we behold as an impressionist dream. Both James IV and James V attacked this Douglas stronghold in force, and both failed either to capture or reduce it, and again it took the superior guns of the Lord Protector to finish the job, plus the skilled pen of Sir Walter Scott to immortalize what was left in *Marmion.* Slightly inland is another massive ruin, lacking the grandeur of Tantallon and its romantic glamour. I refer to Dirleton, in one of Scotland's prettiest villages. I use the word pretty and not bonny, which is more common in the North, because Dirleton is a rare English-feeling place, having been created for the most part by the local Sir Roger de Coverley, and its ruined castle is very much emergent from the lawn, plump in the middle of the village. It was built originally for the Norman family of De Vaux, part of whose huge round tower, linked to smaller ones in what has been described as 'a clustered keep', still dominates the scene. All around is a newer park wall and extremely beautiful garden, which turns the whole thing into an immense folly. Ruskin really would have had a fit here, the very wording of the Ancient Monuments guide would have turned him purple with fury, "The stronghold of the De Vaux stands amidst a lovely flower garden in the heart of the charming hamlet of Dirleton, the most English of Scottish villages". It would be interesting to know who wrote this particular piece as it seems more effusive than most in official publications, and dwells rather less on archaeology than some: but it does make one squirm a little, even if the garden is nice and there is a seventeenth-century bowling green.

The Earls of Wemyss and March are now but were not always the principal lairds in the neighbourhood, indeed they are comparative new-comers when one thinks of the De Vaux, and later of the Setons, who rose to fame under the Stewarts, and especially James VI and Charles I, one becoming Earl of Winton, the other Earl of Dunfermline and Chancellor of the kingdom. Lord Winton built a brand new house for himself in the English style in the second decade of the seventeenth century at Pencaitland. It is replete with jolly, twisted chimney stalks, buckle-quoins and strapwork decoration, elaborate Renaissance details on the dormers and balustrading, and within some sumptuous plaster ceilings. There are no battlements, of course, but several gay, ogee-roofed towers and features borrowed both directly from the South and from the work done for the king at Edinburgh castle in 1617 by the Royal master mason, William Wallace. Indeed Wallace himself is known to have had a hand in the building of Winton. Later, when Charles I decided to tempt fate and come north for his coronation in 1633, a 'King's Room' was prepared at Winton with a magnificent new ceiling displaying the royal coat of arms, the king's cypher, national emblems and the Seton crescent. It is of a higher quality than what went before and includes a quite sophisticated Florentine frieze that has nothing to do with national or local events, but shows the greater standard of taste that pertained then and makes one sad that the arts, which had begun to display a remarkable growth, should have lost their native ethos and become more southern based, as in this case, or Palladian and international after the Restoration.

On the western side of Edinburgh one can see another ceiling in another 'King's Room' obviously by the same hand, or certainly with some of the same moulds, at the House of the Binns. This was and is the home of the Dalyell family, and was partly the creation of one who spent his youth at the Court of James VI and I in London and returned determined to emulate the new fashions, and of a later Dalyell who employed William Burn to tudorize the exterior. The ceilings from the earlier period survive, plus the memory of the great Tam Dalyell, who grew a long white

beard which remained uncut after the execution of King
Charles I as a mark of respect for that martyred monarch.
During the Commonwealth Tam travelled extensively on the
Continent, reaching Russia, where he served the Tzar and
whence he returned home at the Restoration to found what
has become the Royal Scots Greys, the 'grey' referring to
the white winter headgear copied from that worn in Russia.
Tam Dalyell is one of those legendary figures whom the
Covenanters, unwilling to admit as superior (except in so far
as the Devil, never the Almighty, made them), learned to
hate, since he cleaned them up militarily. His boots and
other belongings can still be seen at The Binns, not to
mention a muckle great lump of volcanic rock which the
Infernal one is said to have hurled at him when he beat him
at cards!

Neither The Binns nor Winton House can be described as
castles; they are English buildings to all intents and purposes, but their ceilings had many imitations and repeats
elsewhere in Scotland, not least at Pinkie House, the home of
Chancellor Alexander Seton. The plasterers who operated in
Scotland in Jacobean and Caroline times were the
forerunners of Dunsterfield and Halbert, and were responsible for the Great Hall at Glamis, the drawing-room at
Muchalls, in Kincardineshire, and, perhaps their masterpiece
in little, the dining-room at Craigievar. The moulds undoubtedly reached Aberdeenshire and were used by local
apprentices as well as their itinerant 'masters'. Seton Castle
probably also once possessed plaster ceilings of the period,
but the building is now no more, having been replaced in the
late eighteenth century by Robert Adam's 'Italian' fort-
mansion, which may also have been influenced by his and
his father's work at Fort George, near Inverness, so plain and
monumentally military is it. The castle is privately owned
and cannot be seen except at a distance, or side-ways on by
visitors to the handsome sixteenth-century collegiate kirk in
the grounds. This was the burial place of the Setons and is
now in the care of Ancient Monuments; it is noteworthy for
its broach spire, a curiously early sign of anglicization which
pre-dated the Reformation. There are no crenellations or

*Seton Castle: detail of
entrance; general view*

other gothic features at Seton, which is only medieval in its massing, and symmetrical in a way Robert Adam alone could have achieved without appearing to force the issue. The fenestration is entirely in the usual elegant 'Adam' manner, without a trace of a pointed arch, just one or two bold arrow slits to punctuate the side towers, and the somewhat surprising introduction of a gable end with crowsteps at the centre. The entrance is reached through an outer wall and archway simulating the idea of medieval defences but without using medieval detail.

Alexander Seton, Chancellor to James VI and a courtier in London after the Union of the Crowns in 1603, was the most gifted of his house in learning and cultural pursuits, and his first superb gesture in the architectural field was the creation of a newer and grander Fyvie, in Aberdeenshire, which I shall describe in its proper place. Suffice it to say here that there one will find more notable plaster ceilings and a work in which the builder presaged that of Sir William Bruce in providing symmetry by the simple expedient of repeating existing features, and, as was done at Thirlestane, linking them by a high level arch and central turret. Lord Dunfermline's seat at Pinkie, near Edinburgh, was a simple L-shaped tower with rounded corner turrets on the main structure and rectangular ones on the projecting arm, which the Earl enlarged by a whole new wing, intending to enclose the building within a courtyard. He is thought to have had Hatfield in mind, having been in the company of the Cecils whilst in the South, but if so only a suggestion of what was intended was accomplished. The handsome Jacobean fountain in what would have been the centre of the courtyard is certainly English inspired, also the superb painted Long Gallery. The latter is devoted to classical subjects and colourfully painted in tempera, the present writer having had a small hand in its being left exposed, and where it is, when the house was adapted as part of Loretto boys' school and the Long Gallery proposed as a dormitory. The then headmaster seemed to think that pink-bodied cherubs and naked wenches on the ceiling might disturb his pupils, and wanted them either removed or covered up. Fortunately the

*Pinkie House, Musselburgh*

forces of cultural preservation were alerted in time, the situation saved, and the beautiful ceiling remains intact *in situ*.

There is a 'King's Room' at Pinkie, gay with much the same plasterwork as at Winton and elsewhere, in which Charles I almost certainly slept; and the building stands not far from the site of the Battle of Pinkieheugh in which the Scots were badly mangled by the Earl of Hertford as part of Henry VIII's 'rough wooing' policy. He wanted a union between the child Queen, Marie Stewart, and his ailing weakling of a son, Edward VI, but went about it the wrong way, throwing the Scots further into the arms of France, when a marriage was arranged between their Queen and the Dauphin François de Valois. The latter was weak and ailing as it happened and a Roman Catholic, which meant the protraction of the war with England and the outbreak of fratricidal strife in Scotland between the different religious factions. Douglas Simpson in his booklet, *Scottish Castles*, published by the Stationery Office, blames this, and the 'blight of Calvinism', for the demise of the Scottish style of building, just at a time when its chief flowering was in progress. I wonder, however, if that is the whole story. It is true Calvinism put a stop to free appreciation of the arts and imposed on a naturally demonstrative people curbs that made them into dull, dour folk whose forms of expression became ingoing rather than out, a fact revealed when Scots find themselves living abroad and suddenly liberated from their traditional restraints. These restraints were only traditional in the sense that from about 1560 onwards it was forbidden for Scottish bairns to play at Robin Hood, for girls and boys to walk together under the trees in summer, for there to be decent music in the kirk; and most refinements were counted sinful by a sect that wished to subdue the Scottish temperament, which is neither dull nor dour, but extrovert and impulsive, the very opposite of what we have been told. Indeed, at the very moment of writing, the truth of this is being demonstrated in every possible way, the old restraints having disappeared everywhere except in the remotest outposts, where a rearguard action is being fought under the guise of protecting us from pollution by oil, to preserve outmoded habits and attitudes.

If anyone doubts the essentially outgoing nature of the Scottish character he has only to look at the intricacies of Scottish masonwork and sculpture which even after 'the blight' survived in the making and carving of gravestones and the ornamenting of the houses of those who enjoyed royal favour and could afford to show a little independence from the ministers of the kirk; Craigievar, with its fake cannon, corbels and turrets, and its rich plasterwork, is a triumph of frivolity and fun in a cold climate inhabited by supposedly unimaginative, miserable men, whose whole beings were governed by the doleful recitation of the psalms and the fight for survival. It is a false picture, of course: Craigievar was built under the episcopalian ascendancy in any case; but the point I am trying to make is that whoever was in the ascendancy the capacity and will to have this fun was there all the time and still is. That is what one sees in much of the Scottish vernacular, and what one misses when that vernacular merely copies foreign styles which the imitators do not understand and are not really familiar with. In a great house like Winton it works reasonably well because both owner and mason were high up in the establishment of the day and to some extent cognizant of the prevailing fashion, and the same is true, perhaps truer, at Pinkie, where Chancellor Seton had personal experience of life in another country; but such patronage came to an end in the very same century, while the ordinary man, who has always imitated those with more means or power than himself, was apparently happy to follow the anglicization programme that was, perhaps, inevitable once the United Kingdom came into existence, and more especially after the Union of the Parliaments in 1707, after which date one can scarcely speak of a Scottish vernacular at all.

One is tempted to try and conjure up just what might have happened in the cultural field given slightly different circumstances. For example, had King Charles' and his father's religious policy succeeded and Scotland continued to have bishops in the kirk and acquired a wider, more moderate ecclesiastical outlook, and not descended to in-fighting over 'prelacy' and such futilities as to whether the public reciting of the collect for the day constituted saying Mass or not, which was the excuse for a riot in the High Kirk of St Giles in Edinburgh and the immediate cause of the so-called 'Bishops' War'. We would have had a happier country without the memory of 'the blood of the martyrs', and a more interesting one artistically after the middle of the seventeenth century. One thinks of George Jamesone, the 'Scottish Van Dyck', or John Napier of Merchiston, the inventor of logarithms, of Montrose, naturally, whose heart the Napiers treasured for centuries, of William Drummond of Hawthornden, who with Jamesone arranged the festivities for King Charles' Coronation and whose seat in Midlothian was the venue for a visit by Ben Jonson to compliment the poet personally on his *Teares on the death of Meliades*, which was written on the untimely demise of Henry, Prince of Wales and inspired Milton's *Lycidas*. Drummond's sister married Sir John Scot of Scotstarvit whose Montaigne-like existence in his tower house in Fife was enlivened by gatherings of other cavaliers and poets. The list might also include Sir Thomas Urquhart of Cromarty, the first to translate Rabelais into English, who died of a fit of laughter on hearing of the Restoration of Charles II in 1660, and Sir William Alexander, founder of Nova Scotia, poet and courtier whose country seat at Menstrie, near Stirling, has been restored by the local Council and the National Trust and boasts a splendid Nova Scotia Room with the coats of arms of all but two of the baronets created between the years 1625 and 1707. Alexander was Secretary of State for Scotland and a great friend of Drummond of Hawthornden, who died of grief on hearing of the beheading of the king.

Hawthornden Castle, which is situated at the eastern end of a deep ravine above the North Esk River, almost within sight of Edinburgh in an extremely romantic setting, received a new lease of literary life and interest in the days of Sir Walter Scott, who lived the first years of his marriage in a cottage nearby at Lasswade. Scott had for visitors the Wordsworths and others whom he took on the famous walk along the glen to Roslin, which he made internationally known through his writing and imaginative vision. The former inn at Roslin, now called Collegehill and the home of the caretaker of Rosslyn Chapel, has a visitors list second to none, with the names of the great and the gifted, from Boswell and Johnson to Burns, Queen Victoria and more modern royalty and notabilities. The area is not what it was, very few places are, and the future of Hawthornden Castle is not certain. The old sycamore tree under which the poet and Ben Jonson conversed amiably is still there, however, and flourishing, also a portion of the original tower in which Drummond resided, the bolt barring the gate still being used each evening as he used it to lock himself in. Later buildings have arisen behind, the castle having to be largely rebuilt after its sacking by a mob that came out from Edinburgh in 1688, but the contents include Robert Bruce's two-handed sword, or claymore, which was worn on the back and drawn by placing both hands upon it, pulling it out and using at once with deadly effect. Some caves along the path to Roslin are said to have sheltered both Wallace and Bruce; they are partly artificial and have certainly provided shelter for important fugitives, if not the two great national heroes themselves.

Rosslyn has a castle as well as a celebrated Chapel where the St Clairs, according to Scott, were buried in their armour. The family were Earls of Orkney, as well as Lords of many other places and the holders of numerous orders, British and foreign; indeed, we are told the recitation of the St Clair titles would bore a Spanish grandee. Hertford damaged Rosslyn Castle considerably, and Cromwell furthered the work of destruction, so that all that remains today is a seventeenth-century house built on the foundations of the old castle, the ruins of which are extensive and impressive and greatly appealed to early nineteenth-century visitors, they complementing an excursion to the Chapel. Parts of the drawbridge and gatehouse survive, and there are six storeys of dungeons below the existing courtyard, the whole being supported by a remarkable range of round-headed buttresses. The Caroline house is worth having a look at and its tea room patronising if only to enjoy the fine contemporary panelling and decorative plaster ceiling which, for me at any rate, makes a welcome change from the much more ornate and rather confusing themes of fabulous Rosslyn Chapel, which is literally covered with carving, inside and out, much of it subject to controversial interpretation with a decidedly fictional background, making one look elsewhere for relief.

There are a number of castles within, or almost within the boundaries of Edinburgh: Dalhousie, which although a restaurant and modernized retains its original drawbridge slots, and Craigmillar, which is the best known and most important. This is a ruin, but extensive and interesting both as regards its historical associations and unusual plan. One gets a surprise view of it crowning a green hill in the southern suburbs, with housing estates of varying architectural standards all round. The Gilmour family on whose land it stands have for centuries maintained the main structure of this large fortalice and kept in being the few farms that presently

*Dalhousie Castle: entry showing drawbridge housings*

constitute an outpost of Edinburgh's 'Green Belt'. To most Scots at home and abroad, the castle, set against a background of Arthur's Seat and the grey spires and towers of 'Auld Reekie', now rather spoilt by the intervention of concrete boxes in the immediate foreground, will for ever be associated with the name of Mary Stuart, who came here to recover from the murder of Rizzio, and whose favourite retreat Craigmillar was. Not that the castle can have been a particularly happy place, for even as she enjoyed its better air and security her own advisers were plotting another murder therein, one to rid her of Darnley. At first the Regent Moray, her half-brother, Bothwell and Lethington, tried to coax her into divorcing her husband, but when she refused, others, less squeamish, took over. Moray was himself assassinated, and Lethington, although afterwards apprehended and accused of taking part in Darnley's killing was probably not involved in this second scheme, though oddly enough one of the things they show you at Lennoxlove is the box in which the infamous 'Casket Letters' once were. These comprised a 'frame-up' of the Queen and were composed of genuine letters of hers, taken out of context and put together with forgeries in an attempt to make her responsible, for the murder and not those who actually did it. The principal villain in the piece was the Regent Morton, who paid for his crime in due course, though there were hired murderers who escaped, and Bothwell, who played a part in the killing of Darnley for private and personal reasons. Morton and his friends feared a popish plot in which the Queen's consort was supposedly a key figure and so decided to blow him up, while Bothwell wanted him out of the way so as he could marry the Queen. The two plots came together in an oddly fortuitous manner, the victim being already dead before the second party blew up the house, in which he and his valet were thought to be. In fact, the bodies were found lying half naked some distance from the building, unmarked by gunpowder, having probably been smothered and taken away before the charge went off. It would be interesting to know just how well informed Queen Elizabeth was of all this, and which plot she knew about, for she was sent a detailed drawing of the event, showing house and bodies exactly as they were on the fatal night.

It is against this dramatic scenario, and the background of Arthur's Seat and Holyrood, that Craigmillar has such an appeal, but for the student of military architecture it has other attributes, many of them still discernible in its ruins. Craigmillar began life in the fifteenth century as a typical L-shaped tower and was twice considerably enlarged, once after its burning and partial demolition by Hertford in 1547, and again in the seventeenth century when the central tower, already added to and enclosed within walls of *enceinte,* was further strengthened by new outer walls, thus providing a double system of defence to the north and east and west, leaving only the southern aspect exposed; this stood on a rock outcrop and was difficult to approach. In the rebuilding comfortable living quarters replaced the two halls in the fifteenth-century tower, the lord, in this case the Queen, being provided with a private suite and dining-room, not partaking with the rest of the company in the hall as was more usual. There were elaborate precautions against surprise entry, the main door of the tower being tucked away round a corner of the 'L' and watched over by a guard chamber above; a sort of obstacle race was also provided for the unwary in the form of changes in height, unexpected steps and a hole in the ground deliberately left to trip up those unfamiliar with the lay-out. No wonder Craigmillar became the haunt of conspirators and the retreat of a harassed Queen.

The castle is out-of-date for its period because most of what one sees was built in the sixteenth century when the idea of a motte-and-bailey fortress which it is, lacking any gatehouse and consisting in essence of a 'keep' and outer walls, had long been replaced by the castle of *enceinte,* with the 'keep' incorporated within a gatehouse and ancillary buildings attached to the outer walls. Other unusual features are the fact that there are no projecting battlements on the main tower, which rises directly from rocky foundation to roof in complete contrast with the very up-to-date defence walls erected after Hertford's passage, which have elaborate

*Craigmillar Castle: general view; view from south, slightly restored*

and splendid machicolations and crenellations that give them an 'Italian' feel, especially the round corner towers. The illusion is not too fanciful either, as by then Italian military engineers had already thrown walls round the town of Berwick-upon-Tweed and helped create a new citadel at Leith. These heavily corbelled towers and curtain walls do in fact suggest the Castello di Bracciano, near Rome, which impressed both Robert Adam and Sir Walter Scott, and undoubtedly influenced Adam when formulating his castellated style for Culzean and elsewhere. The extramural bastions, if one can speak thus, enclosed a chapel, and a great barn which served as the parish kirk of neighbouring Liberton in Jacobean times. Both survive, also a circular doocot at the north-eastern corner incorporated in a defence tower. Doocots and their possession played a significant part in Scotland in the old days. Their ostensible purpose was to provide winter feeding, but as more and more of them were built the crown decided to control and license their existence. They became because of this a status symbol, notably in the seventeenth century, and even later, when it was an offence to pull one down and to do so was thought to bring bad luck on the demolisher. This accounts for the remarkable number of doocots that remain in eastern Scotland, particularly in Fife and the Lothians, where the fields of grain were plentiful, and there were more bonnet lairds as well as large estate owners, to profit by them. The doocots take various forms, the commonest being rectangular and provided with a lean-to roof, but there are many 'beehive' dovecots, with domed roofs, and double ones, depending on the size of the house and the extent of the property and licence. In Georgian times the doocots were often quite decorative, with urns and other features suitable to current taste and they are mostly now protected under preservation orders, though I know of one at Billowness, near Anstruther, which was wantonly pulled down against the pleas of the local amenity society on the excuse that it was dangerous. What happens is that owners do not repair the doocots until it is too late and they really are dangerous. It is all a bit specious really and people should see through it more often. Clearly in such

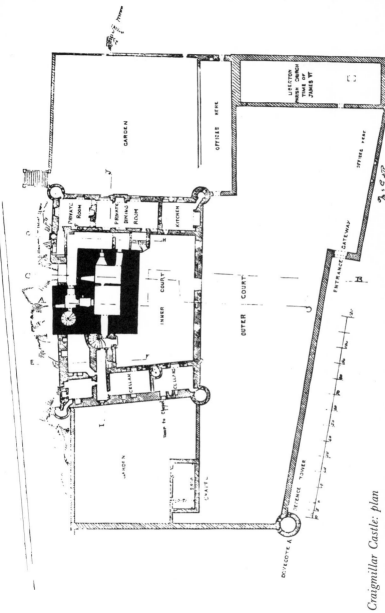

Craigmillar Castle: plan

a case no antiquated superstitions inhibit the demolishers!

A lot of the internal fittings at Craigmillar have survived, the stone window seats in the baronial hall being notable, and the big open fireplace with its moulded canopy support and columns; but the wooden floor that formerly divided the now 25-feet-high vaulted chamber of two storeys seems to have come down very low for such a room, nearly 40 by 20 feet on the ground but only 12 feet from floor to ceiling. In fact the corbels for this exist and only just clear the window openings and the top of the chimney canopy. The proportions were obviously bad, and the effect must have bordered on the claustrophobic. Other corbels, projecting from the outer walls of the south face show that timber hoardings, or fighting platforms, were once there, the door onto them blocked up but still discernible. Other Edinburgh castles include Merchiston, which was a Napier seat and the home of the inventor of logarithms. John Napier was a typical product of his age and of the cavalier society, as opposed to the calvinist, which produced poets and scientists rather than preachers and demagogues. He was not quite a Scottish Leonardo, but he was a 'Renaissance man' and besides inventing logarithms he also produced an early version of a computer, a hydraulic screw, a tank and new mining machinery, while retaining his devotion to religious learning. In this he was perhaps matched in ingenuity, though not in the mathematical sphere, by Sir Thomas Urquhart of Cromarty, who invented a universal language, the details of which were unfortunately stolen from his travelling trunk and used by Cromwell's soldiers to light their pipes.

Merchiston Castle consists of a greatly restored oblong tower, with plain battlements, small bartisans, crowstepped gables and a turreted cap-house, and is preserved as an ornamental centrepiece in the courtyard of a school of technology. There are some interesting ceilings inside, a genuine Charles II plaster one of the kind Dunsterfield and Halbert introduced into Scotland, another, a typical painted ceiling of the Jacobean era, from an old house that had been vacated and installed here for safety; and a third is in the style of the second but actually painted by students from the

*Merchiston Castle, Edinburgh*

Edinburgh College of Art, who had the good sense not to be clever but to simulate an original object, decorating it with geometrical patterns and the armorial devices of the Napiers. Such ceilings were very popular in the second half of the sixteenth century and the early seventeenth, and the subjects ranged from heroic figures of Biblical, Antique or Christian lore, to patterns of rope and foliage, improving mottoes and coats of arms. Sir Archibald Napier of Merchiston, John's father, lived at Lauriston Castle, on the western side of the city, a much less folly-like structure though having been altered from time to time and added to in the nineteenth century. Lauriston stands in a charming park beside the Firth of Forth and was the birthplace in the late seventeenth century of John Law, the financier and founder of the Banque Nationale de France, which went bankrupt with a big bang, ruining half of France and Law himself, who died penniless in Venice.

In the lea of the Pentland Hills lie Bonaly Tower, Malleny and Baberton. The first was the retreat in his retirement of Lord Cockburn, judge and recorder of his times and namesake of Edinburgh's oldest amenity society. The Tower is now turned into flats and is only interesting for its site and its associations. Malleny is an attractive seventeenth-century laird's house with a circular staircase tower, and a garden that is open to the public by arrangement with the National Trust for Scotland. Baberton is a small L-shaped edifice right on the edge of the moors, bleak and lonely in winter and used as a hunting lodge by James VI and I. Then there is Craigcrook, another retreat on the Bonaly model, on the north side of the city; again of uncertain age but much less spoilt, retaining a touch of the Gothic Revival atmosphere it had in the days of Lord Jeffrey, Cockburn's friend and fellow judge, a backer of the *Edinburgh Review*, which supported the Whigs. Jeffrey's literary parties in the grounds were famous for their good company, good wine and good conversation, and the guests included those of rival political persuasions, such as Scott and Christopher North, the latter Professor of Moral Philosophy at Edinburgh University and with Scott a contributor to *Blackwood's Magazine*, the Tory organ. The

*Edinburgh Castle, from the Grassmarket*

castle may have some older parts and has been bought by a firm of architects who have restored it as their offices.

None of these retreats, however, can compare in fame and glory with Edinburgh Castle, though Baberton at least, and possibly Merchiston are quite as old in their main parts, for Edinburgh Castle is modern as castles go, having supplanted a mainly timber erection which was burnt by Robert Bruce in the fourteenth century. Then all but Queen Margaret's tiny romanesque Chapel, which was built of stone, perished. Bruce's son, David II, was responsible for the first stone tower, in the late fourteenth century, but even that has disappeared from view, engulfed under the semicircular, or 'Half-Moon' battery which Regent Morton built to protect the castle from the adherents of Mary, Queen of Scots, when the renaissance entrance to the Portcullis Tower was made with Morton's Douglas 'heart' taking precedence over the royal coat of arms. The tower, now replaced in its upper storeys by a modern reconstruction, is known today as the Argyll Tower because in it the first Marquis and his son, the ninth Earl of that name, were held prisoner before their executions. It is perhaps worth recalling that neither suffered the indignities heaped upon their adversary Montrose, who was paraded before the populace in a cart which was made to stop in front of the Argyll family seated on the balcony of Moray House, to be insulted by them, even spat upon by Lady Argyll, a Morton by birth; and subsequently the King's Lieutenant-General died the death of a felon, by hanging, drawing and quartering. In contrast, both Argylls were beheaded by 'The Maiden', or Scottish guillotine, both being guilty of treason, having borne arms against the king, a fact that is often overlooked when tearful stories are told about them.

The present gatehouse of the castle is entirely modern, completed by Sir Robert Lorimer in this century, with the addition of two fine statues in niches on either side of the entrance of Bruce and Wallace respectively. In the seventeenth century it was proposed to build a 'forework', or outer defence on the star-pattern as developed by Vauban, but this was never done, though there is still a deep ditch dividing the castle from the esplanade, one part of which is Nova Scotian territory, a reminder of the practice of taking 'Sasine', or formal possession of symbolic earth by holders of property there. The castle esplanade is the scene of a celebrated military tattoo, when seats and stands make it impossible to take photographs from about mid-June until the end of September, which is when visitors principally wish to do so, while the actual performances make life unbearable for folk living within a quarter of a mile of it. In fact, all the marching and counter-marching, banging of drums and so on has so weakened the castle foundations that for the past decade engineers have been busy grouting the rock and making the place safe for future tattoos, which might perhaps be produced better on a larger stage, say in Holyrood Park, where there could be pitched battles and other recreations of the past such as they have at Aldershot. Morton's 'Half-Moon' Battery, heightened in the seventeenth century by Robert Mylne, master mason to Charles II and builder of most of Holyrood House under the supervision of Sir William Bruce, is perhaps the finest and most authentic part of Edinburgh Castle, apart from Queen Margaret's

*Edinburgh Castle, the 'palace' and battery*

Chapel, and makes a splendid background for military parades. Above it rises the Palace Block, or King's Lodgings, which was mostly the work of James VI when he had it restored and partly rebuilt for his homecoming in 1617; though it still contains the little room in which he was born and the Crown Room in which the Honours of Scotland are, the crown remodelled for James V, the sceptre and sword given to James IV by the Pope, and the ensigns of the Orders of the Thistle and Garter which belonged to James VII and II, which he took into exile in 1688. These were returned by his grandson, the last Stuart, Cardinal York, brother of Prince Charlie, together with an expandable ring, said to have been last used at the Scottish coronation of Charles I in 1633.

One of the most exciting moments in the life of Sir Walter Scott, and one of his grandest and most dramatic achievements, was his rediscovery of the Scottish Regalia, the 'Honours Three', which had lain hidden in an old box in the Castle and forgotten ever since they were used ceremonially for the last Riding of the Scottish Parliament in 1707, (the ceremonial procession on horseback at the opening of Parliament). Previously these precious objects, Scotland's symbols of separateness and royal status, narrowly escaped Oliver Cromwell's clutches when orders were given that they should be wrested from the Governor of Dunnottar Castle at all costs. The Minister's wife of nearby Kineff and the Governor's wife, Mrs Ogilvy, between them managed to remove the crown, sceptre and sword (no easy task when one sees the sword) and hide them under the floor of Kineff Kirk, where they remained safe and sound until the Restoration, and their return to Edinburgh. Previously they had been used at the impromptu Coronation of a reluctant Charles II at Scone, in 1651, at Hogmanay, when the king, depicted in a contemporary English cartoon as having his nose held to the grindstone by the Scots, was obliged to listen to a dreary two-hour sermon and have the crown of his ancestors placed on his head by the repulsive Argyll. 'The Honours' were last used ceremonially in 1953 for the Coronation visit of Her Majesty the Queen, when they were brought from Edinburgh Castle and presented to her in St Giles' High Kirk, the Duke of Hamilton bearing the crown, Lord Home holding the sword of State and the Earl of Crawford the sceptre.

One side of the old courtyard at Edinburgh Castle is now occupied by the Scottish National War Memorial, again the work of Sir Robert Lorimer, in which the architect used decorative features taken from Stirling Castle and other buildings to create a not unsatisfactory silhouette when seen with the rest of the castle on its rock above Princes Street. One of the few authentic portions left facing this courtyard is the Banqueting Hall, which has its main elevation to the south, the walls rising directly from a precipice above the Grassmarket. It was built in the late fifteenth century by James IV and retains its original hammer-beam roof, preserved through having been enclosed behind latter-day plaster, and displaying on its carved items a number of interesting subjects, such as the king himself, his queen, Margaret Tudor, their initials and cyphers and religious emblems of the pre-Reformation era. When James VI had the castle restored for his 'salmond-like' return home, he sent up plasterers from the South to assist William Wallace, his Edinburgh mason, and it was undoubtedly some of these who became itinerant and made other plaster ceilings in the northern kingdom. In the library at Kellie, in Fife, for instance, plasterers from York were known to have been employed on a similar ceiling, since lost, and the same moulds went elsewhere. At the highest point of the castle rock, beside Queen Margaret's Chapel, rescued from service as a munitions store and now restored to religious purposes, is the odd-looking gun called Mons, or Mollance, Meg, which may or may not have been made by the Royal Gunsmith to James II of the Fiery Face and used at the siege of Threave Castle, in Galloway. One thing is certain, it exploded when firing a salute to the departing James, Duke of Albany and York, the future James VII and II, and the last monarch in the native Stuart line to rule over us.

The Yorkshire plasterers almost certainly were responsible for some of the strapwork ceilings in Moray House in the Canongate, whilst they were busy at the castle, and they or their apprentices went to The Binns in West Lothian. This Jacobean house has a good site, sheltered from the north by a long, low hill and facing due south. From the top of the hill, now marked by a look-out tower-cum-folly, the eye takes in most of the length and breadth of the Firth of Forth, from central Scotland almost to the open sea. The Highlands are not far away, indeed one can see how the Ochils, rounded and grassy for most of their length, suddenly turn rugged and bracken covered, with outcrops of rock and heather, where the geological fault, which is the true division between Highland and Lowland, not any fanciful notion about clans or tartan, occurs. Below one Blackness Castle juts out into the sea in the shape of a ship. It was one of the four Scottish fortresses that were to remain repaired and garrisoned after the Union of 1707, Edinburgh, Stirling and Dumbarton being the others. MacGibbon and Ross do not have much to say about Blackness largely because they could not get into it, the castle still being army property in their day, and adapted to modern defence purposes and seemingly lacking in original features. Since then there has been a transformation and the Ancient Monuments people have worked

*Blackness Castle on the Firth of Forth*

wonders with what the army left them, removing outer coatings, like a picture restorer removes varnish and repaintings from a portrait, to reveal a not too greatly damaged original underneath, placing it on 'a velvet lawn', as is their wont, but not as a ruin. Its shape is undoubtedly its most remarkable attribute, and when seen from a distance resembles a telescoped version of an oil tanker, with 'prow' projected towards the waves on a small peninsula, the funnel represented by a fattish but much higher erection at the 'stern'. Blackness is still severely defensive-looking and by no means reminiscent of having made a home for anyone at any time; it was, after all, a prison, before being militarized, and its sea-gate is guarded by a strong iron yett of traditional pattern. The surroundings could be, and probably were, more salubrious before the sea turned black and brown and even red from pollution, the shore littered with dead animal and piscatorial debris in an area which was once famous for its oysters. If one found an oyster here today one would certainly not eat it. Yet the immediate inland area is pleasant enough, the Crown Property on which the castle stands extending to grazing land where both public and sheep are permitted, and the distant prospect is attractive provided one avoids Rosyth and the power station and oil refineries round Grangemouth.

Within sight of Blackness is the Hopetoun Estate, whose park wall runs down to the sea and whose origins are very much older than the mansion which Sir William Bruce began at the end of the seventeenth century. In fact there was a Roman fort on the most prominent hill in the view, and below it is the Kirk of Abercorn in which can be seen a Danish hog-back tombstone and the broken cross of a Pictish bishop, rescued from doing service as part of a bridge. The Picts were reduced to impotence by the Scots, who came from Ulster, in much the same manner as the grey squirrel has extinguished the red in this country; they were never decisively defeated in battle but gradually pushed further and further south until their last resort was as allies of the Saxons, when the Firth of Forth became the 'Scottish Sea', and Edinburgh the capital of Northumbria. The Bishop at

*Midhope Castle on the Hopetoun estate*

Abercorn was a 'tame' Pict, allied to the sassenach, or sas-
sunach, which is only the Gaelic name for a Saxon, and the
kirk was his cathedral. Hopetoun House, the seat of the
Marquess of Linlithgow, is just across the park, with the
castle mound within the grounds, and the family burial aisle,
designed by Sir William Bruce in 1708, is attached to the
kirk. Still on the estate is Midhope Castle, which I have seen
deteriorate and half collapse over the last fifteen years so as
to become almost unrecognizable for what it was. It is an old
castle, with a keep-like tower at its western end, tall with
steep roof added in the sixteenth century, when the conical
caps to the corner turrets were lopped off to become oversailed, with the roof running straight on over them. At its
eastern end are two homogenous extensions, both of the
seventeenth century, when Midhope Castle was still the
residence of the Earls of Linlithgow, Keepers of Linlithgow
Palace under Charles II. Their name was Livingstone, not
Hope, which is confusing. The present Hope owners came
here from Fife, and before that from Holland, in the seven-

teenth century. There is a fine classical doorway to the six-storeyed tower, which has the feel of Bruce but perhaps predates his arrival on the Hopetoun Estate which was not before 1696. He probably, however, designed the handsome entrance gateway to the walled courtyard, now the victim of farm tractors, which have simply been used to knock the wall down wherever entrance was required.

Midhope Castle, which the first Marquess of Linlithgow thought at one time of restoring, was inhabited until the war, when it became the plaything of the Fire Service and others who ruined it and let the weather in, so that dry-rot appeared and the woodwork had to be removed and destroyed. The roof is now off, the splendid panelling and Queen Anne staircase have all had to be burned and the place is an empty shell, not merely decayed, but ready for the bulldozers. It is very sad and none of it was necessary. One might add that in the vicinity the Castle of Bonhard was actually removed in the space of a few days by the local farmer, and this despite the fact that permission is supposed to be obtained before doing such things, and a fine of £200 imposed if done without. Of course, the fine is chickenfeed to the average farmer, who can, as is in this case, re-use the stone for his dykes and sheds, and the timber in other ways. I remember visiting Bonhard one week-end, and a fortnight later a roofed, hale building, which only needed minor alterations to make it entirely habitable, had evaporated, leaving 'not a wrack behind'. I do not suppose the Linlithgow Estates would do such a thing at Midhope, but what happens to the castle if it becomes too expensive to maintain, even as a ruin, and something falls on someone and injures them? At Macduff Castle, across in Fife, this happened, or rather the threat of it seemed proved, and the offending portion was dynamited by the local council. It is certainly a problem few of us would care to face, property which is too far gone to be used for anything, fit only as a home for the pigeons and possibly dangerous. Midhope is approached through handsome gates at the end of a drive, or was, one gatepost only remaining intact, the other having its top-piece knocked off, not by the West Lothian Civil Defence this time. The castle could be presented to the nation and maintained in semi-ruinous condition by the Department of the Environment, a case of one Government agency repairing the damage done by another. At least it still exists, which is more than can be said for Bonhard; and what price Grange Pans, which John Fleming describes in his introduction to *Scottish Country Houses Open to the Public?* That was demolished in the reign of Edward VII; which only goes to show how careful one must be when writing about Scottish castles to make sure they are still standing!

The commonest approach to the 'kingdom' of Fife, which was one of the seven sub-kingdoms of Pictland before the Scots arrived, is via the Queensferry, no longer a ferry but a road bridge and railway bridge, bringing one onto a large peninsula whose history of separateness and individuality has not been entirely removed by these links. Witness the fact that the Fifers, almost alone in Britain, succeeded in retaining their regional identity and boundary against the findings of the Wheatley Report and later efforts to divide the county in two, the northern part destined to go to Dundee, the southern to Edinburgh. In some ways it is nicer, certainly more contrasting to enter Fife at its westernmost extremity, where the 'kingdom' marches with Stirlingshire and Clackmannan, and Perthshire is not far away. Here Highland hills drop to meet the Lowlands in one fell swoop and a wild landscape turns into one of well-tended farms and villages and industry, protected as by a natural wall from the North by the hills. The road crosses the Forth by the Kincardine Bridge, with a fascinating long view of Airth Castle and ruined Norman kirk on a rocky eminence at the gates to Stirlingshire, and the massive Clackmannan Tower, seat of the Bruces of that Ilk, rising proudly on the far side of the Forth on its own complementary hill. Once in the 'kingdom' one senses the separateness immediately: it is not just the overall atmosphere, the dialect, red pantiles, long low cottages, harling and Dutch curly-ended gables that make Fife different; it is the complete integration of the landscape and people that is not so apparent in other parts of Scotland, the settled air that is not so obvious in Highland airts nor nearer

Edinburgh. Fife has escaped most of the wars of passage that devastated much of the rest of the country, and almost everything and everybody had come to it by sea, including the Romans and later the Normans, the latter as early as the end of the eleventh century, when the first, the de Candela family from southern Italy, arrived.

After nearly a thousand years these Norman families can now no doubt be reckoned indigenous, many still retain their estates and all have adopted local names or adaptations of them. Their castles, however, have gone except for a few toothy ruins, and they either live in Jacobean manor houses or later mansions. Sir William Bruce's house at Balcaskie, the home of Sir Ralph Anstruther, of the original de Candela line, is a case in point. An L-shaped laird's tower was gradually enlarged to make it symmetrical by the King's architect and more comfortable, then sold when he moved to Kinross and built his masterpiece in the Palladian style, Kinross House. The Anstruthers, who till then had lived in Dreel Castle in Anstruther itself, acquired Balcaskie and have been there ever since. Kinross, of course, gives its name to an adjacent county, a small one that has always been associated with its larger neighbour with whom it shares a sheriff. Loch Leven Castle is its best-known monument, better known than Kinross House, which faces the castle on an island in the middle of the loch. Indeed, Bruce especially chose this site with its view of the ruined tower in which Mary, Queen of Scots was imprisoned and from which she escaped with the aid of the governor's son, as the principal object in the vista from his windows; he even took a medieval stone from the castle and used it as a keystone in one of his garden gazebos, thus perpetuating the links between past and present as he was fond of doing. In summer one can row out to the castle and either fish for pink trout or picnic near where Mary Stuart was forced to abdicate, where she was daily insulted by the governor's wife and finally got away to be defeated at Langside and forced to throw herself on the mercy of an embarrassed Elizabeth Tudor. Loch Leven Castle is not extensive in area and consists of a fourteenth-century tower with uncrenellated

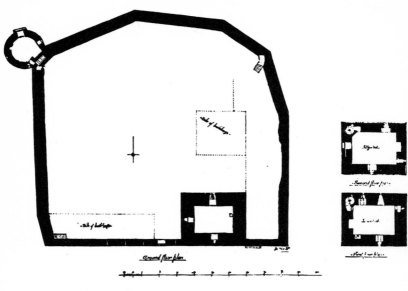

*Loch Leven Castle: plans*

battlements, low bartisans at three corners, and outer
defences, including a wall walk, with links to a smaller,
round tower in which the Queen was held. The original
entrance was by movable ladder to a door on the second
floor, not the first, which is most unusual, and the difference
between the comparative amplitude of the governor's
quarters and the cramped space allotted to Mary Stuart is
particularly noticeable.

Near the northern shore of Loch Leven stands the Castle
of Burleigh, erstwhile seat of the Balfours of that Ilk of which
there were several branches in Fife. The fifteenth-century
tower of the castle is ruined and empty and only one side of
the barmkin, or outer wall, has survived, joining the existing
ruin to a highly intriguing and remarkably complete gatehouse. This dates from the late sixteenth century and is
roofed, with all its windows; it is a symposium in miniature
of Scottish masonic ingenuity of the period and a perfect
example of its kind. The local builder's approach to his work
was obviously intuitive and what happened did so as he went

along rather than as the result of any cohesive plan arrived at in advance. Thus, when an extra stair was required after half the walls had gone up, a bulge was made in the appropriate place and a spiral inserted, the shape and nature of its roofing having to wait until the masons reached the top and saw what was wanted. In essence the Burleigh gatehouse is circular with bends and bulges here and there to accommodate extensions, such as the one for the above-mentioned stair, which does not so much break from the main wall surface as grow out of it, almost imperceptibly, creating a new and interesting shape on the first floor which is neither round nor anything else especially. Above this nominally circular form a polygonal room has been devised by using the thickness of the walls to produce straight sides internally and pushing out externally what remains on corbels. The roof is gable-ended, but without crowsteps, which would have been more normal, and instead the coping is finished smooth. The slating has to conform to the curious pattern produced by gables, bulges and circular base, which converge at slightly different levels and require roofing. It is all done very expeditiously and is a model of Scottish Jacobean building.

Burleigh is plentifully supplied with shot- and shut-holes, so that one could almost make a study of them in its gatehouse. The rounded basement is little more than a pillbox perforated with horizontal slits and entirely devoted to defence, the slits being just a few feet from the ground. Other holes abound higher up, on the stair turret, where one shot-hole is clearly divided so that fire aimed at it will not penetrate, while immediately under the principal window in the four-sided room is a typical shut-hole, not for defence but air and capable of being closed by a small wooden shutter. The castle is built of a pleasant red volcanic stone and stands beside a farmstead where the key may be had by those wishing to visit it. More shut, as opposed to shot, holes may be seen at Tulliebole Castle, again in Kinross-shire, and the seat of Lord Moncreiff. Tulliebole was restored after the war by the late Ian Lindsay together with Aldie Castle, whose estate marches with it. Both have been white harled and look

(left) *Burleigh Castle on the shores of Loch Leven.* (right) *Aldie Castle*

very spick and span in their new state. Aldie was the dream-come-true of a Scotsman working most of his life in the Orient, who as a boy had already made up his mind to buy a castle and live there when he retired. Before he went to this fairly remote corner of Kinross-shire, with its farmlands half hidden under the bield of the Cleish Hills, Aldie was known as a castle, but oddly enough he renamed it the 'House of Aldia', seemingly on the authority of some ancient document. As we have seen, however, whether a laird's tower or a mansion goes by the name of castle or house depends to a large extent on current taste. In Georgian times castles almost disappeared to become houses, while in the Victorian era practically everything was a castle that had a turret, and that concept is mainly accepted today, although no more justifiably.

There can be little doubt that Aldie was built as a castle, its main tower dates from the fifteenth century when it became part of the dowry of Aldia Murray of Tulliebardine, of the same family which in the seventeenth century inherited the Stewart of Atholl lands in Perthshire and their titles. In 1950, just before the recent restoration, Aldie was decayed but not ruined, remnants of the roof sarking remained and it was by no means difficult to imagine it completely repaired. The tower is older at its base than at the top, the three conically capped corner turrets being 'studies' not bartisans, there having been no battlements or other defensive features, and the crowstepped cap-house on the fourth corner merely marked the top of the stairs. Some seventeenth-century additions were attached to the older building and these had to be linked to it somehow, this being done by making a small courtyard and forming a new entrance. The vaulted ground floor, or 'laich hall', was left as a superior garden room in which visitors on open days were given tea if it rained, while the hall proper was opened up to reveal its big fireplace, but no minstrel's gallery. Above are the bedrooms, with the 'studies' making attractive closets and viewpoints. In the garden is a handsome sundial, which does not actually belong here as it was brought from Cramond House, near Edinburgh, having been made for Sir Robert Dickson of Inveresk, but it is contemporary and recalls the origins of Aldie's restorer.

If Aldie has changed from being a castle to a house, Tulliebole might almost be said to have done the reverse, not recently, but when Mr Halliday, an Edinburgh lawyer, bought it in 1608. It was certainly not castellated, had neither turrets nor battlements, shot-holes nor anything else that could be interpreted as defensive, was, in fact, nothing more than a bonnet, or untitled, laird's house which had grown, as many did, from an original tall tower to a second tall tower, with linking central portion. Mr Halliday added to the second tower corner turrets and a small sentry walk, corbelled stairs and a rather obvious shut-hole near the new front door, replete with fine mouldings and panel above bearing the date and the arms of himself and spouse. The fireplace lintel in the hall is worth mentioning specially for it is composed of a single slab of stone more than 11 feet

long, and has for rival only one in the neighbourhood, in the
main room of the contemporary house known as 'The Study',
at Culross, headquarters of the National Trust for Scotland
in West Fife. There painted beams adorn the ceiling,
replacing others long since disappeared, but at Tulliebole the
architect was content with ordinary undecorated beams,
though one feels he might have been justified in mocking-up
some new painted ones, imitative of those in vogue in this
part of Scotland, and indeed throughout the eastern part of
the country, in Jacobean times. On the other hand, there is
a minstrel's gallery or what seems like one, and possibly also
what may be a 'laird's lug', a curious device consisting of a
tiny room in the thickness of the wall, in which the laird
could hide himself and listen in secret to the conversation
going on in the hall below. A commoner device, also sometimes labelled 'secret', usually turns out to be merely the
laird's private stair down to the cellar!

The Moncreiffs, and the Wellwoods into which they
married, have a remarkable record of service to the com-

*Tulliebole: the entrance. Note shut-hole*

munity in the church and the law; one was the judge in the celebrated Madeleine Smith case, and they have the papers at Tulliebole, while another has just retired as Primus of the Scottish Episcopal Church. There are also two Baronetcies of almost the same name, Lord Moncreiff's, which is spelt without an 'e' at the end, and Sir Iain Moncreiffe's of that Ilk, which is. The first Baronetcy was granted to Lord Moncreiff's ancestor in April 1626, and selected visitors may be shown the original insignia, the second was not granted until November 1685, which makes things a trifle complicated for those who do not understand the ways of Scottish heraldry. The present Baron Moncreiff of Moncreiff is a Wellwood Moncreiff, without hyphen, and the following lines were composed by a forbear to keep friends right on the spelling:

> His name it was W
> E double L,
> W double oh! D!

Needless to say, this was to distinguish his family from one that spelt the name with only one 'L'.

Aberdour Castle, on the Fife coast opposite Inchcolme, is described by MacGibbon and Ross as "a Scottish house, as distinguished from a keep or castle". So once again we are up against the problem of nomenclature, though here it is not so much of a problem because there does survive at Aberdour the ruined nucleus of a medieval castle which was superseded, rather than being added to or built around, by newer buildings of a domestic character which the Regent Morton erected in the second half of the sixteenth century. These are crowstepped and in the local vernacular style, generally little different, except perhaps in scale, from many other houses along the coast, in the High Streets and harbour fronts that Billings found so fascinating and in some cases illustrated. The castle is surrounded by gardens, presumably reconstituted by the Ancient Monuments people, since MacGibbon and Ross speak of the buildings being used as piggeries, and describe the chapel "one of the most complete Norman structures in Scotland," as being "in a state of heedless neglect". The Ministry have reroofed the domestic quarters, which are now in part inhabited by a caretaker, who looks after the terraced garden wherein will be found another old bowling green and a fine 'beehive' doocot, of which Fife can boast quite a few. As for the chapel this has been separated from the castle by a high wall and locked gate and become the Parish Kirk of St Fillan and is very popular for weddings, though too small for the grander variety. It belonged in origin to the Abbey of Inchcolme, which itself became the property of the Lords of Aberdour at the Reformation, they acting as Commendators and keeping in repair the living quarters for their own private use. The shape of the ruined tower of Aberdour is unusual, being a parallelogram without right angles, and it, together with the rest of the extensive group of house and kirk, can be seen from the train between Inverkeithing and Kirkcaldy when it stops at Aberdour Station, right under the castle walls.

Visible only at some distance, and when the flag flying on its battlements points the exact position, is Fordel Castle, the home of Nicholas Fairbairn, M.P. This small but interesting fortalice, maintained by its previous owners as a folly in the grounds of their newer mansion, is oblong and tall, with rectangular towers at two opposing corners, making it a version of the Z plan; though the towers are only for stairs and modest in size. One tower retains its battlements, the other has been domesticated and finished with crowstepped gables, but they must have been the same originally. When Mr Fairbairn bought Fordel, from relatives-in-law of the late Lord Attlee, he had to set to work with his own hands to make it habitable again, and try to recreate the once famous formal garden, a Caroline masterpiece of the same date as the chapel, which has also been restored and is used for family occasions. Sir John Henderson of Fordel is, perhaps, the castle's most celebrated laird, he being, with some of the other cavaliers I have listed, somewhat of an eccentric-cum-genius. He was taken prisoner whilst travelling in Africa and sold into slavery in Zanzibar, where he met a dusky princess who was so infatuated with him that she changed her religion and arranged for his escape. She sailed with him as far as Alexandria, where unfortunately she died, and Sir John, returning home to a Scotland torn by religious strife, joined the army and fought valiantly for his king in the Civil War. Fordel's lodging in Inverkeithing was his town house, its turreted stair tower still protruding into the street near the church.

Wemyss Castle does not appear in either Billings or MacGibbon and Ross, though Slezer made an interesting sketch of it, from the sea, which he inadvertently labelled 'Dunnottar', but about which there can be no doubt whatsoever; even the weem, or cave, after which Wemyss is named, is visible. The castle as one sees it today is not only much altered, and restored, but much smaller than it used to be, for since the last war Captain Michael Wemyss and Lady Victoria have achieved their life's ambition by removing the accretions of the Victorian age and reducing the castle, as far as possible, to how Robert Mylne left it in the reign of Charles II. It is, therefore, largely a Restoration house, with flat roofs and Renaissance balustrading, lacking turrets or other castellated features, and furnished with the accumulated possessions of the Wemyss family, one of the oldest in Scotland. An ancestor of Captain Wemyss lost his title to a secondary branch, today represented by the Earl of Wemyss and March, at the time of the Jacobite Rebellion, but he is 'of that Ilk', and a descendant of William IV and Mrs Jordans, whose portrait hangs in the drawing-room. He and his wife did not remove an older bit of the castle, dating from the sixteenth century and rising from medieval foundations, in which Mary, Queen of Scots is said to have had the misfortune of first meeting Lord Darnley. The Restoration of this tower was a major work of reconstruction and resuscitation, but it has been beautifully done and the decoration of the inner court-yard completed by a remarkably imaginative touch by Lady Victoria. Before the war there used to be glass pigeons in various postures around the pond of the Rond Point at the foot of the Champs Elysées, in Paris, which Hitler did not like and had taken away. Shortly after the war Lady Victoria traced them to a bric-à-brac shop in the vicinity and now they are at Wemyss,

*Wemyss Castle: from Slezer's* Theatrum Scotiae; *after restoration*

sitting on the window ledges of the reconstituted courtyard of the old castle. Other French touches are observable in the spacious formal layout of the grounds as recently completed, with beech avenues and statuary in the manner of Vaux-le-Vicomte, and the castle forecourt is paved with unwanted stone setts from the streets of Kirkcaldy.

Very different is Ravenscraig, actually in Kirkcaldy, on a high cliff above the sea. The castle is an uninhabited fortress, the first built in Scotland, possibly in Britain, exclusively for the purpose of withstanding and returning gun fire from cannon. Its two rounded towers, not rounded on all sides and one taller than the other, are grimly blackened with age, and present blank surfaces to the world on the landward façade, having windows on the seaward, where there was a courtyard on a narrow spur of rock running out into the Firth of Forth. Behind these somewhat forbidding towers, 14 feet thick on the landward and pierced by windows with seats on the

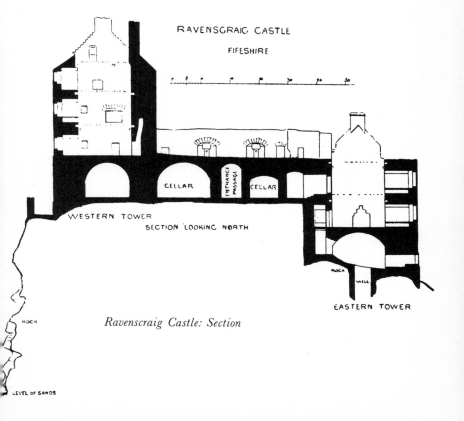

*Ravenscraig Castle: Section*

seaward, life went on much the same as in other castles of the mid-fifteenth century, only here, instead of being defended from high battlements, there was a lower gun-platform on which movable cannon could be deployed. James II of the Fiery Face was the king responsible for this remarkable edifice, the man who loved guns and died from the unscheduled exploding of one. He never saw it completed, though work continued after his death under the aegis of his widow, Mary of Gueldres. That the fine ashlar surfaces of Ravenscraig have never suffered a cannonball to deface them is clear, and the only signs of wear have been occasioned by the near presence of coal mines and the sea air, the latter being almost as much responsible for the blackened patina of the masonry as the former. The castle was exchanged against his will by William St Clair, Earl of Orkney, the builder of Rosslyn, for his castle at Kirkwall, when James III married Margaret of Denmark and wished himself to be Earl, or 'Jarl', of Orkney. In fact Orkney and Shetland were then Danish and offered as security for the dowry promised by the King of Denmark for his daughter on her marriage to the King of Scots. Unfortunately he was hard up and had to put the dowry in pawn, and never redeemed it. Thus towards the end of the fifteenth century Orkney and Shetland were annexed to the Scottish Crown in lieu of the Queen's dowry, though with what legal propriety is difficult to assess. Perhaps under international law it might still be possible for the King of Denmark to redeem the islands?

The records on Ravenscraig show that in 1460 the necessary lands on which the castle was to be built were exchanged for others by two vassals of the Earldom of Fife, which makes one wonder who exactly was the Earl at that time. We all know about Macduff, Shakespeare's Thane, who lived in the twelfth century, but his line died out in the fourteenth, a hundred years before Ravenscraig was begun; and Sir Thomas Innes of Learney, late Lyon King, states in his *Tartans and Clans of the Families of Scotland* that in 1757 the then Earl of Wemyss was 'representer'. This only makes the puzzle worse since at that particular date there was no *de facto* Earl of Wemyss, only a *de jure* one living abroad after having his lands and titles taken from him for his part in the Forty-five Rebellion. Curiously enough too, there existed at that time an Earl of Fife, with the surname of Duff, who lived in Banff, was the banker and landowner who employed William Adam to build Duff House and gained his title for supporting the Duke of Cumberland. His descendant, the sixth Earl of Fife in the Banffshire branch, married Princess Louise, Princess Royal and daughter of Edward VII, when he was created first Duke of Fife; and there is a Duke today, the son of Lord Southesk, who married Princess Maud, the Duchess's daughter and eventual heir. None of this establishes very much, for the Duffs cannot produce any evidence that they derive from the original Thane of Fife, it would be remarkable if they could, and the Wemyss connection is possibly closer since they have lived in the 'kingdom' for many centuries and possess what is left of Macduff Castle.

The Earls of Fife, as such, had a seat at Falkland, the extremely scanty ruins of which survive to the north of the existing Palace, really a Royal Stewart hunting lodge, which was built on its present site in the fifteenth and sixteenth centuries and is still in the hands of a royal keeper, preserved as part of our ancient patrimony by the National Trust for Scotland. It was probably not the scene of the murder by his uncle of the heir to Robert III—the long-lost castle will have witnessed that—when the young man who should have been David III of Scots was left to die of starvation, which he did despite the reputed efforts of local people to pass him food. No, the hunting lodge is a typical Franco-Scottish building with Italianate courtyard and many of the attributes of a *château* by the Loire. It is largely out with this narrative, except to say that in what is now called the Chapel Royal some of the woodwork and fittings date from the sixteenth century, when the 'palace' was completed by Continental craftsman, and the 'chapel', which was then the Great Hall, was divided at one end by an oak screen. This remains *in situ* and is practically the only one left in Scotland, certainly the finest, with splendidly turned balusters that remind one of Castilian examples. The courtyard also boasts Continental

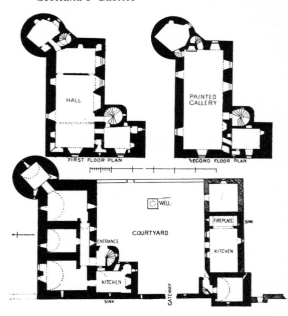

*Earlshall: plans*

work in the series of carved roundels enshrining the busts of heroes of Classical and Biblical lore, the vogue for which covered most of western Europe in Renaissance times. In Scotland it was adapted for woodwork panels and painted ceilings, the 'Hall of the Nine Nobles' at Crathes being a case in point, where three notables from the Old Testament, three from the New and three from the Antique world are represented.

The screen at Falkland was copied and adapted by Sir Robert Lorimer when he restored the building known as Earlshall, in northern Fife, in the late nineteenth century. It was his first job on his own and still one of his most interesting and successful restorations, those at Dunderave, in Argyll, and Balmanno, in Perthshire, running it pretty close. The thing about Earlshall, which replaces both in its name and structure an earlier fortalice, one with obvious connections with real and imagined Earls of Fife, is that Lorimer not only resuscitated a fine old fortified house of the sixteenth century but relaid and replanted the formal garden, merging it into a less formal one based on much the same ideas as Sir Edwin Lutyens and Gertrude Jekyll worked on but which he himself arrived at by his own mental processes. This combined the stiffer, traditional Scottish idea of a garden, which was more Continental in feeling, with the freer, more modern English arrangements made possible by the use of herbaceous borders and a wider variety of plants and shrubs. Thus, we have at Earlshall a splendid formal layout of yew hedges and topiary, blending with something less formal and recognizably modern by the clever use of space and levels and imaginative planting. There have been other recreations of the kind, the Renaissance gardens of Edzell Castle in Angus, and Pitmedden in Aberdeenshire, have both been brought back to life, one by the Department of the Environment and the other by the National Trust for Scotland under the guidance of the late Dr James Richardson, first Inspector for Ancient Monuments in Scotland; but neither attempts to do more than recreate something that was there before, while Lorimer went on to evolve and progress from the earlier forms.

*Earlshall*

This is not the place for a full discussion on the work and life of Sir Robert Lorimer, but since it was principally he who revived the Scottish idiom in architecture and planning after it had been in disrepute or misunderstood for several generations his contribution is significant in relation to the preservation and restoration of Scottish castles which has been such a feature of this century and which has reached a virtual peak since the last war, when more than thirty fortalices have been brought back into operation, mostly with the aid of Government grants. I will have more to say about this later, but there is a very good example of a post-war restoration almost within sight of Earlshall at Pitcullo, so one might as well expound a little here, even if the comparison does seem a bit invidious. Of course, Pitcullo is only small beside Earlshall, and the skill and imagination, possibly also resources, used in its restoration considerably less, but what amazes me about it, and in some of the other castles restored under Government advice and assistance, is the way in which they have actually not been restored. They are mostly roofed

*Pitcullo, after restoration*

and tidied up sufficiently to make them more or less habitable according to legislative standards, the walls harled to cover the joins, with corbels sticking out, obviously, supporting nothing, as at Pitcullo, where even a seventeenth-century wing was entirely demolished, on the grounds that it made the rest of the work dangerous. At Druminnor, in Aberdeenshire, a later structure was removed, good work by Archibald Simpson, which had the opposite effect on the restored portion, rendering it weak for lack of support.

Pitcullo is another former Balfour seat, L-shaped and possessed of a delightful stone lantern at one corner that takes the place of the more usual turret. The present dining room has been made out of a vaulted basement, with enormous fireplace, and is full of character, but one feels instinctively that had Lorimer done this he would have plastered the underside of the vaulting as he did at Balmanno. All of which brings us back once more to the subject of wall coverings, and to the impression that in some cases where the outside walls have been covered over they should, probably, have been left exposed, and inside where they have been exposed it might have been better to cover them. One wishes there was someone of Lorimer's standing living, a real expert and craftsman in the Scottish tradition with sufficient authority to make sure that the right as well as the best thing is done in each case, especially since we are all paying for some of it from public funds. The original idea of harling, for example: was it meant to make a strong contrast with the stonework, as practised today, or not? If one knew Craigievar before its recent reharling and tidying up for the reception of visitors one can remember there being virtually no difference in colour between harling, stone and pink granite drive, the whole recalling, as John Fleming has remarked, an old-fashioned hard tennis court; while at Crathes the harling used to be greyer to match the greyer granite of the stonework, not contrasted at all. Indeed, one suspects that the masons went to considerable pains to match up the various parts in this way. In East Lothian, it is true, they devised a colourful rendering in which the lime, sand, and ballast used in the harling was turned deep orange by the addition of copper wires in the mixture, and this contrasted with the grey stone of the building, or did it? Much of East Lothian is built of red sandstone. Again, in Perthshire one finds a sort of strawberry pink harling on the cottages, which undoubtedly matches the red stone of the district. Limewash, of course, was another thing, and often took the place of harling, it was mostly used on farm buildings and its colour ranged from almost white to creamy yellow, the variations being produced by the proportion of hydraulic lime to hydrated, the former producing creamier finishes, the latter whiter.

One of the major technical problems overcome by the young Lorimer at Earlshall was the repair of the magnificent ceiling in the Long Gallery, which was painted *en grisaille* and rivalled Pinkie. MacGibbon and Ross, who inspected the ceiling before its restoration, deplored its state and wondered how it could be saved. Well, it was saved by taking every bit of painted timber down, replacing the missing bits and doing a little judicious touching up where necessary; and so professionally was this done that today one scarcely knows what is old and what is not. The subject matter is largely armorial, with the emblems of most of the important Scottish families displayed, together with the more usual improving mottoes and legendary allusions, which here displace the heroes of the Bible and Antiquity. Lorimer did not rebuild Earlshall, leaving a partly ruined portion near the entrance more or less as it was, making a little courtyard behind and tidying up the rest, which still had its roof on. The plan is vaguely a 'Z', one says vaguely because the shape of the two diagonally opposed sections is not the same, and one tower in particular ends in a Renaissance top-piece that owes nothing to Scottish precedent, at least not traditional Scottish precedent. It had its inspiration in work done by the royal masons at Falkland, and at Myres Castle, near Auchtermuchty, which was the seat of the King's macer and sergeant-at-arms, who also happened to be his architect. The royal macer was related by marriage to the lairds of Earlshall as well, so it is no wonder that the Renaissance finish to his tower at Myres should have found some reflection there. It

Monimail Tower

Myres Castle, Auchtermuchty

takes the form of a turreted penthouse, projected from a round tower on corbels, but more significantly, it is decorated with Florentine-inspired roundels which not only have their immediate source in Continental work at Falkland, but were repeated again at nearby Monimail, country residence of the Archbishops of St Andrews.

Monimail was the retreat of no less a personage than Cardinal Beaton, or Bethune, himself, who would naturally wish to be as up-to-date as possible and emulate his royal master at Falkland, both here and at his archiepiscopal castle in St Andrews, of which only the toothiest of remains survive, corroding on the sea cliffs, the few evidences of civilized living showing in armorial panels and Renaissance projections that seem daily to become more jewel-like and abstract as the wind and the salt wear them away. At Monimail the principal tower remains intact, with its delicate mouldings and wreathed roundels decorating the parapet. There was still a little old glass in one of the windows a few years ago, and in an antiquated copy of the Edinburgh Architectural Association's sketch book I found measured drawings of a huge candlestick, now gone alas, which was supposed to be in the tower. It could only have been a Pascal candle and must have predated the Reformation. One imagines it once graced the now wholly ruined metropolitan cathedral of St Andrews, for where else would one find a candlestick 4 feet across at the base and nearly 15 feet high?

After the Reformation the archbishops lived in the Hospitium Novum which had been built to receive Mary of Guise, the consort of James V, when she came from France in 1538, and for country residence they moved to Dairsie, a charming spot a few miles inland, not so far from St Andrews as Monimail and guarded by a strong castle. To this haven came Archbishop Spottiswood, the man who crowned Charles I at Holyrood in 1633, building beside the restored castle a delightful little kirk in what he thought was the gothic style; attempting to re-introduce something decent into ecclesiastical architecture after a generation of despoliation and the creation of 'God-boxes'. The kirk has survived, its interior gutted by the Presbyterians, but other-

wise hale, and is the property of the University of St
Andrews. The castle in which Archbishop Spottiswood wrote
his history of Scotland has all but disintegrated, leaving not
much more than one tall round tower with gun-loops at the
foot and doocot at the top. This part of Fife is known at the
Howe, or hole, a name which it no longer deserves since the
hole, a marshy useless basin, was drained to become one of
the most productive areas in the country in the eighteenth
century.

The capital of Fife, Cupar, lies on the edge of the Howe,
with highish hills with a certain Highland flavour between it
and the Firth of Tay. This is a fairly sparsely populated area
which is rarely explored, though it ought to be, not only on
account of its relative emptiness, which is pleasant, but its
remnants of an as yet not too damaged past. Amongst the
small tower houses that survive there one must have special
attention: it is Collairnie, which the visitor might miss
altogether if he was not careful, as it stands in the middle of
farm steadings, off the road, and could easily be mistaken for
a grain silo at a distance. It is important, though, because
preserved in its interior are two timber ceilings decorated
with the armorials of all the Fife families of consequence, the
numerous Balfours, the Wemysses, Anstruthers, Bethunes
and Lindsays, the Normans who developed the 'kingdom' in
the twelfth and thirteenth centuries and ensured that it
enjoyed comparative peace and prosperity. Collairnie was
actually a Barclay castle in origin, and it is curious why
nothing is ever done to save its precious heraldic record from
deterioration. Everyone seems to realize the necessity to do
something but no one is willing to make the first move.

On the other side of Cupar rises the Hill of Tarvit, with
Scotstarvit Tower commanding the Howe from its well-
chosen position. It was the retreat in the seventeenth century
of Sir John Scot of Scotstarvit and the place where he wrote
his *Staggering State of Scots Statesmen* and worked on the maps
which Blaeu of Amsterdam were to publish in 1651. It is
difficult to understand how the 'Scottish Montaigne'
managed to gather all his friends in the political, literary and
artistic world under the roof of this modest and typical tall

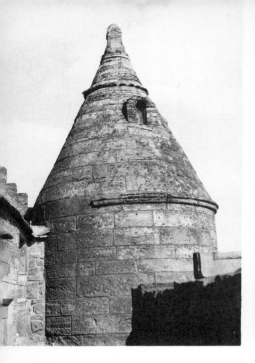

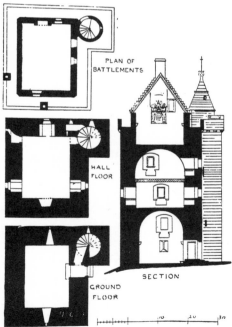

PLAN OF
BATTLEMENTS

HALL
FLOOR

SECTION

GROUND
FLOOR

*Scotstarvit Tower: turret and door
window recess in hall; plans and
section*

tower, which was built as late as 1627. Its plan would be a rectangle but for a small nib containing the spiral staircase and protecting the door, which is on the ground floor. The masonry is regularly coursed and finely wrought. There are no shot- or shut-holes, and the windows are few and tiny. Each room is simply placed above the next, with only the turnpike giving access, and two of the vaulted ceilings survive, the timber floors between them having gone. Also removed is a chimneypiece with the armorial devices and initials of Sir John Scot and his wife, Anne Drummond, sister of the poet. Otherwise the tower is intact and roofed, the cap-house being finished with a conical stone roof, and nearby is a ledge and single opening for pigeons. There is a plain parapet supported on simple corbels and chimney stalks that rise from the outside walls and not at the gable ends, necessitating a flying-buttress-like erection to keep them rigid. The bare rooms, even with their recessed windows and seats, give little impression of any comfort, but one must think of them as being hung with tapestries or curtains, and one, the lord's chamber on the top floor, was panelled, the ceiling beams painted, and there were rugs on the floor and enough furniture.

Further south, towards but not on the coastal strip, is the surprising castle of Balgonie, surprising because its late-medieval tower is complete to the roof, and that was still tiled until a decade or so ago. It was last occupied in the eighteenth century, when Rob Roy MacGregor, a Jacobite free-booter, sacked the place, and after that farmworkers continued to live in the additions and outbuildings right down to modern times. Balgonie was the seat of the Sibbald family, one of whom founded the Royal Botanic Gardens in Edinburgh and was physician to Charles II, but it was purchased in the reign of Charles I by General Alexander Leslie, afterwards first Earl of Leven, a Covenanting soldier who turned his coat more than once and nearly came to grief as a result. He was the offspring of the Captain of the Guard at Blair Castle, in Perthshire, and a 'wench' from Rannoch. He fought for Gustavus Adolphus of Sweden, who made him a Field Marshal, and returning home later offered his sword

*Balgonie Castle, in process of restoration*

to the highest bidder, in the first place the Covenanters, whom he served well in his own tortuous manner, before twice coming to terms with the King, twice swearing never to take up arms against him again, and twice doing so. He eventually partially redeemed his character by walking, in winter, and as an old man, all the way from Balgonie to near Blairgowrie to offer his sword back to the 'White King's' son, Charles II. He then fought at the Battle of Dunbar under his namesake, David Leslie, as an ordinary infantryman, being taken prisoner and put in the Tower of London pending execution. He escaped death through the intervention of Queen Christina of Sweden, and returned to Balgonie, where he died greatly respected, having lived to see the Restoration of the Monarchy in 1660.

Leslie does not seem to have made the old tower his principal habitation, but instead restored some of the outbuildings, and added more, in the Fife vernacular, with crowsteps and red pantiles. Curiously enough it is these, the most recently occupied part of the castle, which are the most ruined today, they following the original line of the *enceinte* which in the time of MacGibbon and Ross was still pierced by a fortified gateway, now 'tummeldoun'. The authors also mention a moat which defended Balgonie on the south, but that is difficult to make out since the land has been given over entirely to farming. The handsome late-medieval tower has been restored as part of Fife's contribution to European Architectural Heritage Year by a friend of mine whose intention is not so much to live there as to use the vaulted rooms as meeting places, and provide accommodation for short visits. After all the walls are enormously thick, 11 feet about, and there is the minimum of window space, each floor being above the other, as at Scotstarvit, and not readily amenable to modern adaptation. Originally a ladder went to the first floor, as was usual in such 'keeps', and there is a separate entrance to the basement, which was not linked to the floor above. Apart from this, access to the upper floors was by an awkward spiral which was replaced by an outer stair when the additions were made and Alexander Leslie came to live there. There is also a fairly long run of barmkin, or outer defence-cum-boundary wall, surviving, easily recognizable from other stone walls dividing the fields by its height and thickness.

The battlements at Balgonie are crenellated, which is rare in Scotland, and there are bartisans at three corners, the fourth being occupied with a cap-house, but no turrets. The corbelling is well preserved and continuous round the base of the parapet and there is a plentiful supply of gargoyles sprouting on all sides. There is no harling intended in the restoration, partly because the stonework is ashlar and in excellent condition and partly because there will be nothing much to cover up; the only doubtful object one might notice here are the crowstepped gables on the old tower, which are unlikely to have been employed on a fourteenth-century defence tower of such strength. The roof was in all probability of stone slabs, not slate, and at a lower pitch than at present, but its raising, crowstepping and slating does not spoil the appearance of this fine building. The slates, incidentally, which came from Angus, by sea, go a delightful sepia shade which improves with weathering and attract a warm yellow lichen.

David Leslie, the other Covenanting general returned from the Swedish service, was of an old Fife family, from Lindores, in the north of the 'kingdom' and his part in the Civil War is almost as tortuous as Alexander's. For instance, it would be interesting to know if his winning of battles against the king and losing those under the royalist banner was purely fortuitous or deliberate. His behaviour at Philiphaugh has been noted, but how he managed to lose at Dunbar is a mystery, unless the evil influence of the ministers was to blame once more, their futile attempts to equate military prowess with godly fervour? In any event, Cromwell's force was tired and small, in a bad position militarily, at Leslie's mercy. Yet it was the latter who was routed, causing the former to declare, "The Lord hath delivered them into our hands". Perhaps He had; but what about Worcester? Leslie again lost the battle for the king; and cynics have suggested that after so poor a showing, and his previous record, instead of being ennobled by a tolerant Charles II David Leslie should have been "hung for his auld wark", a reference to his becoming Lord Newark. Like his name-sake, he built, or rather added to, an older castle which today stands in a dangerous, decaying condition on the edge of the cliffs near St Monans in the East Neuk of Fife. What one sees is a fairly incomprehensible mass of masonry, only partially recognizable as architecture, a mere fragment of the great Dutch gabled 'newark' erected by the retired general survives. More substantial, but of course much smaller, is the fine beehive doocot that matches the castle—on a neighbouring cliff, complete with its rings of pigeon holes, and blocked spaces behind to prevent the birds escaping. In Jacobean times there were more than three hundred doocots in Fife, and James VI, himself superstitious, made it illegal to pull them down; there are still about a hundred listed.

Half way between St Monans and Pittenweem, under the bield of Kellie Law, set back from the coastal plain, but with a good view of it, is Kellie Castle, which for some reason or another does not feature in Billings, though he travelled in these parts and thought very highly of the local architecture, sketching Aberdour, Earlshall and Falkland, even St Monans Kirk and several of the more interesting houses in the East Neuk fishing villages. It is true that Kellie is not battlemented and is more of a large manor, or *château*, like Traquair, but it is a castle and does have plenty of turrets and other baronial features that should have drawn the discriminating Billings. It was decayed at the time, being rescued from falling down by Professor James Lorimer, father of the architect, in the later part of the nineteenth century. He obtained a lease of it from the Earl of Mar and Kellie and set to work to bring the old place back to life, first making it wind- and water-tight and then more comfortable inside. His restoration was actually a renovation, the distinction is important as the inclination to over-restore, even to rebuild, is often very strong and succumbing to it has spoiled many otherwise well-meaning schemes of resuscitation. A castle or house has a personality that ought to be respected by each new owner, and especially those with face-lifting ambitions; as with religion, too much can be worse than too little and Professor Lorimer showed the proper perspective when he made Kellie Castle a home once more, not a too carefully preserved specimen of another age.

There is no harling at Kellie, though plenty of rubble in the masonry and alterations that might conceivably have justified it, in fact I know of no other building of its size and scope with so many alterations and additions showing in the structure, particularly on the garden side, which is a veritable microcosm of the Scottish vernacular in a single elevation that looks more like one side of a street than the façade of a castle. As with most Scottish buildings of the sixteenth and seventeenth centuries the various bulges and breaks in the façade have a utilitarian purpose, several of them denoting stairs within, for in place of corridors separate entry to the rooms is provided by a private stair and lobby. This is a feature shared with Elcho Castle, near Perth, a former seat of the Wemyss's and Maclellan's House, or castle, in

*Kellie Castle: front. Note squinch and, in foreground, doocot with sundial; plans; garden elevation*

Kirkcudbright: the latter by original design since it was built all of a piece, the former having grown that way by degrees and not so interesting to look at as Kellie, its bulges not so attractively disposed, its 'Z' plan so irregular as almost to repel. The disparity between these buildings is clear indication of how Scottish castles generally arrived at their particular forms as much from trial and error as conscious planning, so that the odd combination required to make Elcho and Kellie work produced a happy result in one case and not so happy in the other, while in the case of Maclellan's Castle produced a less wayward and almost perfect solution.

The plan of Kellie actually is more of a 'T' than either a 'Z' or an 'L', the older northern tower, whose base probably dates from the fifteenth century, having been added to on two sides, which is unusual, with a second tower linked to it and a third, possibly once separated and part of an *enceinte*, joined later, in the seventeenth century. The castle belonged in origin to the Seward family, which was Saxon and probably amongst those which came to Scotland with Margaret and Edgar Atheling, the heirs of Alfred the Great, to escape the Norman invaders. Margaret, of course, subsequently married the last Scoto-Pictish king, Malcolm Canmore, and is the Saint Margaret who built the tiny chapel on the castle rock in Edinburgh. Nothing remains of any building the Sewards may have lived in, and it was the Oliphants who built the first stone castle and sold it to the Erskines, in the person of the first Earl of Kellie, in Jacobean times. The earl extended the eastern tower, joined it up to the old northern one and added a new portion to the south, now represented by a handsomely-turreted tower with crowsteps and high-pitched roof, and entered by an elegant scale-and-platt staircase, a rare refinement in seventeenth-century Scotland. Indeed this, the fifth of Kellie's stairs, may not have been installed until the time of the third or fourth earls, who completed the castle as we see it today and possibly employed Sir William Bruce, the King's Architect, and the royal plasterers, on the work, they being busy then, at neighbouring Balcaskie, Bruce's seat. We have already noted how plasterers from York, engaged at Edinburgh Castle, were responsible for the strapwork ceiling in the little library at Kellie; and on closer inspection it will be seen that the chimney stalks at the junction between the north and southern towers rise on a false gable, and in the English Jacobean mode, diagonally placed, as at Winton.

Kellie Castle boasts two squinches, the biggest and most obvious being across the angle between the south-western tower and the long easterly arm. It takes the form of an arch supporting the corbelling of a stair turret that, but for the thrawnness of Scottish masons, might just as well reach to the ground and not require such support. In France a similar device is used when there is a door or window below the corner turret, and then the squinch is camouflaged by a shell-like arch; often decorated as a trellis or some other feature, and called a *trompe*. The other squinch is on the garden side, where there are also a number of Renaissance touches in dormer finials, moulded panels and window surrounds, none of which, however playful, fully prepares one for the elaborate décor of some of the rooms inside. There is some good Restoration panelling in the drawing-room, painted panels in the Dutch manner in the dining-room, and sumptuous plasterwork ceilings not only in the Vine Room, but in several others. Dunsterfield and Halbert almost certainly had a hand in the best examples, and Jacob de Wet painted a central panel in the Vine Room representing the 'Gods in Olympus'. This derives from the ceiling by Mantegna in the Camera degli Sposi in the old palace of the Gonzagas at Mantua, and repeats one in Holyrood except that it is round and not oval; it was for some years in a house in Ireland until traced, and returned to Kellie.

In the nineteenth century there was a dispute over the title of Earl of Mar by which the original earldom, the oldest in Britain and one of the most ancient in Christendom, became separated from that of Mar and Kellie, and it was from the latter that Professor Lorimer rented Kellie Castle when he saved it from wrack and ruin. Robert Lorimer spent his boyhood there and experimented with the layout of the garden and in designing an ogee-roofed gazebo. Less ambitious than at Earlshall he nevertheless achieved a pleasant harmony between traditional Scottish formality and freer modern tastes in which herbs, fruit and vegetables play a decorative part with the flowers and ornamental shrubs in making a delightful walled garden, replete with *jardin secret*, pergolas and other attractions. In 1958, on the death of the twelfth earl, Hew Lorimer, Sir Robert's sculptor son, bought the castle and in 1970 was able to make an arrangement whereby the National Trust took over and maintained it with himself as resident custodian.

# III

# *Stirling, Perth and the Highlands*

NEITHER Stirling nor Perth are actually in the Highlands, but both are gateways to them. Both are county capitals of shires in which at least half of the area is Highland, about two-thirds in Perthshire, and both exude the atmosphere of a meeting place of peoples and cultures. Perth is not a particularly distinguished-looking town, being laid out regularly on flat ground and with few remnants of earlier days, the much restored kirk of St John, where Knox preached one of his most inflammatory sermons, and the former house of the Glover's Guild, referred to by Scott in *The Fair Maid*, are just about all. As some compensation for the flatness of its site Perth has an attractive background to the north, where the first Highland hills reach the Tay, lending themselves to the erection of Rhineland-type follies on appropriate rocky outcrops and a scattering of mock-gothic and pseudo-baronial mansions on the lower slopes. There, is however, little heightening of tension here, not until one follows the Tay valley to Dunkeld and the Forest of Atholl. The Highland line, that geological fault that runs across Scotland at an angle of about forty-five degrees in a south-west to north-easterly direction, begins on the outskirts of Glasgow, at Dumbarton, passes by Callander to cross Stirlingshire before entering Perthshire in Strathearn, reaching the Tay as indicated. Thence it turns more sharply northwards behind Strathmore until it arrives in Kincardineshire and southern Aberdeenshire, where it bends to the north-west, avoiding Banff and Moray and coming down in the middle of Nairn, whose river is usually considered the dividing line. Inverness is called the 'Capital of the

Highlands', though it is scarcely more Highland in feeling than Perth or Stirling, and its immediate environs to the north and east are quite lowland, especially the Black Isle and Beauly Firth. The Highland hills touch the sea in Sutherland, breaking the continuity of the Lowland plain, which is only revived in Caithness, a wholly lowland area, where the inhabitants still speak pretty good Northumbrian English.

Stirling is sited half way between Dumbarton and Perth and almost equidistant also from Glasgow and Edinburgh. It sports a festival of art and drama in imitation of Edinburgh, though less eccentric in character; and like Perth it was once the capital, that being movable depending on where the court happened to be. It is on the Forth, as Perth is on the Tay, at the point where the river ceases to be tidal, is no longer navigable, and where the first bridge crossed in ancient times. To the west the valley of the Forth reaches almost to the shores of Loch Lomond, the easternmost banks of which are in Stirlingshire, as too is the end of the famous Loch Katrine, facts that seem somewhat remote as one walks the busy, workaday streets of Lowland Stirling. Climb the castle hill, on the other hand, past the Kirk of the Halyrude in which Mary, Queen of Scots and her son were crowned, both as infants, to the castle esplanade, with its statue of Robert Bruce set within protective iron spikes, symbolic of the caltrops employed at Bannockburn, and all is changed. The Highlands appear on the horizon and history comes alive, the days of Wallace and Bruce seem but yesterday in such a setting, and one is thrilled in a way quite different from when standing on the esplanade in Edinburgh. So much of the original castle has survived, and the scale of the town below is so much more natural. As one surveys the scene, with the silvery Forth winding its way towards the sea, with the tower of Cambuskenneth Abbey rising in the meadows beside it, one thinks of another battle, that of Sauchieburn, which James III of Scots lost to his rebellious nobles and after which he was murdered by one posing as a confessor. He lies buried in the remains of the choir of the Abbey, with his spouse, Margaret of Denmark; the existing

tomb, replacing one destroyed at the Reformation, was
erected by Queen Victoria.

Before Sauchieburn James III burned the Castle of Airth,
Stirlingshire's easternmost outpost on the Forth. The same
laird was also the possessor of Clackmannan Tower, fourteenth-century redoubt of the Bruces of Clackmannan, seen
to the north of the river. These Bruces were a bastard line
related to the Royal House who received the tower from
David II, son of Robert Bruce, in 1359. They remained in
possession, and living in it, until the end of the eighteenth
century, when the last of them, a lady, amusingly 'knighted'
selected guests with her ancestor's sword. Clackmannan
Tower is one of the best preserved 'keeps' in Scotland, it is a
hundred years older than Borthwick and was originally a
simple rectangle. In the fifteenth century it became L-
shaped, the newer piece actually being taller than the old,
though in much the same style, with lower adjuncts and
heavily machicolated, indented battlements. All this is intact, plus other extensions made in the sixteenth century,
when the tower was made more comfortable inside and
henceforth entered via a handsome Renaissance doorway.
The building is not quite a ruin, only decayed, which
qualifies it for approbation by Messrs Ruskin and Butler,
who both thought ruins fakes, and it has been under repair
for at least a quarter of a century. These repairs have been
occasioned as much by subsidence caused by local coal
mining as anything, and the tower, a small portion of which
collapsed not so long ago, is still not open to the public. On
the other hand, one can walk fairly close up to it and enjoy
its splendid view. Clackmannan Tower stands on a commanding hill in relatively flat country beside the Forth, on
the edge of the little town of the same name that serves as
county capital of Scotland's smallest shire. In its erstwhile
marketplace stands the 'clack', a quaint masonic talisman,
not unlike a very modern war memorial, but lacking any
inscription, which ornaments the place in front of the
Jacobean Town House, itself sporting a gay ogee-roofed
tower of Netherlandish inspiration.

Clackmannan county is more often considered an appen-

*Blackmannan Tower*

*Menstrie Castle: Detail from the Nova Scotia room*

dage of Stirlingshire than of Fife, and in truth it has a
Highland feel on its northern boundary that deserves this
association. The Ochils become Highland near Airthrey,
where the first of the ancient crossings of the Forth is, and
Stirling University has installed itself in the grounds of what
remains of Airthrey Castle, former seat of the Haldanes of
Gleneagles and later the home of Sir Ralph Abercromby of
Aboukir Bay fame. He is thought to have been born in
nearby Menstrie Castle, a much restored wing of which rises
rather oddly from the midst of a council estate in Menstrie
village. Airthrey was designed by Robert Adam in his Scottish castellated style, and the drawings, which survive, show
a transitional stage between the slightly self-conscious use of
turrets and crenellations at Culzean and the balder, more
basically fort-like appearance of Seton. In fact, the principal
façade for Airthrey probably represents the architect's most
satisfactory exercise in the *genre*. Unfortunately it was not
built as designed, the Haldane brothers kept the plan but
employed their own staff on its interpretation, and, as so
frequently happens when the hand of the master is not in
evidence, bungled his scheme, so that when, in the nineteenth century, a Glasgow businessman came along and
Scotch-baronialized the castle the loss was perhaps less than
might otherwise have been the case.

Menstrie was the country seat of Sir William Alexander,
Viscount Canada and first Earl of Stirling. It was he who
suggested to James VI and I the colonization of Nova Scotia
by selling property there, plus titles to go with it, as a means
of filling the royal coffers and bringing aid to the royal cause.
Curiously enough the first Baronetcy was not created until a
month after the demise of King James, in May 1625, and by
far the majority of titles belong to the succeeding reign. Sir
William was both courtier and poet, as well as cavalier, and
Menstrie Castle was a considerable place in its heyday. It
was built around a courtyard and was more of a large manor
house or 'palas' than a castle. The fragment that remains
became the subject of controversy in the 1960s when it was
proposed to demolish it, but in the event the National Trust
for Scotland and the local authority came together and saved

it, commemorating its connection with Sir William Alexander and the baronets of Nova Scotia in a special room set
aside as a memorial to the venture. The walls are decorated
with shields of the holders, except for two, Sir William Bruce
of Kinross, King's Architect, who had only one descendant,
and Sir John de Medina, the 'Scottish Kneller', who was the
last baronet created before the union of the Parliaments in
1707. As most were Caroline in origin a portrait of King
Charles I was bought and placed in the centre of their coats
of arms. With outstanding architectural features Menstrie
Castle is not over-endowed; it was formerly pantiled like a
big farmhouse, and is now slated, a conically-capped turret
surviving at one corner; and the old courtyard entrance
through a rounded arch is interesting because its decoration
includes Renaissance motifs as well as the more traditional
Scottish cable-coursing and columned supports that recall
the Romanesque.

Sir William Alexander's forbears hailed from Argyll and
were Highlanders known by the name of MacAlister, of
which Alexander is the Lowland version. They came to this
part of Scotland from the west in the train of Colin Campbell, first Earl of Argyll, who was Chancellor to James IV of
Scots and the first of his house to involve himself in Lowland
politics. He died before Flodden, in which battle his son was
killed, but in 1489 he rebuilt and renamed one of the most
fascinating castles hereabouts. The King and Court resided
mostly at Stirling and the Earl required secure and commodious quarters not too far away, so he acquired an existing rectangular tower set in a secluded site in a fold of the
Ochils then called Castle Gloume, which he changed to
Castle Campbell by royal proclamation, and enlarged and
embellished in the early Renaissance manner. The castle lies
up a short glen and is built on a rounded hillock at the point
where the Burns of Care and Sorrow join and flow down to
the village of Dollar, which some have equated with dolour,
thus completing a trio of gloomy connotations. It is indeed in
an extraordinary position this renamed castle of the Lords of
Campbell and Lorn, for it is quite invisible from Dollar
itself, though if one knows where to look one can see it from

*Castle Campbell, Dollar:
detail of loggia; general
view*

a greater distance, standing up like an eagle in its eyrie above the bracken and few trees. Behind is open moorland and emptiness, except for sheep; and nothing could be more contrasted than this wild emptiness and the almost suburban air of Dollar, which has become a dormitory and weekend retreat for townfolk from as far away as Glasgow.

The original castle which the first Earl of Argyll acquired is still hale and roofed, consisting of three barrel-vaulted rooms one above the other, and one floored in timber. To it the Earl added a whole new range of buildings at different levels, linking them with a staircase tower and containing courtyard wall. The most attractive feature here is the lovely little arcaded loggia that actually joins the bottom storeys at the foot of the new stair, and which in its refined design and workmanship recalls the Great Hall at Stirling Castle, which was completed a little earlier by Robert Cochrane, Master Mason to James III. Part of Castle Campbell is inhabited by

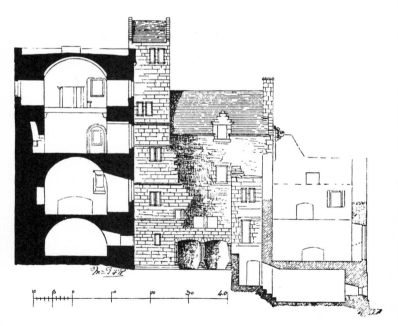

*Castle Campbell: section looking east*

a custodian, and the whole property is maintained by the Department of the Environment on behalf of the National Trust for Scotland to whom it was made over in 1950. The Campbells were ambitious and soon lost their Highland attributes, taking the side of Knox, who stayed at the castle, and the Lords of the Congregation against Mary of Guise; and again in cavalier times the eighth Earl and first Marquis was responsible for the pantomime crowning of Charles II at Scone in 1651 and the hanging, drawing and quartering of Montrose not long afterwards. He himself suffered, but with a cleaner death, at the Restoration, while his son, the ninth Earl, paid a similar price for supporting the Duke of Monmouth against James VII and II. The Massacre of Glencoe is normally laid at the door of the Campbells, though it was a Dalrymple, the Earl of Stair, who actually engineered it, and to this day there are many Scots who regard all Campbells with suspicion. Be this as it may, the first Duke of Argyll (though he took the Hanoverian side in 1715, and led the army that fought the Jacobites under the Earl of Mar at Sheriffmuir, between Castle Campbell and Stirling) was a moderate man and strove for political peace and economic progress. He almost fell over backwards in an effort not to carry on the struggle with Mar too conclusively, and it is odd that the latter, who could have defeated him, having superior forces, broke off the engagement at a critical moment and allowed the first Jacobite Rebellion to collapse.

The position of Stirling Castle is reminiscent of that of Edinburgh, but the town being smaller and the site more open one sees it better, and especially from the south and west where, despite the encroachment of housing estates, there are still fields in the immediate foreground. The buildings sit proudly on a rocky spur jutting out into the plain and are approached, like Edinburgh, via a long, steep High Street lined with old houses, many of them recently restored and on the whole more authentic than most in Edinburgh's celebrated 'Royal Mile'; the house of James IV's tailor, for instance; and on one side of the formerly cobbled, now alas tar-macadamed, central square is the Burgh Tolbooth, with a neat tower and cupola added by Sir William

*Stirling Castle from the west, the King's Knot in the foreground*

Bruce in 1703. The road turns sharply east to west near its summit, beside the tall, flamboyant apse of the Kirk of the Halyrude, then passes a quaint, corroded-looking mass of dark masonry and extravagant carving which is called 'Mar's Wark'. This crumbling façade was begun but never finished in the time of James VI, by the Earl of Mar whose Countess had charge of the boy king, and he sought to emulate the rich Continental sculpture of the Palace Block at the Castle. Nothing could be less like its model, which was the work of skilled craftsmen imported by Mary of Guise, who created in Stirling a good replica of a French *château* of the period, with twisted columns, Italian-inspired detail and some quite remarkable statuary, including the first nudes seen in Scotland. The Earl of Mar's wall of 'fenestrated-sculpture' is coarse and clumsy and was done after the French masons and their assistants had departed. The Earls of Mar were, and still are, Keepers of the Castle, and it is interesting to note that in the days of Charles II the Duke of Lauderdale attempted to buy the then Earl out, in order that the King might have sole control of his own establishment, but without success.

Opposite 'Mar's Wark' is Argyll's Lodging, a very different piece of architecture. It was built in Charles I's time by Sir William Alexander and is the most perfect example of a private Renaissance town dwelling in Scotland. It is not dissimilar in arrangement from a French *hôtel*, with high wall to the street and central rusticated gateway, a minor version of the Luxembourg, with arms coming out from a central *corps de logis*, itself rich in Italianate sculpture and gay with conical turrets and ornate dormer finials that give the place a more picturesque, native appearance. The name comes from the residence there in the second half of the seventeenth century, of the ninth Earl of Argyll, in the days before he turned against James VII and II, who actually stayed in the house when Duke of York. It is not a castle, of course, but could almost be one if transplanted into the country and bereft of its enclosed entrance court. It is now a Youth Hostel, and with its odd neighbour across the street prepares one for the greater architectural and historical glories of Stirling Castle on whose doorstep they stand.

The former royal fortress and palace is protected by latter-day defences erected in the eighteenth century, when the conical caps to the twin towers of the gatehouse, dating from the fifteenth century, were lopped off and replaced by prosaic crenellations and un-Scottish battlements. The army are gradually being eased out of the castle, the Argylls having their officers' mess and museum there, but otherwise the various quarters and notably the Great Hall, which was the masterpiece of James III's architectural favourite, Robert Cochrane, and one of the first buildings in Britain to display Renaissance features, is in the progress of demilitarization. It will be years before the work of restoration is finished and even then the hall cannot be returned to its original condition, as the hammer-beam roof it once had, minstrels' gallery and other features have gone; but at least the external masonry is capable of being revealed in something like its old form, and the partitions and floors inserted by the military removed. A preview of what can be done is already visible in

*Stirling Castle: corner of the Great Hall; iron yett*

a portion of the Palace Block, built a century later in the reign of James V. This was formerly ceiled with a coffered ceiling in oak, decorated with carved roundels depicting the heroes of Antiquity, the Bible and sixteenth century sovereigns, a few of which have survived but not *in situ*. They were still there in the mid-eighteenth century until one fell and injured a soldier, when it was proposed to burn the lot. Fortunately most of them were rescued in time by the governor of Stirling prison, and apart from three, which are in the Museum of Antiquities in Edinburgh, they may be seen in the Smith Institute in Stirling. Two of the three exceptions are said to represent James V and Mary of Guise respectively, the third is of a joyous cherub, or *putto*.

Of more ancient buildings there are few at Stirling, though there has been a castle of some sort on the site for many centuries, certainly long before the days of James II, his son and grandson, with which it is usually associated. It was in a room in the castle that one of the many bloody acts in the feud between the Stewarts and the Douglases was enacted, when William, eighth Earl of Douglas, was murdered by the king on the excuse that he was plotting to overthrow the royal power. The small room in which this is thought to have occurred is shown to visitors, with the window from which the body of the luckless Douglas was thrown by James II's attendants. Many years afterwards a skeleton was found outside and supposed to be that of the murdered earl. This same nobleman's brother had taken part in a grand tournament under the castle walls a few years earlier, when Burgundian knights tilted with Scots and fought each other *à outrance*; and the castle also witnessed the remarkable exploits of a misguided priest who, inspired by the discoveries of Leonardo da Vinci, jumped from the battlements and attempted to fly. He fell to the ground, but was not badly hurt, and when he repeated the demonstration he again survived. The scene was probably near the King's Knot, one of the first formal gardens laid out in Scotland, in which a series of rising and diminishing terraces were built to make an artificial mound, or *monte*, and surrounded by walks and alleys in which peacocks and·cranes and other exotic birds strolled freely. The shape of the King's Knot can still be made out below the castle on its southern side, now wholly grassed over but distinguishable just the same.

The best-preserved and most recently restored part of Stirling Castle is the Chapel which James VI and I rebuilt for the christening of his eldest son, Henry, future Prince of Wales, in 1594. An older building had functioned as Chapel Royal and Collegiate Kirk, and supported the first Scottish Choir School, or Sang Schule, a special concern of James III, who was extremely fond of liturgical music, sung or played, and which has its only counterpart in modern Scotland in St Mary's Cathedral Music School in Edinburgh. The Stirling school came to grief largely on account of the king's too great encouragement of artists in an age when such pursuits were considered secondary to war; and in the end the king and his cultural associates were all murdered by jealous nobles. However, nothing that occurred in that older Chapel Royal could have surpassed the expensive and glittering show put on by James VI in order to impress not only his own subjects with his wealth and power but folk in England and in the world at large. He spent as much as £100,000 on the rebuilding and furnishing of the Chapel, on the splendid baptism ceremony and subsequent banquet in the Great Hall; and amongst those present was the Earl of Sussex, who carried the infant Prince Henry to the font and no doubt reported to his royal mistress in London every nuance and detail of the event. After serving a variety of purposes, including that of dance hall for the Argylls, the Chapel Royal has now been cleared of its more secular impedimenta and made into a memorial to the regiment which garrisoned Stirling Castle for so long. It is a Renaissance structure of considerable refinement, with a rounded arched doorway in the middle of the main façade, and inside a handsome Florentine frieze and fine timber roof. Suitable royal portraits adorn the walls, plus regimental banners,: the total effect, if not entirely religious, at least invoking the atmosphere of a school or college hall.

Throughout the fourteenth and fifteenth centuries the Stewarts were plagued by feuds, not only with the Douglases, who were as powerful as they were, but with other nobles and pressure groups including their own relatives. The fact is they were not of royal origin and gained the throne through the marriage of Robert the Steward to Marjory Bruce. They did not imagine they would succeed the hero of Bannockburn or his son as rulers of Scotland, if rule is the right word for the extraordinary muddling along through murder and blackmail, with the occasional period of relative stability that characterizes the first two hundred years of Royal Stewart history. One could expatiate at some length on the subject of Stewart inability to govern, or how this race of Breton immigrants, established in Scotland in the wake of the Anglo-Norman penetration, came eventually to command such loyalty and provide so much readable history, and who were amongst the most cultured monarchs in Europe. Suffice to say that when the son of Robert the Steward became king, as Robert II, he was related to and not in any marked degree different from the rest of the Scottish

nobles of the Norman ascendancy. It was not until his
grandson, James I of Scots, married Joan Beaufort, of the
Plantagenet line in England, and made a determined effort
to set up firm government in Scotland and create a viable
and widely acceptable monarchical system that the Stewarts
could be said to be either royal or in command of any
kingdom.

Robert II was succeeded in his old age by Robert III, who
left everything to his more forceful brother, the Duke of
Albany, and it was the Duke of Albany who acquiesced in
and did nothing to end the imprisonment of his rival and
nephew, James I, in England. The boy king languished in
the south for eighteen years, ostensibly as the ward first of
Henry IV and then of Henry V, until funds were found in
Scotland to pay for that wardship, really ransom money, and
he returned home. One of his first acts was to cut off the
heads of Albany's son and grandsons. They had lived in the
great castle of Doune, which they built. It stands at the
junction of two rivers, the Teith and the Ardoch, but not in
an elevated position like Castle Campbell. Doune is the finest
and best-preserved specimen of a late fourteenth-century
castle of *enceinte* in Scotland, its erection coinciding with the
imprisonment of James I at Windsor Castle and with the
height of the Hundred Years' War, when a Scots Guard was
set up in France under Charles VII to fight the English and
in which almost every well-known Scottish family was
represented. Henry V actually took his young Scottish charge
to the Continent with him to witness the Battle of Agincourt,
and it was after seeing how the English archers decimated
the French cavalry that James made a vow never to let that
happen in his country. When he came home again he introduced 'wappinschaws', or armed contests on the Swiss
model, and these usually occurred on Sundays, after church,
in place of football, which was banned in order to promote
military preparedness. The period of the Hundred Years'
War marked an important phase in the celebrated Auld
Alliance between France and Scotland, and there can
be little doubt that French influence prevailed both in
ecclesiastical and military architecture in Scotland at the

*Doune Castle, a Moray seat: general view; view from the south-west, with some suggested restorations*

time, Doune Castle being a good example in the military field.

MacGibbon and Ross show Doune as it was before its partial restoration by the Earl of Moray in 1883, though their volume came out a year or two later. The authors also give a conjectural restoration of their own which is not too thorough to defy credibility and is considerably more natural looking (if one can use the phrase in respect of the building) than the over-thorough restoration that occurred at contemporary Pierrefonds under the guidance of that archrestorer, but undoubted expert, Monsieur Viollet-le-Duc. I mention Pierrefonds specifically as even our friends MacGibbon and Ross admit similarities between this huge for-

*Doune Castle: plan of first floor*

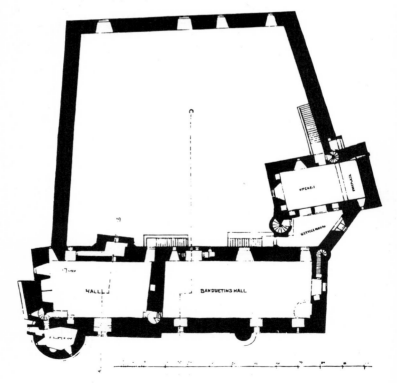

*Doune Castle: view in Service Room*

tress in the Forest of Compiègne and Doune. The similarities
are both visual and on plan, the latter, however, providing
the most obvious links. This shows no keep as such but a
strongly fortified gatehouse, attached to but not opening
directly into a lower range of buildings the principal of
which is the banqueting hall; and this adjoins the kitchen
and guest rooms, running round a bend of the main walls.
The whole area of the castle is enclosed within these outer
walls, to which gatehouse, hall and kitchens are attached. It
has been suggested that other buildings were intended to be
added, including a chapel, the possible position of which
being marked by a gothic window that survives. The actual
chapel, really only a private oratory, was contained within a
slight projection of the inner face of the gatehouse, with an
opening into the private quarters of the lord and his lady, on
the second floor of his solar, or hall. As in other castles of the
period passages and spiral stairs are formed in the thickness
of the masonry, one down to the lord's wine cellar, while
three outer staircases, originally covered, reached to the first
floors on the courtyard side.

The Earl of Moray's restoration was not for the purpose of

making the castle habitable again, but merely to render it
wind- and watertight and to recreate the essentials of a
fifteenth-century interior, especially of the banqueting hall,
whose timber roof was replaced, so that one can see today
exactly how the fortress-cum-manor, which Doune was,
functioned. Particularly notable are the arrangements
between the hall and the kitchen, a triangular-shaped area
being used both as back-hall and reception room, where
goods as well as people came, rather than to the lord's
quarters, or straight into the great hall. A small spiral led
guests up to their rooms above the kitchen, and some
remarkable hatches exist between the kitchen and service
area, the arches being what in France would qualify as *anses
de panier,* or basket-handles. Such features are rare in
Scotland and virtually unknown in England, where flat
arches either come to a small point at the centre, as in the
lintels to chimneypieces in the Cardinal Wolsey parts of
Hampton Court, or were literally flat, as in the perpen-
dicular style, not gently elliptical as here. The same form of
arch is used over the gothic fireplaces in the lord's hall and
private room, also in a guest room over the kitchen, but the
smoke from the fire in the middle of the floor of the
banqueting hall went out through the timber roof. In the
kitchen a special hole in the stone vaulting was made above
the big open range, and there were louvres in the ceiling as
well for ventilation. Sanitation was not neglected at Doune
and *garderobes,* or small lavatories, were provided in the
thickness of the walls. Over the pend under the fortified
gatehouse a further refinement existed in the lord's secret
room, from which he could see what was going on in the hall
without himself being seen.

Work at Doune ended with the execution of Murdoch,
second Duke of Albany, his progeny and their associate the
Earl of Lennox, in 1424. The first Duke had been responsible, or so it was thought, for the murder of the king's
brother, David, Duke of Rothesay, at Falkland, and Murdoch and the Lennoxes were in league to usurp the royal
power and keep the king in captivity in England as long as
possible. They were done to death at Stirling by the royal

command, but the memory of it was to remain and rankle in Lennox hearts so that when Henry, Lord Darnley, whose father was Earl of Lennox, married Mary, Queen of Scots, he did so as much out of revenge, or at any rate in an attempt to get even with her, as anything else. This explains some of his odd behaviour; it also explains the sad story of his niece, Arabella Stewart, whom James VI of Scots and I of England prevented from marrying and so producing heirs, the title and lands of Lennox thus staying in Royal Stewart hands. They passed in due course to the descendants of Charles II, including property in France as well as Scotland. The Earls of Moray are Royal Stewarts on the bastard side and have possessed Doune uninterruptedly since the sixteenth century, the estate becoming the inheritance of the Earl's eldest son, Lord Doune. The most recent holder succeeded to the Moray Earldom in 1974, having added to the attractions of the castle and park by creating a very fine museum of old cars rivalling that at Beaulieu.

The village of Doune, still keeping its ancient mercat, or market cross, used to be well known for its pistols, which were made there, but today it is a quiet retreat and what little importance attaches to the district has passed to neighbouring Dunblane, whose beautiful cathedral entranced Ruskin. This was the see of the saintly Bishop Leighton, who attempted to bring Presbyterian and Episcopalian together in the mid-seventeenth century, and failed, his principal memorial in Dunblane being the library he founded and left to the cathedral, it being the oldest, but not free, library in Scotland. In the cathedral, which has been restored more than once and most recently by the late Sir Robert Lorimer, will be found the three slab tombs of the Drummond sisters, and notably of Margaret Drummond, who was reputedly married to James IV of Scots and 'removed', presumably by poisoning, with her sisters, so that he could marry Margaret Tudor. It is the sort of legend that cannot easily be proved true or untrue, though Lord Ancaster, who lives at Drummond Castle and inherited the Drummond estates through marriage, has the relevant documents and has offered to let me examine them. The

Drummonds are traditionally supposed to have accompanied Margaret Atheling and her brother Edgar when they fled to Scotland from the Normans at the end of the eleventh century, having previously found refuge in Hungary; and the first Drummond is said to have been the captain of the ship bringing them to our shores, hence the wavy lines on the Drummond coat of arms. Be this as it may, the family is of pre-Norman origin and the story may very well be correct in essence.

Drummond Castle, which lies just over the watershed from the Forth valley in that of the Earn, has been much altered down the centuries, but the base of a medieval tower has survived and now serves as entrance gateway and small museum. It stands on a rocky eminence which on one side, to the north, remains rustic and wild, but on the other looks onto a magnificent Italian garden, This was originally laid out in the reign of Charles II by a member of the Mylne family, who worked in Perthshire as well as at Holyrood and in the Lowlands generally, recreated for a visit by Queen Victoria and again resuscitated after the last war. As one approaches the castle from the north the lochan, or small lake, one sees in the fields, recalls the temporary occupation of the grounds by government troops during the Forty-five, the memory of which was so nauseating to the Jacobite dowager Duchess of Perth that she had the area where they encamped flooded to eradicate it. She was the widow of one of James VII and II's most avid supporters, married into a family whose loyalty went so far as conversion to the same papist religion as the king. 'His faith hath saved him' was the cynical remark of a contemporary when the Earl, soon to become Duke, followed the royal lead. He was, in fact, the one *de facto* Duke, the others existing only in exile on the Continent and not recognized in Britain. They married into Continental families and it was not until the nineteenth century that the disabilities pertaining to such persons were lifted; and not until the middle of the same century that the Perths, accepted as earls but not as dukes, returned to their ancestral domains, or to part of them, for Lord Ancaster generously made over the Dower House of Stobhall, or

*Drummond Castle, from the Italian garden*

Stobschaw, to the present Earl, who has restored it nicely and made it an easier and more convenient home than Drummond Castle itself.

Drummond was largely destroyed by Cromwell so that its first rebuilding came at the Restoration and was much modified in Victorian times, the gatehouse and lower portion of the original tower remaining as a record of what had gone before, embellished with new battlements in approved baronial style. Alongside rose the present fairly modest mansion, not the grandiose affair proposed by Sir Charles Barry, architect of the Houses of Parliament, in which Drummond would have become a vast Italian *castello*; the drawings exist and suggest a scheme which for once would not have entirely destroyed the character of the old 'keep' and its surroundings, and which would certainly have been in harmony with the Italian garden. The 'keep' had retained its double yett, or iron gates, plus other features that would perhaps have gone quite well in a sturdy Florentine fortress, which is more than can be said for the turreted house that was built instead—it is scarcely complimentary to the large formal garden that fills the valley below. The family had other visitors besides Queen Victoria (who was entertained to a banquet in the midst of this splendid garden) in the persons of Charles X of France and later the Empress Eugénie, who was a frequent guest; and although the building in which they were housed is itself not outstandingly authentic it does contain some very interesting objects. The documents concerning James IV's marriage to Margaret Drummond have been mentioned, but there are also fine portraits: a Jamesone of Charles I, a Hondthorst, which I identified, of Sophie, younger daughter of Elizabeth 'the Winter Queen' and mother of George I, and an Allan Ramsay of Charles Edward in checked plaid copied from a miniature by Sir Robert Strange.

Stobhall is nearer Perth, on the banks of the Tay, and if not a castle is at least a fortified house. I say house because the main building is no more than that, dating from the mid-eighteenth century and not very different in appearance from any other Scotch house of the period; almost a but-and-ben, with upper floor in the roof lit with dormer windows, and stair rising directly from the door. Beyond, under a pend, is its principal feature in the form of a pre-Reformation chapel and priest's house, the latter turreted and tall in the sixteenth-century manner and once the retreat of Ruskin and Mr and Mrs Millais, in the days when naïvety and permissiveness were in their infancy and wife-swapping not yet a Home Counties amusement. The chapel is gothic and replete with stone *mensa*, or altar, and delightful aumbry, or wall cupboard for keeping the sacramental vessels and altar wine in. It has a wooden door ventilated with fretwork louvres. The ceiling is the *pièce de résistance*, being painted all over with portraits of contemporary kings and potentates and their arms and insignia, dating from the reign of Charles I but retouched and possibly repainted in the nineteenth century. This was not a funerary building of any kind and the burial chapel of the Drummonds, which has survived

intact, with iron bars guarding the open windows and earth
floor, is at Innerpeffray, beside the library founded by David
Drummond, Lord Madderty. The library dates from a few
years later than Bishop Leighton's at Dunblane but is free,
the oldest in Scotland.

There are a number of mortuary chapels in Strathearn, the
one at Gleneagles being the oldest and traditionally founded
by St Mungo, or Kentigern, first Bishop of Glasgow. Its
present form is that of a simple crowstepped shed, restored
this century in memory of Bishop Chinnery Haldane of
Argyll and the Isles, and it stands between the House of
Gleneagles and the ruins of the hoary pile that preceded it,
in the glen of the church, or eagles, which territory has been
in the possession of the Haldanes of that Ilk for seven
hundred years. Another Norman family whose estate
marched with Gleneagles were the Murrays of Tulliebardine,
ancestors of the Dukes of Atholl, who founded a slightly
larger collegiate kirk in the vicinity which has survived to
this day unaltered and structurally perfect. It dates from the
fifteenth century having been built by Sir David Murray in
1446 and is fortified around its squat square tower with
loopholes. Crowstepped in the vernacular like St Mungo's at
Gleneagles the transepts, nave and altar space of its cross
plan are equal in area. The church is not used, indeed it has
remained undamaged because it was not a parish kirk but a
private establishment maintained by its builders, and it is
now in the care of the Department of the Environment.

The Murrays now reside elsewhere in the country, the
Tulliebardine branch merging with the Stewarts of Atholl
and having their seat at Blair Castle, while another branch,
represented by the Earl of Mansfield, lives at Scone. The
eldest son of Lord Mansfield is Viscount Stormont, which is
an interesting connection both as regards the title itself and
its territorial derivation, for in Scotland it is still considered
important to try and keep land and name together. It makes
heraldry so much simpler and avoids hyphens, which in any
case have no official place north of the Border though used
indiscriminately as status symbols amongst the uninitiated.
With the viscountcy of Stormont goes one of the most in-

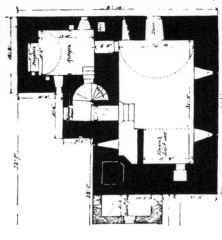

*Stobhall: the Priest's Tower*

*Balvaird Castle: plan of ground floor;*
*general view of the castle, a Murray seat*

triguing of ruined castles in Perthshire, Balvaird, which MacGibbon and Ross place in 'Fifeshire', though it is just inside the Perthshire boundary, in a hidden site between northern Fife and Strathearn. The surroundings are curiously deserted and wild, yet within a quarter of a mile of a turn in the road that brings lowland warmth and well-being to this seemingly remote and Highland-looking spot above Glen Farg. Ostensibly L-shaped on plan Balvaird has a separate tower in the angle containing stair and entrance, suggesting a very early version of Craigievar, where, however, the similarities cease, for its skyline, remarkably intact for a building that has been empty for so long, boasts crenellated battlements with open bartisans; and on top of the angle tower is built a higher replica as a cap-house, with its own chimney-stalk and corner bartisans, a veritable miniature of the main structure.

The older part of Balvaird was built by Sir Andrew Murray, a son of Sir William Murray of Tulliebardine, who married Margaret Barclay, heiress of Balvaird, both of whose arms appear over the entrance at the foot of the spiral staircase. Later additions included a new outer entrance and barmkin wall to the fifteenth-century structure in 1567, and oddly enough these adjuncts are more ruinous than the earlier work. Being of so comparatively late a date for a defensive building a number of refinements occur, presaging those of the less warlike Jacobean period, when decorative corbelling, elaborate chimneystalks and rich armorial carving was used, not as here to frighten off would-be assailants but to impress the neighbours. A particularly unusual feature at Balvaird is the arrangement for the ventilation and swilling out of water closets, by the provision of a spout and flue in the thickness of the wall, and movable stone at the base for the removal of waste. A successor to the first Murray laird, the Reverend Andrew Murray, parson at Abdie, was created Baron Balvaird by King Charles I for his moderate attitude towards the royal ecclesiastical policy, much to the fury of some of his more militant fellow ministers; and his son inherited the viscountcy of Stormont, which as we have seen goes with the Murray earldom of Mansfield. If it did not, no

*Balmanno Castle, Bridge of Earn, restored by Lorimer*

doubt the present viscount would be happy to sell Balvaird to a would-be restorer, for it is still not beyond redemption. Unfortunately there is no made-up road to it, and no services, which might cost as much to install as the actual work of restoration, but every time one passes one feels sorry to see so splendid a place unoccupied.

Still on the borders of Perthshire and Fife, and not far from Bridge of Earn, is the white, harled castle of Balmanno, made white and harled by Sir Robert Lorimer when he restored it in 1916. This was also a Murray house, but descended to farm use, until its complete renovation as a modernized laird's tower made it one of Lorimer's best and most successful rejuvenations. Earlshall was the first and Dunderave the second in a happy group of imaginative restorations. If Balmanno lacks the robustness of Dunderave, and is perhaps less authentic in its newness than Earlshall, it nevertheless has much to teach the restorers of today, many of whom, whilst deploring Lorimer's liberties with the Scottish baronial style, have much less appreciation of the living traditions of Scottish architecture and seem more concerned with archaeology than the evolution of native methods. It is true that here the architect added things that were not there before, especially in the ogee-roofed turret with which he crowned the stair tower, and he framed the *tout ensemble* with side wings and an entirely new courtyard and gatehouse; but why not if it improved the overall effect and made the building more upstanding and beautiful than it had been without materially altering the plan and general shape.

Lorimer was very keen on the surprise view of buildings, and at Earlshall he had already created a new approach with his gatehouse, but not in the same form as here, not a forecourt that is, and the castle itself is different and needed different treatment. The new entrance block is low and unobtrusive, constructed and finished in rough stone, not harled, while the castle stands at a slightly higher level, at the far side of the court, from which it is divided by a few steps and balustrading. The walled garden has also been remade, with sundial and gazebos, the latter roofed ogee fashion with fancy animal carvings on the copings which, admittedly, are not to everyone's taste. There are precedents for something of the sort, though not in quite the same context. At Cawdor, for instance, there is a large chimneypiece with a lintel carved with foxes smoking, cats playing violins and monkeys blowing horns, huntsmen, mermaids and hounds; but they are not grotesque in an unpleasant way, nor Walt Disney-ish in a cloying way, which is almost true of some of Lorimer's animal sculpture. Still, the clever restoration of the castle proper is not much affected by the stone oddities in the garden. The plan is an L-shaped one, and like Balvaird, Balmanno has a stair tower in the angle, old photographs showing that it was harled before restoration and presumably that was one reason why Lorimer decided it should be harled afterwards, as well as to hide 'improvements'. When he did harl he did so with thought and refinement, and students of good detail should notice how, instead of bringing the harling over the crowsteps, as has been done by government departments and others since the war, he stopped it against a narrow stone margin, making a neat and attractive finish. He did this in the Balcarres estate office for Lord Crawford, at Colinsburgh, where he also made a plinth of rough masonry at the foot of the building so as not to run the harling right to the ground, where it gets all dirty and splashed. These touches are the kind of thing that enhance the vernacular and are complementary to it.

It may be noted that at Balmanno the window sashes mostly diminish from ground floor to the top storeys, and the ogee-capped turret on the stair tower is completed with a nice big cock and weather vane. The barrel-vaulted basements, which in their original form would have been out with the normal living quarters, have been brought into use without resort to over sophistication or folksy tricks, the ceilings and walls being plastered, not left looking like a cave or the interior of a railway tunnel, only the tooled stonework around the doors and chimneypieces being exposed.

The plasterwork at Balmanno is in any case notable, and includes a splendid Jacobean ceiling in one of the smaller bedrooms clearly inspired by that of the little library at

Kellie, which Lorimer of course knew intimately as his father's. Again, a coved ceiling at the top of the stairs, and a more magnificent one in the drawing-room, replete with heavily moulded circular feature, are in the seventeenth-century manner, the drawing-room related to the Dunsterfield and Halbert tradition. One might add that such distinctive finishes are not confined to the larger, more important subjects but appear in a number of minor ways: oak panels hiding the central heating pipes, for example, are carved and fretted with novel designs reminiscent of the ventilation decor on the aumbry door in the chapel at Stobhall.

Balvaird stands on high ground above Glen Farg, Balmanno on low ground at the northern entrance to the same glen, while across the valley of the Earn, beyond Moncreiffe Hill and down by the River Tay itself, lies Elcho, one of the least visited but most interesting of the later Scottish castles. It is described in the Ancient Monuments book as a 'fortified manor', the fortified portion consisting of a square tower containing a fine and uncommonly wide ceremonial stair-case, which leads to the hall and principal apartments on the first floor. This tower is capped with battlements and guarded by a curious sentry box with coved stone roof. The rest of Elcho is more in line with Kellie, that is, domestic looking, with crowstepped gables and high pitched roofs pierced by dormers with carved stone finials; and there are four divergently shaped towers on the river side, two rounded and topped with projecting rectangular features, and two rectangular all the way up, one of these indicating an enormous chimney in the kitchen wing. The others mark the position of separate staircases that rise to bedrooms on the upper floors, each room boasting its own private lobby and lavatory. Like Kellie there are at least five staircases in Elcho Castle, and besides them a corridor or passage links the rooms on the ground floor, so that an almost modern conception of amenity and privacy is provided. The plan of Elcho is actually a long rectangle with a big fortified stair tower at one corner and a smaller purely domestic one at another, with all along the narrowside, facing the Tay, an

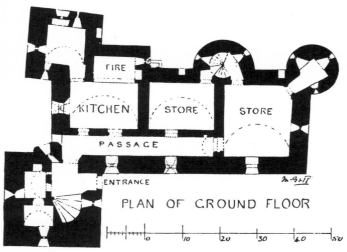

*Elcho Castle: general view. Note iron bars to windows; plan of ground floor*

array of towers and turrets which, while suggesting the garden elevation at Kellie, is much less pleasantly disposed, proving once more that the happy effects sometimes arrived at in Scottish castellated architecture are often as much a matter of chance as they are of deliberate design. Elcho is uninhabited but roofed and well maintained by the Department of the Environment. It is noted for having kept on its main front the original iron bars protecting the windows, and around the basement a series of gun-loops run like a menacing frieze. In truth there was an older fortalice on the site, one ruined round tower of which, also well supplied with loops, stands isolated from the main building as the land falls towards the river. The castle was constructed from stones quarried on its north side, the scars being still visible, but finer masonry, timber and other materials came by water, for at this point the Tay is navigable and a connecting ditch was made to bring the boats right up to the foot of the castle walls.

Huntingtower, on the west side of Perth, gives the impression at first of being in the same mould as Elcho, but this is only an impression and brought about by the roughness of the unharled, local stone and a certain gauntness consequent upon that. In fact, Huntingtower, which was originally called Ruthven Castle and was the seat of the Earls of Gowrie, is not at all like Elcho, being much more, at least as far as the development of its plan is concerned, akin to Traquair. It was built in stages, with two end features eventually linked to make the existing house, which is another 'fortified manor'. In the beginning Ruthven Castle consisted of a free-standing tower with a slight bulge at one corner showing where the staircase came, and above bartisans and a cap-house. A plain rectangular tower was added in the late fifteenth century, now represented by the hall, and these buildings were separated by a gap of some ten feet. In the seventeenth century the gap was filled in, but not very conclusively as anyone can see when approaching the castle: the junction with the older towers being roofed at a different level and in a different manner, lacking battlements, bartisans, corbelling or waterspouts, and having no crowsteps

*Huntingtower, formerly Ruthven Castle, seat of the Gowries*

either. The story goes that the young lady of the house, caught with her lover in one of the detached towers, was obliged to leap back to the other, at a height of sixty feet above the ground, in order to escape detection from her mother. Whether the gap was joined as a result of this episode or not no one knows, but it is supposed so and the story is in keeping with the rather more dramatic history of Huntingtower as compared to Elcho, which has hardly any history at all.

The Gowries miscalculated in the reign of James VI of Scots when they imitated earlier kidnappers of royalty and held the boy king captive at their castle in order that they might control the kingdom through him. James, for all his faults and apparent physical weakness, was really the first of his race to master the rebellious nobles, and their contenders for power after the Reformation, an arrogant kirk, which had it in mind to become a law unto itself, like some modern Trade Unions. He must have learned how to deal with this unholy combination through experiences such as the one that occurred here, which preyed on his memory and affected his later actions as King of England as well as Scotland. Indeed, Shakespeare is said to have written *Macbeth* after a visit to the North when he was made aware of the course of the 'Gowrie Conspiracy', and the king's getting the better of his enemies. In practice the young James was cleverer than his captors and one day, announcing a hunting expedition, never returned, at least not straight away, but waited his opportunity and disposed of the entire Gowrie clan some four years later, in 1600, when the family were lured to a house in Perth and there all killed, the king inventing another plot against his life as the excuse. Ruthven was renamed Huntingtower, the earldom abolished and the remains of the unfortunate victims publicly hanged. It may be recalled that it had been Lord Ruthven, father of the first Earl of Gowrie, who assisted in the murder of Rizzio, so that King James' action was not wholly unexpected in any event.

Huntingtower remained royal property until Charles I bestowed it on William Murray, son of the minister at Dysart, and former 'whipping boy' when the king was still Duke of York. Murray became the first Earl of Dysart and was the father of the notorious Bessie Dysart, Duchess of Lauderdale, whom we have already encountered. The Earl subsequently offered the property to James, second Earl of Tulliebardine, whence Huntingtower passed to the Dukes of Atholl. It is remarkable internally for its mural paintings and early plasterwork, some of the latter also painted. The beams in the old Hall, however, are the most important feature. These display striking geometrical patterns mostly in black and white, but also with backgrounds of yellow and red, and are amongst the earliest examples of their kind in Scotland. Fairly similar work at Traquair was recently uncovered, dating from the first half of the sixteenth century, while traces of even older and freer patterns showing animal and human grotesques suggest the subject matter of a late gothic tapestry from the valley of the Loire. The eastern tower is now a caretaker's house, and is interestingly capped with a doocot on the battlements.

From Huntingtower the line of the Highland hills is not
far distant. It can be seen as one leaves Perth for Dunkeld,
sweeping across the horizon in an easterly direction towards
Angus and Aberdeenshire. Behind it there are comparatively
few castles in anything like their original state, mostly ruins
left to decay or ruins so thoroughly rebuilt as to be almost
unrecognizable for what they once were. The Highland area
has always been fairly empty and controlled by its chiefs,
with occasional periods when the royal authority made itself
felt, only to be broken by sorties into the Lowlands on the
part of the Highlanders whenever a sign of weakness appeared. The Romans ignored the Highlands, but not the
Normans, and some of the finest Norman remains in the
country are yet to be found in the west of Scotland, at Castle
Sween, in Argyll, for example, the thick crumbling walls of
which are thought to date from the twelfth century and to
represent the earliest work of their kind in the North. Even
Duart, the much restored and virtually rebuilt seat of the
Macleans on Mull, rises from Norman foundations of the
thirteenth century, certainly the *enceinte,* which is also true of
Duntrune, amongst the claimants to be the oldest inhabited
castle in Scotland. The *enceinte* there has later-day crenellations along its top and the inhabited portion was actually
built in the seventeenth century. More authentic, though
ruined, is Dunstaffnage, which is undergoing repair by the
Ministry of Public Works and not open to the public. This
Argyllshire fortress, one of several in the Campbell country,
is again largely of the thirteenth century and a castle of
*enceinte,* with, besides its walls and towers, an Early English
chapel, which distinction it shares with Kildrummie, many
miles to the east in Aberdeenshire. Kildrummie has been
called 'The Queen of Highland Castles', but geographically
speaking it stands, like most of the others, on the perimeter
of the Highlands rather than in them, and is only Highland
in the way it guards against Highland encroachment. It was
the creation of Gilbert de Moravia, of the same family which
gave its name to the County of Moray, where their principal
seat, Duffus Castle, is now collapsed but splendidly chunky
in its strewed remains. They were the ancestors of the Dukes

of Atholl and Sutherland, and in common with many ancient families hereabouts were probably Normans, but quickly assimilated.

Policing the Highlands was usually done on behalf of the king by 'planted' feudal barons, but by the later Middle Ages this had degenerated into mere family rivalry and the king himself was obliged to come and see what could be done to redress the balance. James II conferred the royal earldom of Atholl upon his half-brother James Stewart of Balvenie in 1477, he setting up his headquarters in what was left of a feudal castle begun by John Comyn, father of the man Bruce slew in the Kirk of the Greyfriars in Dumfries. Today 'Comyn's Tower' forms the nucleus of Blair Castle, modern seat of the Duke of Atholl. The first Stewart earl succeeded in keeping at bay the rebellious Lord of the Isles, John Macdonald, but a state of intermittent insurrection lasted almost until the days of the Forty-five, when at Culloden the Highland power set-up was finally broken. James VI and I, as we have seen, combined coercion with offers of preferment in an effort to pacify his kingdom, Lowland and Highland, English, Scots and Irish. The Borders he subdued pretty effectively, and much of the Highlands, realizing that what the average Highland chief desired most of all was recognition of his own position and appropriate honours to go with it. Thus, the Macleods of Dunvegan benefited from their chief's going to court and assisting rather than opposing the royal cause, Dunvegan Castle being the only one in the West Highlands which has been occupied by the same family since its founding, though much altered in appearance and largely a nineteenth-century edifice as one sees it today. Sir Rory Macleod, the Jacobean courtier, has left his mark on the architecture here and there, features of his addition to the original tower protruding from Victorian battlements and Georgian fenestration.

Other supporters of the royal authority were less successful in their efforts than the young chief of the Macleods, and James Menzies of Menzies suffered so much from "vicket and perversit clannis of the Hielands", that his health was affected and he became so worried and ill that the king gave him permission to eat meat in Lent. This in itself may seem a little surprising to those who were brought up in a Protestant-orienated society which eschewed religious feasts and fasts, for the period under discussion antedates the Reformation settlement in Scotland and the abolition of the Roman obedience north of the Border. It confirms, however, that Presbyterianism as such did not triumph in the first decades of the new order but later, after the death of John Knox and towards the end of the reign of James VI, and even then it was soon eclipsed by Episcopacy. Poor old James Menzies lived at Castle Menzies, on the north side of the Tay near Aberfeldy. The building survives, having been ruthlessly restored in modern times to become the Menzies Clan headquarters. What a pity Sir Robert Menzies, former Prime Minister of Australia, did not retire there, or at least make part of it his home—it might have been rendered less gloomy and not so empty looking. The question of the pronunciation of the name Menzies is rather ineresting, Sir Robert having given up all attempts at imitation of the existing Scottish version, which comes out roughly as 'mingies', and resorting to a straight 'menzies', as spelt. On the other hand the name was originally Meyners, from Robert de Meyners, the Norman ancestor of this family which now considers itself Highland.

Castle Menzies, like most of the others, is on the Highland fringe, its nearest neighbour, on the south side of the Tay, being Grantully, which is a Stewart house built on the familiar 'Z' plan: that is, a rectangle, or near square, with towers placed diagonally at two corners, in this case oblong instead of round additions, or one of each. Grantully Castle has been altered to some extent: there is a chapel which is new and a corner turret which is clearly of the nineteenth-century Scotch Baronial persuasion. The unusual feature about the place is the siting of the stair tower, which instead of rising in the angle, by the entrance, is on its own on the outer face of the building and capped with a seventeenth-century ogee roof, which gives the castle its special look. On the western side of these two seats is Taymouth Castle, on Loch Tay, in the Highlands proper. The whole area was

*Grantully Castle: showing the stair turret*

*Blair Castle: redesigned by Bryce in the nineteenth century*

Campbell property until quite recently, belonging to the Marquises and Earls of Breadalbane, or braid Alban, and stretching right across Scotland from Perthshire to Argyll. Taymouth Castle was the culminating expression in stone of the engrandisment and gradual move eastwards from Loch Awe which began in the fifteenth century, when the Campbells of Glenorchy established themselves here. They were a remarkable family, especially in the seventeenth century, when Sir Duncan and Sir Colin Campbell lived, and between them built Barcaldine Castle in Argyllshire, an L-shaped turreted mansion with conically capped 'studies', and improved and enlarged Taymouth in Perthshire. Sir Colin was a great traveller and patron of the arts and the friend of George Jamesone, the Aberdeenshire portrait painter who has been called the 'Scottish Van Dyck'.

There used to be at Taymouth Castle, which is now institutionalized and in any case was Gothickized beyond recognition in the last century, an amusing family tree showing Sir Colin and his forbears, painted by Jamesone, with roundel miniatures of his patron and others pendant from the branches, and the first Campbell of Glenorchy seated at the foot. These Campbells were ostensibly cavaliers and not covenanting by inclination, though the first Earl of Breadalbane, Sir John Campbell of Glenorchy, has gone down in history as 'slippery John' on account of his ambiguous political activities, while one of his brethren, Captain Campbell of Glen Lyon, was the instrument of William of Orange and his evil adviser, Sir John Dalrymple, later Earl of Stair, in perpetrating the Massacre of Glencoe, when the Campbells took revenge on their traditional enemies the MacDonalds. The artistic streak displayed by the first Earl's father and grandfather re-appeared in his successors, one of whom was the re-introducer of Palladianism into England after the baroque phase under Wren and Vanbrugh, and the author of *Vitruvius Britannicus*; though I am assured by Sir Iain Moncreiffe of that Ilk that this was not the Hon. Colin Campbell, Yr, son of 'slippery John', who with Sir Iain's own ancestor, Thomas Moncreiffe, went to Italy aged sixteen in the year 1695, in the company of the Reverend David

Moncreiffe, former Minister at Anstruther Easter, and signed the visitor's book at Padua when visiting the Palladian villas. The bill, which is extant, includes 'going to Padua, 0009 Lire O Soldi. At Padua 14 days and $1\frac{1}{2}$ day afterwards meat lodging etc. 0057 Lire O Soldi'. In Glen Lyon incidentally, one of the most beautiful in Scotland, is Meggernie Castle, a simple tower with rectangular corner turrets in place of the more usual rounded ones. This castle still recalls the savage history of the region. It is attached to a more modern hunting lodge.

The Battle of Killiecrankie was fought near Pitlochry on 28th July 1689, when Graham of Claverhouse, Viscount Dundee, the 'Bonnie Dundee' of the popular ballad, was killed at the head of his cavalry at the moment of victory. Thus the cause of James VII and II collapsed almost at a blow, and apart from some skirmishing around Dunkeld Cathedral and the house of the second Marquis of Atholl, later first Duke, it was not until 1715 that a further serious attempt was made to restore the Stuarts. Dundee had spent the previous night at Blair Castle and was brought back and buried in St Bride's Kirk at Old Blair on 30th July. His breastplate and part of his helmet are preserved in the Tulliebardine Room in the castle. Another reminder of the curiously interwoven history of Blair, its earls and dukes, is the sketch in the same room of Nairne House, near Stanley, on the outskirts of Perth, which has written on the back: "The House of Nairne-or Strathord—built by William Lord Nairne and destroyed by his nephew James Duke of Atholl". The latter was the second Duke and acquired that title, through the second son of the first, while his elder brother was alive, by advocating the Hanoverian cause. William Marquis of Tulliebardine, the true heir, was recognized as *de jure* Duke by the Jacobites. The *de facto* Duke inherited the Sovereignty of the Isle of Man, becoming 'king' of that island through his descent from Lady Amelia Stanley, daughter of the seventh Earl of Derby and Charlotte de la Trémoille, heroine of Scott's novel *Peveril of the Peak*. He was a strong supporter of law and order and of the Georgian monarchy. His nephew, the builder of Nairne House, Sir William

Bruce's last and largest design, was on the other side, as were all his family; they suffered considerably from two successive acts of attainder, one after the 1715 rebellion and another after the Forty-five, but returning from France later were prevented from buying back their old home by the second Duke of Atholl, who kept the bidding going while his nephew's friends had deliberately kept it down.

Finally he obtained the property, which he proceeded to demolish, only the central cupola being saved and presented to the James VI Hospital in Perth, where it still is. Lady Nairne was an interesting person and one of the first women architects. A pupil of Sir William Bruce, she designed the Court House at Logierait, near Blair, and made some improvements at Blair Castle itself.

The castle does not appear in either MacGibbon and Ross or Billings; in the latter's day it was still the Georgian mansion the second Duke had made it in the mid-eighteenth century, and although it was re-baronialized in the nineteenth, Messrs MacGibbon and Ross probably thought there was nothing much left that was original. They were probably right, but in its various transformations Blair Castle is of interest as showing to perfection the fate of so many Highland fortresses which have survived as inhabited buildings and not fallen into complete ruin or adopted for mundane uses. Less dramatically or picturesquely sited than Dunvegan, which sits comfortably but evocatively astride a rocky saddle on the western seaboard, Blair nevertheless has a more authentic architectural look, and its battlements and turrets, even if they were put back in Victorian times, have a romantic glow about them that is slightly more convincing than Dunvegan's over-simplified castellations in the southern English manner. Comyn's Tower, now rendered Cumming's, is the oldest bit of Blair, but only its lower storeys, for the upper two replace those removed by the second Duke of Atholl in his Georgianization of the building when the castle became, in fact as well as name, a gentleman's country house. It belonged to a larger edifice which grew around an *enceinte,* or barmkin wall, and included a lord's solar, or hall, and other adjuncts, as with the normal castle of the fourteenth and fifteenth centuries. It was then the seat of the first Stewart Earl of Atholl, who was executed in 1437 for his part in the murder of James I of Scots at Perth. This castle, being quasi-royal, had some important visitors, including Edward III of England, and later James V of Scots and his daughter Mary, both of whom were entertained in lavish style, when a whole new timber 'palace' was erected in the grounds for their reception. Enormous quantities of game were slaughtered, indeed there was so much killing as to suggest callous competition; more than a thousand birds and deer, wild boar and wolves being done to death on each occasion.

In fact, Blair was more of a hunting lodge than an ancestral pile, especially in the days of the first Murray earls, who lived mostly at Dunkeld, the house there being rebuilt by Sir William Bruce after damage incurred during the civil wars. It was one of the seats sketched by the ubiquitous John Slezer in his views of Scotland. Later it was intended to build an Atholl 'palace', and this was begun, but has since been abandoned for Blair and the name 'Atholl Palace' now pertains to a grandiose hotel at Pitlochry. One of the most curious things to occur in the metamorphosis of the castle was the setting up therein of a ceremonial staircase in the manner of Sir William Bruce, possibly inspired by Nairne, if not then by that in Dunkeld House, which dates from the middle of the eighteenth century, while displaying all the old-fashioned features of the Queen Anne period. It was designed by a Mr Winter, employed on the Atholl Estate, and is called the 'picture staircase' because its panelled walls are lined with ancestral portraits, and notably those of the celebrated Charlotte de la Trémoille and her husband, the Earl of Derby, and a vast de Wet of John, second Earl and first Marquis of Atholl dressed as a Roman general, a guise quite popular at the time, the mode evolving through Charles II's adoption of it in imitation of Louis XIV. A detailed list of the treasures of Blair is not our concern, but one might mention the existence of a room full of Hondthorsts devoted to Elizabeth, 'the Winter Queen' of Bohemia, and most of her remarkable family, including Prince Rupert; and the magnificent plaster decoration of the

*Blair Castle: the Picture Staircase*

larger state rooms made for the second Duke, the dining room being the work of Thomas Clayton, plasterer to William Adam, with rustic panels in the style of Hubert Robert by the Scottish artist Charles Steuart. It may be worth adding in this context the influence of James Macpherson, alias 'Ossian', who was at the time gathering material for his poems in the neighbourhood, and that a folly erected near Dunkeld, now called 'The Hermitage' and maintained by the National Trust for Scotland, used to be known as 'Ossian's Hall'. There is another, jollier folly in the grounds of Blair Castle, one wall thick and representing a sham fort, heavily crenellated and pierced by gothic arches from the top of which flew in Georgian times, the three-legged banner of the Kings of Man.

While these mid-eighteenth century improvements were going on and the castle transformed into a country mansion, Blair actually changed hands more than once, as the tide of rebellion passed to and fro over the Highlands. Lord George Murray, Prince Charlie's general, was the younger brother of James, the *de facto* second Duke, and William Marquis of Tulliebardine. Both landed with the Prince in 1745, and Lord George engaged his own Atholl Highlanders at Blair in a siege of his ancestral home. Prince Charlie stayed in the castle on two occasions, and a number of souvenirs of this visit are on view in the Tulliebardine room. After Culloden the 'Jacobite General' retired to the Continent, where he died in Holland in 1760, while his elder brother William was taken prisoner trying to escape and died in the Tower of London in 1746. The Atholl Highlanders who fought in the battle and suffered badly survive as a military unit to this day, having been paraded before Queen Victoria at Blair on her visit of 1844, when they were presented with special colours and permitted to continue to carry arms, the only remaining private army in Britain; just as Blair Castle is the last private fortress to have suffered a siege in these islands. Sir David Bryce was set to work to re-baronialize Blair House, as it then was, in 1869, at which time the Second Empire was still in existence and its chief restorer of castles, Monsieur Viollet-le-Duc, was still busy re-medievalizing the *châteaux* of France. In view of this, and of the visit of the Empress Eugénie to the Duke of Atholl in 1860, it is surprising how sympathetic Bryce's work is, especially when one considers contemporary models such as Pierrefonds in France and Balmoral in Scotland. He succeeded in restoring Blair to something approaching a genuine Scottish castle, albeit one existing in the imagination, by putting back the missing upper storeys of 'Cumming's Tower', raising the general height of the Georgian mansion and adding an array of battlements and turrets to produce a more varied skyline. At the centre he constructed a small replica of Bruce's arched feature at Thirlestane, which itself owed something to the work of the first Earl of Dunfermline at Fyvie, in Aberdeenshire. In this way his resuscitation of Blair respects the native tradition more than most Victorian recreations and produces a restrained overall effect which nevertheless succeeds in suggesting its disparate history.

Beyond Blair the Forest of Atholl declines into a species of Scottish tundra before one reaches the northern slopes of the Grampians and Speyside, where the trees return in a harsh expansive landscape, rocky and reminiscent of the more desolate parts of central Spain, hot and midge-ridden in summer, cold and icy in winter, but clear, and a paradise for Scottish skiers. In such a setting one does not expect to find many castles, architecture being mainly represented by modern sports complexes and by a number of plain but well designed eighteenth-century parish kirks, often with classically inspired bell-cots, their only really decorative feature. As for antiquity this may be found in graveyards, where the names of clansmen long since dead tell of years of internecine strife, of religious and dynastic conflicts and of enforced emigration. The Highland clans were more persistently at war with one another even than the Borderers, they were just as cruel and unforgiving and went on struggling for two centuries after the Borders had quietened down, fighting each other, and for or against the authorities in Edinburgh, in 1715, 1719 and 1745, when a last-ditch revolt on behalf of the exiled Stuarts, whom they had resisted when in power, ended in utter failure and the final dispersal of the clans.

One might add that fighting being in the blood many of the chiefs and their retainers were by 1745 already engaged in the Hanoverian interest, a monument to the Black Watch at Aberfeldy commemorating this co-operation; and at Culloden there were as many Highlanders ranged against Prince Charlie as on his side, and most of these gave their support more in an attempt to set the clock back than out of any deep-rooted belief in the wisdom of the Stuarts!

The Forty-five rendered practically every Highland fortalice empty or ruined, the exceptions belonging to those who had made their peace with the House of Hanover, such as the Macleod's of Dunvegan, and other buildings were taken over and adapted as military outposts, such as Corgarff and Braemar Castles. The first consists of a tall laird's tower of defence, once a Gordon redoubt, which the army surrounded with a protective star-shaped outer wall, rectangular to Braemar's square enclosure. Corgarff lies on the road over the mountains from Donside, in Aberdeenshire, to the Moray Firth area and was used as a staging post for troops en route for Fort George, the great Vauban-like fort built near Inverness after 1745 to make sure the Highlanders never again threatened the peace of the neighbourhood. It is in the care of the Department of the Environment and can be seen at any time. Allied to it, but stronger and much more interesting is the Castle of Mar, also called Braemar, in the Dee Valley not far from Balmoral. It stands in Farquharson country, but was built by the Earls of Mar in the sixteenth century, burnt down by the Farquharsons, witnessed the raising of the Jacobite Standard in 1715, and was restored and strengthened by the British Army in 1748. It is an L-shaped castle of traditional pattern, with semi-circular stair tower in the entrant angle, and would once have been crowned with pepper-pot turrets where today crenellations of proverbial southern English pattern prevail. The lower floors are still barrel vaulted and the castle retains its iron yett, or gate. In recent years it has been rescued from decay by a modern generation of Farquharsons, whose seat, Invercauld House, is in the vicinity, and made into an attractive dwelling. Around the old 'L' is a star-shaped outer wall,

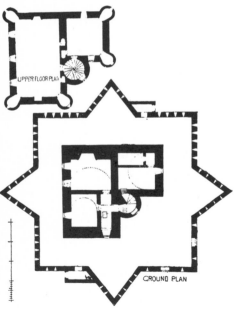

UPPER FLOOR PLAN

GROUND PLAN

*Mar, or Braemar Castle, militarized in the eighteenth century: general view; plans*

dating from the second half of the eighteenth century, with gun-loops and more crenellations, which, however, taken with the unifying white harling that covers all, does not leave the castle entirely lacking in character, especially in its wooded setting. Braemar is certainly more evocative as a Highland fortress than Balmoral, which has an undoubted institutional look inherent in the Prince Consort's search for perfection and too-deliberate study of the local vernacular as applied to castellated architecture. Abergeldie, once on the royal estate but now back in Gordon hands, is a better example in the native style, its hunting lodge additions joined to a genuine old castle which retains its crowsteps, turrets and projecting stair tower topped by a Georgian, but not wholly uncomplimentary cupola. Abergeldie was the home for a time of the Empress Eugénie and later of the Prince and Princess of Wales, the future Edward VII and Queen Alexandra.

Still in the same region, not far from the main road and railway through Strathspey, at Aviemore, are Ruthven Barracks. Hardly a castle, though built as one by Alexander Stewart, Earl of Buchan, a bastard of Robert II and known as the 'Wolf of Badenoch' on account of his rapacity and general lawlessness. Only the motte on which 'The Wolf' built his raiding post remains, and the remnants of a replacement erected by the Gordons of Huntly, as rapacious and lawless as their predecessors, are submerged in the present ruined barracks. The guiding hand in these works of pacification was, of course, the great General, later Field Marshal Wade, the man who thought of himself as following in the steps of Caesar in his road laying, bridge building and policing of the untamed Highlands. The immediate cause of the building of Ruthven Barracks was the little-known revolt that occurred in 1719, when the Jacobites, aided by Cardinal Alberoni and the Spaniards, made an abortive attempt to make up for their failure in 1715, only to find themselves besieged in a single fortress, the highly scenographic Eilean Donan Castle, island seat of the Mackenzies of Kintail. This is on the west coast of Inverness-shire, opposite Skye, and once the besieged, Scots and Spaniards, had been allowed by a tolerant government to escape abroad, the castle was demolished by naval bombardment. Eilean Donan has since been completely rebuilt and may be visited. It is linked to the mainland by a bridge and is considered a tourist 'must' for visitors to north-west Scotland.

The barracks at Ruthven witnessed the last Jacobite muster in 1746 by the clans who did not reach Culloden in time for the battle, and who hoped, by encouraging Prince Charlie to continue the fight, to extract better terms for themselves, now that they no longer expected they could win. The logic of this was that they had succeeded by continued resistance in 1689 in obtaining some amelioration of the conditions of peace, though it has to be admitted that not long afterwards the government broke its word and Glencoe ensued. Charles Edward rejected the idea and took to the hills instead, when four thousand clansmen, after burning down Ruthven, dispersed to their remote fastnesses.

Fort George, near Inverness, was intended as the answer to future possible risings, and is not only the finest and most comprehensive fortress of its kind in Britain but one of the best in Europe. From the first it was too big ever to have invited attack from the Highlanders, yet inadequate against a serious attack from abroad, and in the event was never attacked by anyone from land or sea. It was designed by Col. William Skinner at the behest of the notorious 'Butcher Cumberland', the 'Sweet William' of British horticultural nomenclature, with the Adam family as contractors, which may seem odd to us, but was perfectly normal in the eighteenth century. William Adam held the post of master mason in North Britain to the Board of Ordnance, which position his eldest son John inherited on his death in 1748. The idea was to replace defunct or unsatisfactory older forts and especially the one at Inverness, the first Fort George, which had been captured by the Jacobites and burned by them before Culloden. Fort Augustus had surrendered after a powder magazine had exploded and was no longer considered adequate, while Fort William was likewise captured and rendered ineffective by Prince Charlie's men.

Fort William was older than the others and named after

that Dutch Prince who was largely responsible for permitting the Campbells to wreak their vengeance on the MacDonalds of Glencoe in 1689, and whose writ in the Highlands was shakier than that of any ruler since the days of the early Stewarts. The fort was built near the very much older Inverlochy Castle, a building so ancient in origin that arguments have not yet ceased as to whether the existing ruins date from the fifteenth century or the thirteenth. They form a roughly rectangular enclosure with round towers at the corners, one serving as the main building and being slightly fatter than the rest. In its way Inverlochy suggests the later fortresses in its simplicity of plan and the open court within for marshalling soldiers; and its outer face is starkly bare except for strategically placed arrow-slits which most authorities say are medieval. The castle came to the Comyns, Edward I's chief supporters in the North, and played a part in the Wars of Independence in the fourteenth century. It is, on the other hand, very much a ruin and has been ever since the days of Montrose, who, making use of many of the Highland castles and redoubts in much the same manner as Wade did a century afterwards, defeated the Marquis of Argyll there, that chief of the Campbells who had previously fled by sea from his seat at Inveraray, leaving his clan and family to their fate. He now witnessed the decimation of the remainder of his supporters, Highland and Lowland, remaining in his boat and sailing away down Loch Linnhe just in time to save himself from the victorious royalists.

Fort Augustus was given up by the army in the nineteenth century and is now a Benedictine monastery, while the Fort at Inverness, actually of Cromwellian origin, no longer exists but for a small reminder near the harbour. It was pentagonal, as the new Fort George is, and related to its successor both on plan and in military ideas. Indeed, the old Fort at Inverness, one of several built during the Commonwealth, others being at Leith, Ayr and Lerwick, in Shetland, must have been something like Tilbury Fort on the Thames, which, in common with the walls of Berwick-on-Tweed, was the creation of Italian engineers, though later strengthened and enlarged by Bernard de Gomme for Charles II. These pentagonal forts had at each corner an arrowhead bastion, and at both Tilbury and Inverness they were surrounded by water. The later work, however, included a ravelin, or freestanding projection that covered the entrance. It stood beyond the moat and was connected to the main defences by a drawbridge. It was this arrangement that was applied at the new Fort George, which is actually sited on a narrow peninsula jutting out into the Moray Firth opposite Chanonry Point, where the ferry to the Black Isle used to ply. It is almost impossible to appreciate the form and extent of this amazing layout except from the air or by studying a plan, for Fort George is not only defended by a projecting ravelin, or V-shaped outwork, but by a long grassy slope, or glacis, which, commencing on a line near the top of the battlements, but divided from them by a ditch or subsidiary moat, reaches down in front to a distance of 165 feet, thus almost completely hiding the buildings behind. In fact, but for some amusing little sentry boxes, turreted and corbelled out at salient points in the fortifications, one would scarcely see anything much to suggest a mighty fortress. These sentry boxes, linked to the barracks by deeply set paths in the fighting platforms, are Continental, not Scottish in design, despite their similarity to the turrets of real castles, and were employed extensively by John Romer, Wade's military engineer; they remind one of examples on Spanish and Portuguese forts in America and Africa, and are to be found ornamenting the eighteenth-century additions to Dumbarton, Edinburgh and Stirling Castles.

Fort George is not precisely pentagonal on plan, but with its ravelin and ditch, the latter arranged for taking water but never filled, and extended northern section thrusting like an extra arrow out into the sea, it fills the entire peninsula on which it is built, its walls being washed by the waves at high tide. There was a small port made at the southern end of the ferry which was adapted for military as well as civilian use, and this was defended by a Sally Port, while within the enclosure are the simple but dignified late-Georgian barracks, the governor's house, chapel and stores. Work began in 1749 and went on until 1763, when the chapel was

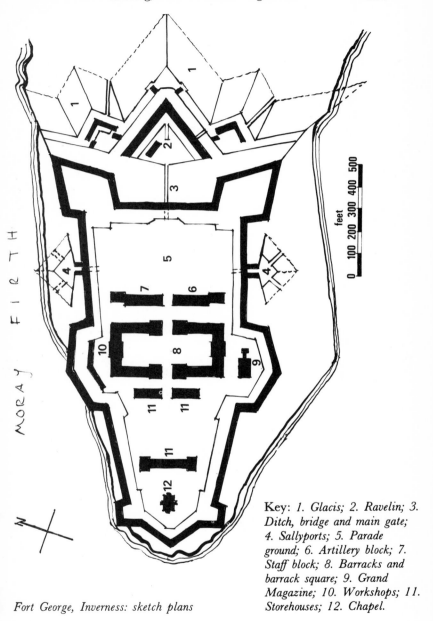

MORAY FIRTH

Key: *1. Glacis; 2. Ravelin; 3.
Ditch, bridge and main gate;
4. Sallyports; 5. Parade
ground; 6. Artillery block; 7.
Staff block; 8. Barracks and
barrack square; 9. Grand
Magazine; 10. Workshops; 11.
Storehouses; 12. Chapel.*

*Fort George, Inverness: sketch plans*

built, and Fort George was garrisoned by troops from 1770 onwards, becoming in due course a point for embarkation and mustering. Eventually the Seaforth Highlanders, raised as part of an act of gratitude by Kenneth Mackenzie of Kintail after he had been created first Earl of Seaforth and relieved of the attainder on his property for taking part in the Forty-five, came to the Fort semi-permanently, remaining there until 1961, when an amalgamation with the Camerons resulted in the creation of the Queen's Own Highlanders. They marched out together in 1964, but Fort George is still used as a barracks, under the care of the Department of the Environment, with some of it open to the public. The Chapel has been restored, rather oddly internally, where the formerly central double-decker pulpit, a relic of low church Anglicanism, is now set to one side to conform to what can only be described as high church Presbyterianism! The Stationery Office publish an interesting and instructive 'wee bookie' on Fort George which includes a list of military-architectural terms and descriptions which are invaluable to the visitor; there are also several plans and good illustrations. Other old forts under government care include Fort Charlotte, overlooking the harbour at Lerwick, on the mainland of Shetland, which is pentagonal on plan and possessed of projecting bastions. It was designed by John Mylne, architect, master mason and captain of the pioneers to Charles I and Charles II, though it may have been begun by Cromwell and was obviously strengthened later.

Henry Mackenzie, 'The Man of Feeling', who knew Hume as a boy and was Scott's friend as a man, who led the enquiry into the authenticity or otherwise of James Macpherson's 'Ossian' and gave Robert Burns his first big leg up in the literary world, had for mother a Rose of Kilravock, one of the oldest and most prolific of north-eastern gentle families. They have lived in the same district since the Norman Conquest and their chief inhabits a castle the original tower of which was built in 1460, the charter granting permission to erect it being extant. Mackenzie's Rose grandparents had a house in Nairn, where more than forty provosts had been of the same name, and it was there, when on a visit to the work at Fort George, that he met the young Robert Adam, who designed a house for his grand-father which, although never built, Mackenzie reckoned was the first from the hand of that architectural genius. The most popular name amongst the numerous Rose clan was Hugh, from Hughune de Rose, who was responsible for the first tower of defence at Kilravock, to Hugh Rose who was killed in the capture of Inverness from the Jacobites. Funnily enough he welcomed both Prince Charles Edward and the Duke of Cumberland, one before Culloden the other after, Cumberland exclaiming, "I hear you've been entertaining my cousin". We are on the borderland between Highland and Lowland, the River Nairn, which flows at the foot of Kilravock Castle, usually being considered the division, thus making Nairn town half Highland and half Lowland, the river flowing through the middle. Interestingly too, Hughune de Rose's Charter was obtained not from the King of Scots but John, Lord of the Isles, while the charter for neigh-bouring Calder, or Cawdor, on the Lowland side of the Nairn and dated only six years earlier, came from the King, James II of the Fiery Face, who died in 1460 at the siege of Roxburgh. The Lords of the Isles became respectable in 1476, when the same John MacDonald was recognized as a peer of the realm; and some twenty years later he surren-dered this title to the King, James IV, so that the Lordship of the Isles was merged with the royal titles and is today held by H.R.H. The Prince of Wales.

The erection of both towers of defence, Calder and Kilravock, within six years of each other and probably by the same masons, is interesting on a number of counts. Both families have remained *in situ* ever since and the 'keeps' make intriguing comparison. Kilravock has not been altered to any great extent since the middle of the fifteenth century, the present dwelling house being an addition which leaves Hughune de Rose's tower intact, while Calder, which became Cawdor for a reason I will explain, has been so greatly altered as to be only original in its shell and lower storeys; the open bartisans at parapet level were raised and provided with conical stone caps in the reign of Charles I,

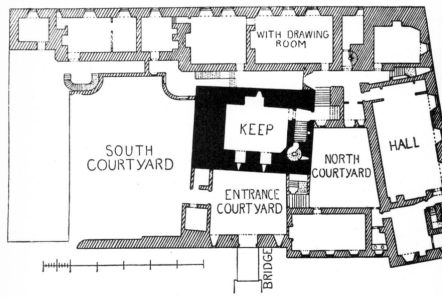

*Cawdor Castle: view of the 'keep'; plan*

larger windows were inserted and after the Restoration an entirely new mansion was erected within the original *enceinte*. Happily the drawbridge at Cawdor remains; it is the only old one left in Scotland, and the general character of the castle is uniquely evocative and baronial. It is set in the most placid-looking of villages, in nicely wooded countryside; seeing all the prosperous farms around one would scarcely imagine that it was here that Duncan may have been murdered, and that the heiress of Thane John, Muriel Calder, whose mother was a Rose of Kilravock, would have been abducted by the Campbells of Argyll, one of whom married her and founded the present family of Cawdor. The episode is well enough known, how a tulchan, or straw-stuffed dummy of the girl was made as a decoy, and six Campbells sacrificed in the pursuit to make sure she was not recaptured by her uncles. Muriel was a red-head and her nurse is supposed to have marked her in some way so as to be able to identify her, but so far as the Earl of Argyll was concerned he is reported to have declared that so long as there was a ginger-headed lass on either bank of Loch Awe there would be an heiress to Cawdor, which is the Lowland pronunciation of Calder. The reason for the change in spelling is not known for certain, but Nigel Tranter in his volume on the North-east in the series *The Queen's Scotland* makes the suggestion that Shakespeare may be responsible, otherwise why should the literate world at large call Calder, Cawdor, and Earl Cawdor be accepted in place of the old Thanes of Calder? Could it be that the Bard of Avon did visit Scotland at the behest of James VI and I, reached the neighbourhood of Nairn, and even placed his blasted heath on the future site of Culloden? It would seem he might have done and heard the local people pronounce Calder as Cawdor and written it down accordingly. Alternatively he may merely have heard the King himself speak of Cawdor when he meant Calder.

The existing arrangement of Cawdor Castle, with outer walls intact, drawbridge, central keep and seventeenth-century house within the *enceinte,* is not dissimilar from what Glamis Castle must have been at about the same time, and before the Earl of Strathmore and Kinghorne started unbaronializing his seat and created what Slezer calls 'Glammis House'. Curious that there should be this similarity when one recalls that Glamis also has Shakespearean associations. There are a number of non-Shakespearean things at Cawdor as well, things that give the castle its special *cachet*. Down in the depths of the dungeon upon which its old tower is built stands the decayed trunk of the tree beside which an ass, according to legend, left to stop where it would, and laden with William Calder's kist of gold, halted, thus choosing the site for its master. Another souvenir of the past is the great iron yett which guards the original internal entrance to the tower of defence but which is older than Cawdor, coming from Lochindorb Castle, in Moray, once a seat of 'The Wolf of Badenoch', but later of Archibald Douglas, Earl of Moray, who defied the king and was brought to heel by William, Thane of Calder, James II's Chamberlain beyond the Spey. His castle was demolished in 1455. Cawdor is one of those rare houses which despite punitive taxation and other disabilities have not only been continuously lived in, but by the same family and its descendants, whose records are complete. Even the contents as listed in old documents can still be seen in the rooms and notably those dating from the time of Sir John Campbell, the husband of Muriel Calder, and of Sir Hugh, his grandson, who married Henrietta Stewart in the second half of the seventeenth century. The monograms of these latter appear on a rather heavy-looking, baroque chimneypiece held up by bewigged caryatids and decorated with quaint figures. Much quainter, and also better displayed, is the larger chimneypiece bearing the arms of Sir John and Lady Muriel, whose lintel is famous for its carved hunting scenes, grotesque birds, mermaids, goats and other animals, one looking like a koala bear playing the violin, another astride a broom, and two foxes smoking pipes. This dates the chimneypiece precisely to the end of the sixteenth century, but how clever of the mason to record the discovery of tobacco so soon after the event.

Neither Cawdor nor Kilravock are regularly open to the public, Cawdor almost never, but both can be seen from outside and Kilravock is open on Wednesday afternoons by

*Castle Grant. The chief's piper with castle in background*

appointment with Miss Rose, who also runs a selective guest house in the castle. It is best seen from the far side of the Nairn River, when its old stone tower with simple corbelling and sturdy battlements stand up nicely beside the newer mansion. In Kilravock is a fascinating self-portrait by the locally based artist named Richard Waitt, whose truer profession seems to have been as painter of armorials, he being responsible amongst other things for the splendid achievement of the first Earl of Hopetoun on the ceiling of the laird's loft in the kirk at Abercorn, which dates from 1707 and in the restoration of which I played a part. Waitt also painted a very vivid and accurate representation of a royal archer of the Queen's bodyguard in Scotland, replete in tartan trews and jacket, the tartan being armorial in this context. Nor did he confine himself to these and allied subjects but depicted for posterity Highland folk at their various occupations at a time when change was in the air and the old way of life about to disappear. At Castle Grant, Speyside, seat of the Earls of Seafield, he painted the laird and his retainers; a hen wife and the chief's piper are memorable, the piper blowing into a most picturesque-looking object, half-bagpipes and half-endless sausage-machine, with Castle Grant in the background. This fortalice is now empty and neglected, and has been for a long time, the Grants having married into the Lowland Ogilvies and gone to live at Cullen House by the Moray Firth, becoming Lowland themselves and taking their possessions with them.

In the reign of Queen Anne, Brigadier Alexander Grant was Constable of Edinburgh Castle, and his portrait by Waitt is amongst others at Cullen. The Grants had been hereditary Constables of Castle Urquhart on Loch Ness for many years, that is, since the King's order prevailed, but when the Lord of the Isles held sway the Constable was Tearlach, ancestor of the Macleans of Dochgarroch, or Clan Tearlach, whose present head, the Reverend Donald Maclean, has recently returned to live near Inverness. Castle Urquhart is one of the most photographed monuments in the North, being one of the few striking memorials in stone to a turbulent history that survives in sufficient state of wholeness

*Castle Urquhart on Loch Ness*

to invite inspection. It rises most evocatively from two spurs of a rocky promontory at what is probably the most beautiful point on the loch, below the main road through the Great Glen and near where the monster is generally supposed to appear. The position is a 'natural' for a fort or castle, and there was a fort here in primitive times, the mound on which it stood is still there, though today crowned with much later masonry, ruinous and not very high. Below, near the edge of the loch the level of which was raised when the Caledonian Canal was built, stand other remnants in an equally incomplete state, the castle having been the subject of numerous attacks, and notably during the Forty-five after which it was blown up. At the northern end of these remains is a taller, better preserved laird's tower, once held by the Grant constables before they became Ogilvies and Lowland. The base stands on a castle erected by the ubiquitous Comyns, and Edward I himself strengthened and occupied

Castle Urquhart, which shows how thorough his hold on Scotland was at the height of his power, reaching to the very heart of the Highlands. The Department of the Environment take good care of the ruins which now have to share pride of place with 'Nessie' during the tourist season.

Inverness is a big, sprawling county, stretching from the Moray Firth to the Western Isles, most of which lie within its boundaries; and the families who had their fastnesses within its confines themselves occupied territory on both sides of the east-west divide. The Stewarts, for example, whose much-rebuilt castle on the way to Fort George, was recorded by Billings in the early nineteenth century as minus its floors and roof, and the prey to vandalism. Today, Castle Stewart is again empty, and its windows are boarded up. The most interesting thing about it is its late date and the way in which an ostensible 'Z' has been adapted to produce sym-metry, as required in Caroline times. Thus the two corner towers, instead of being diagonally placed appear on the same elevation. Otherwise it is a Scottish castle of the late sixteenth century that has strayed into the seventeenth and has had its tall, wimple-capped turrets heightened to produce a decorative rather than a defensive effect, a case of picturesqueness to order, like Glamis.

Another family with both east and west connections is, of course, the Clan Maclean, the western branch of which is now represented by Lord Maclean, Chamberlain to H.M. The Queen, whose seat is Duart Castle, on the Island of Mull. The further west one goes the fewer the castles in any state of authenticity. Duart was rebuilt on the foundations of any early Norman castle of *enceinte,* some of the old walling still being visible. It is open to the public in summer, its charter dating from the thirteenth century, when the outer walls were already in existence. The clan were staunch royalists, thus their seat was the scene of fighting towards the end of the seventeenth century, when the Campbells took revenge on them, and again in the Forty-five, when the chief was taken prisoner and housed in the Tower of London, his lands not coming back to his descendants until 1911, when what was left of the castle was rebuilt as one sees it today.

On Skye there is Dunvegan, wholly Georgian and Victorian in external appearance except for minor touches here and there of the castle built by Sir Roderick Macleod, courtier to James VI in the late sixteenth and early seventeenth centuries; but it contains interesting relics of a family that has managed to avoid too much involvement in the troubles of the Fifteen and Forty-five and so managed to hang on to its patrimony. The so-called Fairy Flag, said to have been given to one of the Macleods by a fairy whom he married, is on view, together with a fifteenth-century silver chalice and Sir Roderick's Jacobean drinking horn. Those who care to seek it out will also find the remnants of what was once the original sea gate, an opening onto the wider world that permitted the chiefs to remain free and supplied with the necessities of life when turmoil raged on the mainland.

The Island of Barra boasts the third in a series of well-known western castles, but unlike Dunvegan it has not been continuously occupied and unlike Duart it has not had to be entirely rebuilt. The Castle of Kisimul, which stands dramatically on a small island in Castle Bay, is not as old as the others, though the MacNeil chief who lives there would probably deny this. It is difficult to see how he can do so, however, when his family did not arrive on the scene until the mid-fifteenth century, and only began building the castle then. Indeed, experts are agreed that its corbelling and other defensive features cannot possibly date from before that time. There is a well-protected sea-gate, and sufficient of the old walls remained standing after Kisimul's desertion in the nineteenth century for the late Robert Lister MacNeil of Barra, an American by birth, to start restoring the seat of his ancestors, tidying up the battlements and constructing a house for himself against the inner walls. Externally the castle looks more of a fort than a habitable seat, an effect strengthened by its romantic setting and the rude walls of its masonry, but inside is the twentieth-century home of the present chief whose forbears thought so highly of themselves that after dinner their trumpeter would mount the battlements to announce to the world that since MacNeil himself had dined the rest could now do likewise!

Dubbed 'Capital of the Highlands' and enclosed on the north and west by majestic mountains, snow-capped in winter but actually protective and providing a mild climate generally, Inverness is very Lowland in character. It possesses an Episcopal cathedral reminiscent of a miniature Notre Dame, designed by the local architect, Alexander Ross, and a red-sandstone castle in Tudor style designed by William Burn standing on the site of something older destroyed by Cromwell. The fact that a statue of Flora Macdonald graces the terraces beside this imported recreation only partially removes one's belief that the Celtic nature of Inverness (where the best English, incidentally, is supposed to be spoken) has worn rather thin. The town has now become the hub of the fast-developing industrial North and is suffering a sea-change at the moment. It is almost as English as it must have been when Cromwell's soldiers first imparted the cockney accent to its denizens and will soon be very prosperous and go-ahead indeed. The Black Isle, which is not really an island but more of a *presqu'île,* is rapidly becoming desirable as a dormitory area for newcomers and is undoubtedly Lowland in history and character; it has been wholly occupied by the same human species for at least a thousand years, settled when the rest of Lowland Scotland was. It has three castles worth mentioning and one, at Cromarty, which is now no more.

Ruined Castle Craig is said to have been the summer palace of the Bishops of Ross, whose cathedral was at Fortrose, but one wonders if this is correct. Fortrose itself is a delightful little town retaining remnants of both its cathedral and ecclesiastical housing, and much more attractive than Castle Craig, which was obviously more of a strong point and faces north on a remote stretch of the Cromarty Firth. It appears in gothic letters on the Ordnance Survey map, which neither Kilcoy, nor Redcastle, the other two, do; and it would be interesting to know the reason for the distinction. Redcastle, crumbling and decayed but not without possibilities, stands on the site of the thirteenth-century redoubt of David, Earl of Huntingdon, brother of King William the

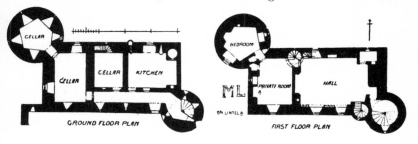

*Kilcoy Castle: plans*

Lion, while Kilcoy, admittedly a seventeenth-century building, was a seat of the Mackenzies of Kintail. Kilcoy has been restored and can be seen on special garden-opening days in the summer. Its plan is crudely 'Z', being compounded of a rectangular main structure with round towers at two opposing corners, one larger than the other and the smaller containing the main stair. A curious feature is the way in which rectangular projections making square-shaped rooms on the top are corbelled out without mastering the face of the semi-circular tower below, while another small angle turret to contain a separate little stair above bursts out most unexpectedly. Kilcoy sports large horizontal and vertical gun loops, symptomatic of the lawlessness prevailing in the North. It has early Gothic Revival dormers with armorial sculpture in the tympana, and inside a big chimneypiece, which although finer in its detail and later in date recalls to some extent that at Cawdor, with its greyhounds, mermaids playing harps, and roundels decorated with clan heraldry.

Kilcoy, despite its apparent neglect by the Ordnance Survey people, is described in detail in MacGibbon and Ross, while the neighbouring Mackenzie seat on the 'mainland', Castle Leod, is not, though marked in gothic on the map! It belongs to the Earl of Cromartie, who is also Baron Macleod, he being descended from Sir Roderick Mackenzie who married Margaret Macleod of Lewis in 1616. Castle Leod began life in its present form about the year 1600, when an L-shaped tower was built, with open bartisans and sentry walks, but was much altered after the marriage of

Sir Rorie, or Roderick, to his Macleod bride, when most of the space in the re-entrant area was filled in, and a new entrance made with scale-and-platt staircase replacing the old spiral. Two of the open bartisans were turned into 'studies' and given conically capped extinguisher roofs, and the main roof level raised, the newer face acquiring handsome dormer windows and some brave Renaissance sculpture. The corbelling at Castle Leod is rich and elaborate, being composed on the main front of two rows, divided by a cable course and set chequer-wise to make a varied pattern. The old castle is roofed and has furniture in it, but is not permanently inhabited, there being a Victorian house discreetly hiding behind it, almost unseen as one approaches the place from the long avenue, and quite invisible the last time I went there, when Castle Leod rose dramatically from the mists of February, like the backcloth to some improbable Scotch opera by Donizetti. It is actually built of a warm, pinkish stone and is stately rather than dramatic, with clipped yews and green lawns as befits a house near the douce nineteenth-century spa of Strathpeffer. The castle is not open to the public, as a notice at the gates clearly announces, but the Earl of Cromartie does allow interested parties in on proper application. He is the descendant of Sir George Mackenzie, who as Viscount Tarbet was Justice General of Scotland in the reign of James VII and II, and who succeeded not only in maintaining his position under William of Orange, but was made Secretary of State by Queen Anne, when the earldom was conferred. He is not to be confused with Sir George Mackenzie of Rosehaugh, his contemporary and also a celebrated lawyer, founder of the Advocates' Library in Edinburgh and friend of John Evelyn. His estate on the Black Isle also still functions.

# IV

# *The North-east*

I̲N̲ S̲O̲M̲E̲ W̲A̲Y̲S̲ the North-east of Scotland is the most Scottish part of the country, most Scottish because its way of life, architecture and general atmosphere have, until the advent of North Sea Oil, been mercifully free from dominating external pressures; and the North-east has preserved in-dividual trade and cultural links at least as close with Scandinavia as the rest of the United Kingdom. This is partly geographical, for if one draws a line straight out into the German Ocean from Aberdeen it will make land somewhere about Bergen; and what is true of Aberdeen is still more so further north. Once when I complained to my tailor about the cost of a repair he said, "Don't blame me, I'm not a Scotsman, I come from Aberdeen", which is, of course, an Aberdonian joke. Seriously, though, he has a point, and displayed a touch of that uninhibited self-assurance that characterizes the North-east. One is reminded, for instance, of the remark of the Provost of Aberdeen to the late Jan Masaryk when offering him the Freedom of the City: "Convey our greetings to your King Peter. Tell him he's welcome anytime. Ye ken our motto, Bon Accord". The fact is the north-eastern counties are far enough away from both London and Edinburgh to have developed their own commercial and cultural contacts and to have enjoyed until quite recently a measure of local independence not always noticeable to the same extent in other parts of Scotland. The advent of oil has increased commercial independence, but it poses a cultural threat that the Scottish Nationalists have been quick to make political capital out of. The probability of their being able, or even willing to slow down the oil programme does not detract from the significance of the fact that they are strongest in the North-east, where before oil they were weakest. This sort of protest is not new, either, for in the days of the Covenant, the University Doctors at Aberdeen denounced that document as contrary to the laws of God and man, and again, in 1689, when the first General Assembly of the existing Presbyterian Kirk was held in Edinburgh, there was a noticeable absence of representatives from north of the Tay, 'the Granite city' being and indeed remaining an Episcopalian stronghold.

Naturally, the North-east is not just Aberdeen, the episcopal diocese itself incorporating Orkney and Shetland; and this confirms associations that have existed with the islands ever since they were annexed by the Scottish Crown at the end of the fifteenth century. The old Castle at Kirkwall which James III of Scots then acquired by forced exchange with the St Clair, or Sinclair, Earls of Orkney, is no more, replaced by the magnificent palace of Earl Patrick, which the Ancient Monuments book describes as "the most mature and accomplished piece of Renaissance architecture left in Scotland". The builder was the son of Robert Stewart, bastard of James V of Scots, and the palace he built dates from the first decade of the seventeenth century. It is not a castle, and it is a ruin, never having been finished before the Earl and his sons were executed for treason, the son first, the father after a delay during which he was taught to recite the Lord's Prayer, a knowledge of which had somehow previously escaped him. What really seems incredible is that this apparently ignorant man should have been responsible for the erection of so much fine Renaissance architecture. A word of explanation, therefore, would seem clearly necessary.

Robert Stewart acquired the Crown Rights in Orkney and Shetland shortly before the marriage of Darnley to his half-sister, Mary, Queen of Scots, in 1565, and both he and his son Patrick used their position and power to squeeze every penny from the poor islanders, depriving the small gentry of their land and turning them into slaves, tampering with the weights and measures and manipulating the law as it suited them. Patrick was probably the greater scoundrel, but also the greatest builder with a remarkable understanding of the art of architecture. It is a pity his masterpiece in Kirkwall is a ruin, despite suggestions that it might be restored for some official purpose, but its ruin is not complete and is important in the story of the development of the domestic style in Scotland, particularly in the North-east. Robert, the elder Stewart Earl of Orkney, has his chief ornament in stone in a more sinister edifice, or so it would appear, at Noltland Castle, the first 'l' silent, situated on the Island of Westray. This is another ruin, but like the other has an historical and cultural relevance beyond both its site and condition. Noltland is the most northern castle mentioned by Billings in his splendid book and it is a tribute to that author's assiduousness and genuine interest in Scottish architecture that he should have ventured so far. It is not the most northerly castle in the United Kingdom: that is Scalloway, in Shetland, which was built by Earl Patrick to control the inhabitants and keep them under subjection. No doubt Billings might even have reached Scalloway had that pile suggested any particularly unusual features, but it does not, except in the expertness of its workmanship, and refined details, which are all hallmarks of Earl Patrick's architectural ploys. It is L-shaped and possessed of the usual corner turrets and rich Jacobean corbelling, with small shot-holes ingeniously secreted between the corbels, another of the Earl's specialities. Professor Gordon Donaldson of Edinburgh University, a Shetlander by origin, has suggested that Scalloway's tall, well proportioned form may have inspired some of the more famous Aberdeenshire castles, but I am afraid this cannot be substantiated; Crathes, which he specifically mentions, was completed ten years before Scalloway was begun, and even Craigievar, which is more or less contemporary, is not so different from its neighbours as to warrant a search for derivatives in the Shetland Isles.

Noltland pre-dates the earliest of these by about a quarter of a century, and is different from every one of them in history and design. Ostensibly it was begun by Gilbert Balfour of Westray for his own use towards the end of the 1560s, and left incomplete in 1573; Balfour ending his life in Sweden, on the scaffold, having been implicated in a plot to murder the Swedish king. He had two brothers also involved in nefarious activities of one sort or another, Sir James

Balfour, the most notorious, being 'art and part' in the murder of Cardinal Beaton in 1546, for which he, in the unlikely company of a young John Knox, served sentence in the French galleys. Later, he and his brothers played a role in the murder of Darnley, the whole story of which has never been unfolded and perhaps never will be. In any event, so far as Gilbert Balfour is concerned, in 1564, the same year in which Robert Stewart obtained the Crown Rights in Orkney and Shetland, he relinquished the post of Master of Queen Mary's Household and became Sheriff Principal of the islands, having earlier received the lands of Noltland in Westray from his brother-in-law, Adam Bothwell, Bishop of Orkney. Oddly enough by 1567 he was no longer Sheriff Principal, that office having gone to Robert Stewart, who in 1568 removed the Bishop from his palace, giving him in exchange the revenues of the Abbey of Holyrood of which he was Commendator, or secular abbot. The Orcadian Eric Linklater, in his history of *The Royal House of Scotland,* relates all these moves to a master plan by the Stewart Earl in which Balfour of Westray merely acted the part of a blind, and notably in the building of a mighty fortress at Noltland which could perform either an aggressive or defensive purpose depending upon the success or otherwise of his patron's tyrannical progress.

The dates seem to fit in with Linklater's thesis for Noltland, which, notwithstanding the possibility of its having had some other existence before 1570, was still unfinished in 1573; and not long after this Robert Stewart was arrested and taken into custody "for the safety of the realm", spending two years under lock and key at Linlithgow before being allowed to return to Orkney. Noltland is a vast and menacing-looking fort, its vacant walls pierced not with windows but gun-loops which form a pattern of holes suggestive more of a man o'war than a building of stone and lime. It could never have been a house for living in, and was clearly not intended as such. It is Z-shaped on plan, with square towers at opposite corners one of which contains what is probably the most remarkable staircase in Scotland; and it is this staircase that brings us back to the wider links

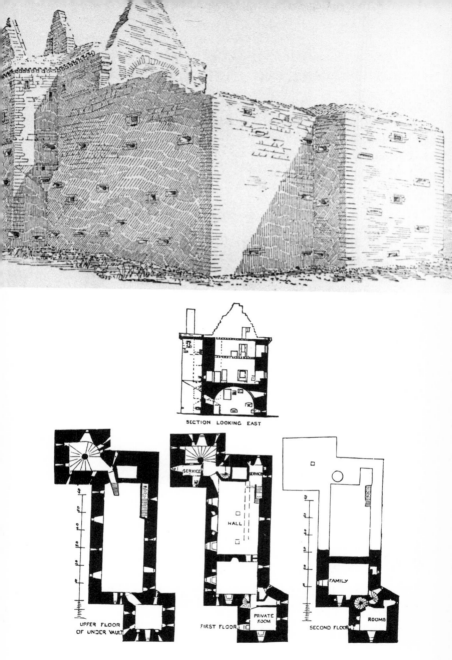

SECTION LOOKING EAST

UPPER FLOOR
OF UNDER VAULT

SERVICE    SERVICE

HALL

FIRST FLOOR    PRIVATE
ROOM

FAMILY

SECOND FLOOR    ROOMS

*Noltland Castle: view from the north-west; section*

between the different parts of the North-east, for there is only one comparable staircase in the country, at Fyvie Castle in Aberdeenshire. This was the creation of Alexander Seton, first Lord Fyvie and later Earl of Dunfermline, Chancellor under James VI. What we are looking for is a key to the great building works of the Stewart Earls of Orkney, their sources of inspiration on the mainland of Scotland and possibly on the Continent. Otherwise it is difficult to understand the extreme perfection of the work, especially when one knows that the masons employed were local, not foreigners.

Donaldson connects Scalloway and Kirkwall with the Aberdeenshire castles, but if he is right, surely it was not the islands that influenced the mainland, but the other way round; and in the case of the two superb staircases at Noltland and Fyvie, it may be that they both derive from the same Continental model and not from each other. Certainly the one at Fyvie is generally considered to derive from French precedents, possibly from the Tour desMinimes at Amboise, which was built by Charles VIII large enough for cavaliers to climb without dismounting, a conceit first conceived by Duke Frederico da Montefeltro at Urbino. othe reduced height of Noltland and Fyvie, plus the supporting arches that occur at regular intervals in the ascent, would probably preclude mounting on horseback, though the steps at Noltland are nearly 8 feet across and each is made of a single block of stone, while the central newel is wide enough to hide a man inside. Fyvie is more ornamental and gaily decorated with Renaissance details, but at Noltland the staircase is defensive and functional, the walls pitted with shot-holes, and the newel ending in a little guard room. Both ascents are right-handed, which is in keeping with the period, and spacious to a degree. MacGibbon and Ross discount the French influence, on what grounds one cannot say, for where else are there precedents for such ambitious and ingenious creations? And, of course, Robert Stewart was partly educated on the Continent. Patrick's refinements may have sources nearer home, in his own inherent architectural good taste, which was proverbial in his family, legitimate and otherwise, and in his having the means to emulate the greatest in the land, including the king.

If we take the beautiful oriel windows of the Earl's Palace at Kirkwall we find they are echoed not only in some of the coastal ruins in nearby Caithness erected by contemporaries, that would be only natural, but in the palace which the first Marquis of Huntly built in 1602, one year before Alexander Seton constructed the grand staircase at Fyvie; and the Setons and the Huntlys, or Gordons, were close kinsmen. Huntly had come to grief earlier when James VI, in one of his forays against recalcitrant subjects, made a progress to the North in the course of which Huntly Castle was destroyed, when the Marquis, still only Earl, went into exile on the Continent. His wife was the daughter of Esmé Stewart, Seigneur d'Aubigny, a descendant of John Stewart of Darnley who in the days of Joan of Arc had been made Constable of the Scots Guard to Charles VII, and received from that king the lands and *château* of Aubigny-sur-Nère, near Bourges, in reward for his services. There can be little doubt at all that the rebuilding of Huntly Castle in *château* style resulted from these and other Continental associations. The family again came to grief through their constancy to the cause of Charles I, when the Jacobean rebuilding itself fell victim to a new despoliation, since when it has remained roofless and empty. Fortunately, enough of the seventeenth-century 'palace' survives for us to get some idea of what a fine place it was, and to confirm its French features: the row of oriels at fourth-floor level have distinct affinities with Blois, for instance, while the larger oriel, projecting from a big round tower, is much on the lines of those at the Earl's Palace in Kirkwall. A novel device is the mock window in one of the chimneystalks. This undoubtedly owes its origins to the Palais Jacques Coeur in Bourges, where not only are there mock windows, but mock servants and other personages leaning out of them.

The Gordons were amongst the most numerous and vicious of all the north-eastern clans, part Norman, part Highland. They are today represented by the Duke of Richmond and Gordon, who is Duc d'Aubigny in the French

*Bog o' Gight (Gordon Castle) from Slezer's* Theatrum Scotiae

peerage and whose huge Gothic Revival castle near Fochabers has been reduced to minimal proportions, the Gordon Lennox family residing in an outbuilding; the Marquis of Aberdeen, better known as Archie Gordon, who lives near London but whose seat if he chose would be Haddo House; and the Marquis of Huntly, 'Cock o' the North', who inhabits ancillary buildings beside the remains of Aboyne Castle on Deeside. Gordon Castle is on the site of the ancient Bog o' Gight, which appears in Slezer under Inveraro, while Haddo is an eighteenth-century mansion designed by William Adam not far from the ruins of the Castle of the Gordons of Gight, or Gecht, the main line of which died out in the person of Katherine Gordon, mother of Lord Byron. Archie Gordon has spoken evocatively on the wireless about their murderous behaviour and addiction to wizardry, and compared past wildness in the Gordon family with present tameness and respectability.

The Setons and Gordons did not arrive in the North from the Borders until the second half of the fifteenth century, when much of the land had already been parcelled out amongst earlier settlers, Stewarts, Douglases and Murrays, and they settled themselves on the fringes of the Highlands where they could command the plain and fend off attack from the hills. A typical Gordon redoubt of this sort is Glenbucket Castle, in upper Donside, not far from Kildrummie. It dates from the late sixteenth century and is notable for its squinches, or arched supports for stair turrets, which in this case have no corbelling, unlike those at Kellie, and are much more like real French *trompes,* though lacking decoration in the alcoves below. Glenbucket is Z-shaped with

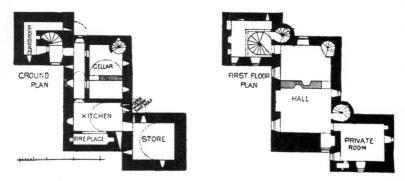

*Glenbucket Castle: plans*

rectangular towers at the opposing angles and was intact and inhabited until the Forty-five, when its laird, having survived Culloden, was forced to flee the country. It is in the care of the Department of the Environment and is interesting to compare with Kildrummie, which is medieval and grand, not in the vernacular, being the creation of the Norman Gilbert de Moravia, mason-bishop of Caithness. It too saw service in the Jacobite wars, having previously become a seat of the Earls of Mar, and in 1715 it was reduced to the extensive ruin it is today.

The de Moravia family were descended from Freskin, a common ancestor of the Dukes of Atholl and Sutherland, who may have been Flemish but arrived in the wake of the Norman penetration of north-eastern Scotland. By the thirteenth century Freskin's grandson, Hugh de Moravia, was already in possession of large areas of Sutherland, while other descendants remained in the South, notably William de Moravia, a kinsman of the great Gilbert, who designed Bothwell Castle, in Lanarkshire, finer even than Kildrummie and dismantled in 1336 by the Scots to prevent its recapture by the English. Gilbert founded the Cathedral of the Diocese of Caithness, of which he was first bishop and a completely reconstructed version of this building exists at Dornoch, episcopal capital and county town of Sutherland. Across the road from it is a wing and a tower of the former bishop's palace, which after several reductions and adaptations is now the Castle Hotel. Although only a small remnant of what was once a bigger, courtyard edifice the little palace is quite scenographic, and an ornament in a county where there are so few roofed or hale fortalices of any kind. To the medieval period perhaps only the lower masonry can be said to belong, the rest comprising a modest Jacobean laird's tower, albeit with interesting crowsteps finished with gablets, a feature usually associated with ecclesiastical buildings, and two open bartisans which, however, have no apparent access from any sentry walk or battlements. Dornoch Castle qualifies for inclusion in MacGibbon and Ross, which Dunrobin does not. This is the most northerly inhabited castle regularly open to the public, and the seat of Freskin's Sutherland descendants. It is probably the oldest continuously lived-in castle of any size in Scotland, of its rivals only Drum Castle, near Aberdeen, can be taken seriously, and that consists of a medieval 'keep' attached to but not part of a seventeenth-century house. The position at Dunrobin is different, for there the old tower is right in the middle of the larger castle, which encases it rather like the circles in the bark of a tree. Actually, very few people know this old bit exists; it is difficult to see and is shut in by successive layers of architecture ranging from sixteenth and seventeenth-century additions to the nineteenth-century redesigning of the whole castle by Sir Charles Barry, architect of the Houses of

Parliament at Westminster. Dunrobin is large and decidedly baronial, but in a playful, pre-Balmoral style, more French and less German, with excessively tall wimpled roofs, possibly the tallest and most amusing in Britain, and highly romantic-looking turrets that reflect themselves in the pool in the centre of the Italian garden exactly as they should do, like the turrets of a dream castle. There are also ogee roofs from the Restoration period giving a flavour of Thirlestane and a whole suite of rooms in Sir Robert Lorimer's mature manner, more robust than Barry's and less whimsical.

Dunrobin's site is sheltered, though right on the North Sea, and the gardens and woods around are lush in a manner one would scarcely expect in so northerly a spot. The plant life cannot, of course, quite compare with that of Culzean, where palms grow out of doors and edible oranges in the greenhouse, but that is on the west coast. Yet the rocky situation is not dissimilar and the mildness of the climate due to the influence of the Gulf Stream and the protection

*Dunrobin Castle: redesigned by Barry*

of mountains immediately behind the castle. Not so the Castle of Mey, which is not open to the public but is well known as the summer residence of H.M. The Queen Mother, who graciously opens the gardens when not at home. These gardens were already famous in Jacobean times and highly praised for their fruit, which, however, was grown against high walls, the same that protected the rest of the garden from snell winds and frosts, for Mey, originally called Barrogile and one of the numerous Sinclair seats in Caithness, is really very exposed, facing north across the Pentland Firth to Orkney. The building is not unlike a larger version of the bishop's palace at Dornoch, only more has happened to it, particularly in the nineteenth century when its walls and bartisans were heightened and crenellated and its turrets had their conical caps removed. It is a proper castle just the same, built on the 'Z' plan, and throughout most of its earlier history enjoyed an episcopal connection, coming to the Sinclairs through purchase from the last pre-Reformation Bishop of Caithness.

It is a moot point as to whether the County of Moray gave its name to the de Moravia family or vice versa; certainly the Murrays are related to the present Earl of Moray, whose name is Stewart, and the territorial designation has always prevailed, even in the days of James II of the Fiery Face, when the Earl was a Douglas. Moray boasts one of the best climates in Scotland, vying with East Lothian in productivity and sunshine, a fact discernible in the settled look and warmth of Elgin and Haddington, the respective county towns. Haddington cannot boast the great cathedral of Elgin, though it does have Scott's 'Lamp o' the Lothians', St Mary's Collegiate Kirk; but Elgin Cathedral was, before its collapse, the most beautiful in Scotland, having on more than one occasion risen from its ashes more resplendent than before. It celebrated its seventh centenary in 1974, when pilgrimages were made from all over the diocese, which today includes Caithness and Ross, and has its modern cathedral in Inverness. Gilbert de Moravia was actually Archdeacon of Moray in the days when the Cathedral was still situated at Spynie, between Elgin and the coast, and his family had their seat at Duffus, nearby. The latter is not only ruined but literally 'tummeldoun', for a huge chunk of masonry has slipped away from the rest and lies precariously on the edge of the motte ready to slip further at any moment. This makes one think of the Château de Coucy near Soissons, which has links with Scotland through the marriage of Marie de Coucy to Alexander II, but which owes its cyclopean disarray not to the vagaries of time but to the Kaiser's guns in the First World War. Though sited on the old Moravian mound and surrounded by an enormously wide fosse or ditch, Duffus actually dates from a later period, as does the former bishop's palace at Spynie, the ruined 'keep' of which is younger than the *enceinte* and magnificent late thirteenth-century gateway. This was rebuilt by Bishop Innes of Moray after the sacking of both palace and cathedral by the 'Wolf of Badenoch', when masons of superior ability and experience were employed, possibly from Lincoln or even from France.

A mile or two to the east of Elgin is Coxton Tower, another Innes venture but dating from the mid-seventeenth century. With Scotstarvit in Fife and Amisfield in Dumfriesshire, it forms one of a trio of perfectly preserved laird's towers of the Jacobean and Carolean eras, with its own peculiarities of construction and use of defensive features. The tower is square and on four floors, all vaulted, the vaulting alternating in direction at each storey, barrel shaped on the three lower floors and pointed on top. Rectangular, crenellated bartisans project at two opposite corners, while from the others conically capped turrets protrude; the gables are crowstepped and there are three chimneystalks, one rising directly from the eaves, the others at the gable ends. The entire building is of stone, roof, ceiling and floors, and the fenestration minimal. Iron bars guard every opening, and the door, on the first floor and formerly reached via a movable ladder but now by a stone forestair, is protected inside by the usual iron yett, or gate. The arms of Innes appear over the entrance and inside the tower. The lower space was reserved for animals and communication with the room above provided by means of a hole in the vaulted ceiling,

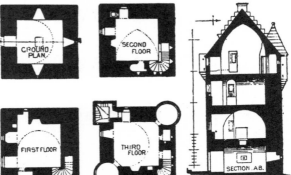

*Coxton Tower, Elgin: general view; plans and section*

thenceforth by stairs contained within the thickness of the walls. What purpose this sturdy but inconvenient little building could have been intended to serve in the second part of the reign of Charles I must remain conjectural. There are those who say it was never meant to be lived in, except possibly in times of stress, while others maintain that the date over the door, 1644, is not that of the original building and is, therefore, misleading. All the facts seem to point, however, to that date being correct, and Coxton being built as a retreat and strong point in an area which, even in the seventeenth century, and indeed in the eighteenth, was still plagued by family feuds and fears of invasion, and did not finally calm down until after the Forty-five.

Coxton Tower stands at one side of the driveway leading to a small country mansion and is not open to the public. It was occupied by tenants in the nineteenth century but today gives more the appearance of a folly than anything else. It contrasts vividly with Innes House, in the same district, which was built between 1640 and 1653 and is a good example of what one might call the Winton style: that is, of imported English provenance as to features such as Jacobean strapwork, Renaissance balustrading and ornamental chimneystalks, and especially those placed diagonally to each other in sets of three, as at Winton, and also in one case at Kellie. Curiously enough the plan of Innes House remains that of the traditional L-shaped laird's tower, and the master mason in charge was none other than William Aytoun, who worked at Heriot's Hospital in Edinburgh. There are no elaborate plaster ceilings in the house such as one might have expected, though some of the same craftsmen were employed elsewhere in the neighbourhood, and notably at Brodie Castle, near Forres, where there exists a fine ceiling of 1640 in which the traditional moulds were adapted to an older, vaulted room. Brodie, which suffered much at the hands of William Burn in Victorian times, retains the nucleus of an older fortalice in which the Brodies of that Ilk have resided since its building in the fifteenth century. It is occasionally open to the public, when visitors will see a fine fretwork ceiling in the Restoration manner, suggesting that either

Dunsterfield and Halbert themselves actually reached Moray or that their best apprentices did; and Brodie is the most northerly castle in which original plasterwork of this kind is to be found.

Just over the Banffshire boundary, outside Dufftown, are the extensive ruins of Balvenie, which has the distinction of being associated with the more important local familes, from the Comyns, who supported Edward I of England, to the Douglas Earls of Moray, the Stewart Earls of Atholl and latterly the Inneses. It has been empty and open to the winds since the Forty-five when the Government garrisoned it, but retains portions built as long ago as the thirteenth century, and larger, better-preserved parts dating from the sixteenth and seventeenth, including fine stair turrets facing the courtyard. Above the entrance to the older of these appear the arms of John, Lord Forbes, and his wife, Katherine Stewart; she was the daughter of John Stewart of Balvenie, himself the son of Joan Beaufort, widow of James I of Scots and therefore half-brother of James II of the Fiery Face, who made him Earl of Atholl and Lord of Balvenie in 1457. It was he who was afterwards commissioned by James III to head off a revolt by the Lord of the Isles, the king speeding him on his way with the words, "Furth fortune and fill the fetters", which is still the motto of the Atholl family. Balvenie is in the care of the Department of the Environment and a visit to it can conveniently and interestingly be combined with one to Auchendoun, a much more ruinous survival of the Middle Ages though a late specimen and built by Robert Cochrane, master mason and favourite of James III, who made him Earl of Mar, hence his appearance in the North. The main feature of Auchendoun's emaciated, somewhat enigmatic condition is the refined gothic vaulting in what was once the hall, this clearly being the work of a master, though also the result of trial and error, as can be seen in the double springing to one vault, and its replacement by a geometrically more correct one. To Cochrane is usually attributed the Great Hall of Stirling Castle, but if so it must have been after Auchendoun and his experimental vaulting there, vaulting incidentally, that may have inspired two sixteenth-century recreations, at Towie Barclay, in Aberdeenshire, and Balbegno, in Kincardineshire, which we will come to in due course.

Banffshire used to be very much a land of castles, and like the Laich o'Moray it benefits from the last lick of the Gulf Stream, and protection behind from the mountains. The county town has been a little capital of sorts for some time, and notably since the Duffs, formerly bankers in Elgin, became Earls of Fife in a new line, married into royalty and became dukes. They built Duff House at Banff, employing William Adam on the project, and this acted as the focal point for a miniature court. Most of this is now a mere memory, the Dukes of Fife have gone, and the local gentry who built houses in the vicinity for themselves have gone also. Yet Banff is full of good architecture of varying periods, one Georgian example standing on the site of the castle, and others, down by the harbour, recalling small country fortalices of the Jacobean era. A particularly good example was built in the nearby village of Fordyce by Thomas Menzies, ex-Lord Provost of Aberdeen, as a place of retiral and retreat, after becoming involved in a number of contentious disputes. This probably accounts for some of the pretty obvious defensive items in his 'town castle': the rows of shot-holes, five together in one case, and the heavy oak door studded with nails. A typical shut, as opposed to shot, hole can be seen immediately below a window of one of the corner turrets, and these and other details can be studied at fairly close quarters, as the 'castle' is at a crossroads in the middle of Fordyce and without any barrier between it and the passer-by. Roughly L-shaped, with stair tower making the smaller arm, it has been divided and added to, to make tenements, but is otherwise intact and its features include the whole array of Jacobean baronial treatment on a small scale, from conically capped corner turrets to elaborate corbelling (a dozen courses being counted beneath the semicircular projection in the entrant angle) to crowsteps and swept dormers, armorial devices and a delicately wreathed Renaissance roundel with Provost Menzies' monogram on a corner turret.

*Fordyce, the 'castle': corner turret or 'study'; general view*

The valley of the Deveron, which flows into the sea at Banff and has in the last century silted up the harbour mouth and reduced the town's capacity as a port and fishing centre, is dotted with small noble houses and castles, of which Craigston, an old Urquhart of Cromarty seat, is contemporaneous with Fyvie and inhabited by the family who built it between 1604 and 1607. Another is Inchdrewer, former seat of the Ogilvies which, after being ruined since 1713, has been restored by a descendant of the then owner, Lord Banff, a much disliked man who earned the hatred of a local youth by whom he was murdered, the castle being set on fire to cover up the deed. Inchdrewer mostly dates from a reconstruction undertaken in the eighteenth century when the old L-shaped tower was altered to make a more comfortable house and became a rectangle with a projection in the middle. It has now been made even more convenient by Mr Robin de la Lanne Mirrlees, a name he adopted partly to obtain funds for the castle's restoration from abroad. Mr Mirrlees, who has described it as "the most beautiful castle in Scotland and the most comfortable one", was formerly Rouge Dragon Pursuivant at the College of Heralds in London and has succeeded in his task without too much interference from official bodies. The result can be seen at a discreet distance from the road, rising in its renewed, unharled masonry from the midst of surrounding fields rather like some knightly tower in an illuminated manuscript.

Craigston Castle, on the eastern side of the Deveron, was built in the first decade of the seventeenth century by John Urquhart, Tutor of Cromarty, that is to say, uncle and guardian of the heir to the House of Cromarty. He was the grandfather of Sir Thomas Urquhart, translator of Rabelais, inventor of a universal language and a family tree taking the Urquharts back to Adam and giving the world a precise age. Part of Sir Thomas's library has been brought together and housed in a top room of Craigston, the rest was lost during the Civil War; the superiority of Cromarty went to another family in the eighteenth century and nothing now remains of Cromarty Castle. Craigston's principal feature is its great *arc de triomphe* over the front entrance, which is obviously derived

*Craigston Castle*

from Alexander Seton's centrepiece at Fyvie, and was possibly the creation of the same masons, the dates being almost identical. Where Craigston differs is in the considerable depth of the arch, which makes it much more decorative than structural, and especially so since it only supports a single balcony high up. The amusingly sculptured corbels at the four corners of the castle are also ornamental, supporting no turrets, rectangular or semi-circular. In the same playful but slightly rude spirit is the carving on the balcony above the arch, which is divided into five panels, richly moulded and containing roundel figures of four jousting knights and a piper, in the middle, the whole being supported on particularly deep and elaborate corbelling, itself sprouting four large animal gargoyles of grotesque design. There is a modern porch and the interior has been altered considerably with much original panelling redistributed around as internal shutters and serving other purposes for which it was not intended. Surviving complete panels show Mary, Queen of Scots, James VI and I, Hector and David, the last two once forming part of the traditional triple series of Antique, Old Testament and Christian lore found in Jacobean castles in stone, wood, painting or tapestry. In the eighteenth century William Adam, then engaged by the Earl of Fife at Duff House, produced a fan-like design for a formal garden at Craigston, but it was not carried out and instead the grounds were romanticized *à la* Capability Brown, when 'gothic' bridges and other items appeared, though the very attractive doocot, now restored and re-inhabited by doves after many years of neglect, is seventeenth century.

Craigston's architectural links with Fyvie are clear, but even if the same masons did work at both castles, they are very different in scale and affect, which only goes to show how imaginative and individual were the tastes of the lairds and those whom they employed. Between the two one will find Delgatie, and Towie Barclay, both in northern Aberdeenshire, near Turriff and both different again, though with at least one important feature in common, their groined and vaulted ceilings which are not medieval but Jacobean recreations. What seems to have happened is that when the timber roofs of the first floor halls were being replaced this was done in stone, hence the vaulting here and in one or two other notable cases. The date of the new work at Delgatie is post-1570, at Towie Barclay 1593, when Patrick Barclay, a strong supporter of Mary, Queen of Scots, was laird, and suffered much for his loyalty. Indeed the Barclays, who originated in England and arrived in the North via Fife, where their arms appear amongst those of the other Fife gentry on the painted ceiling of Collairnie Castle, founded a celebrated overseas branch in Russia, where Field-Marshal Barclay de Tolly was the man who defeated Napoleon in 1812. Their Aberdeenshire seat went to wrack and ruin and in 1792 the top storeys were removed, leaving the barrel-vaulted laich hall and groined upper one as curious memorials to the renewed interest in ecclesiastical architecture that occurred in early seventeenth century Scotland, when Episcopacy temporarily triumphed over Presbyterianism. The present proprietors when they came were presented with quite a problem, for the living quarters had long since disappeared and the building reduced to extremely unsatisfactory proportions. However, they have made a really good job of it, nicely restoring the Jacobean portion, finishing the roof with fake but not unsympathetic battlements and corner turrets, and a little house for themselves alongside. One can go and see it if one wishes to since the work was done with a Government grant and is on the list of places open by appointment.

Delgatie needed no restoration, it has been inhabited more or less continuously since the sixteenth century, though not all the time by the same family who built it. I know Turriff and that bit of the country from my childhood, having been brought up as a very small boy at Cummineston, where my father was Pisky rector and exorcised the ghost at Delgatie. In those days the castle was still owned by the Ainslies of whom Mrs Ainslie was Russian and of the Orthodox faith. It was she who insisted on my father coming along with bell, book and candle and getting rid of the ghost. He seems to have been successful as I asked Lady Erroll, whose family, the Hays of Erroll, belong there, and she assured me there was no sign of any ghost now. At the moment Delgatie is in the possession of Captain Hay of Hayfield, who opens it to the public in summer. It has been enlarged and altered quite a lot, with a seventeenth-century house attached to one side of the squarish old tower, a junction that even the unifying use of harling has not wholly obliterated. The tower retains its open sentry walk and bartisans supported by fine corbelling, in which the favoured cable course is introduced, and there are the vaulted rooms, barrel vaulted in the basement, groin vaulted above. Painted ceilings are another attraction at Delgatie, while the eighteenth-century Gothic-Revival outbuildings, including a most attractive 'medieval' doocot, do not spoil the overall effect in the slightest.

One cannot see Fyvie unless one is a guest there or manages to slip in beside the butcher or baker as he drives his delivery van up the drive. The castle is quite invisible from the road or anywhere else due to its low position, shrouding woods and high park wall. Apart from the small mound on which the castle stands the site is flat and marshy, Fyvie being protected by the River Ythan on whose banks it rises. Both MacGibbon and Ross and Billings are slightly critical of the present appearance of Fyvie which they, rightly on the whole, think untypical of the period and forced when compared to other castles in the North-east. What they really mean is that Fyvie did not evolve but was made into its present perfectionist mould deliberately, and without much consideration for convenience of planning, largely to satisfy the fashion for symmetry. In this it succeeds, the central feature, with its twin turrets, joined above the entrance at a height of more than forty feet, capped by gables and amusing sculpture, including Lord Fyvie's trumpeter, forms the linking feature between the older Preston Tower, which dates from the end of the fourteenth century, and the Meldrum Tower, which probably only dates from the sixteenth century. Symmetry is achieved thereby and the exercise is undoubtedly unique in any Scottish building of the early Jacobean period, when the Renaissance had just arrived and its details had barely been digested even by so grand and gifted a person as Chancellor Seton. Thus, while the 1603 façade follows contemporary taste in its external symmetry, the details remain gothic; and internally the loss of convenience is immediately obvious in the poor entrance, which leads into a long narrow passage and is nowhere near either the staircase or the usual offices. In fact, the marvellous grand staircase, with its rare French Renaissance affinities, comes right at the far end of another wing, itself now reached via a new and more commodious entry erected in the nineteenth century.

There is thought to have been a very much older building on the same site which was visited by Edward I of England, but of it nothing remains to bear witness to that visit; there is also an engaging story about the trumpeter whose effigy crowns the gable of the Seton entrance. His name was Andrew Lammie, whom the miller of Tiftie's daughter loved in the eighteenth century. She was prevented from marrying

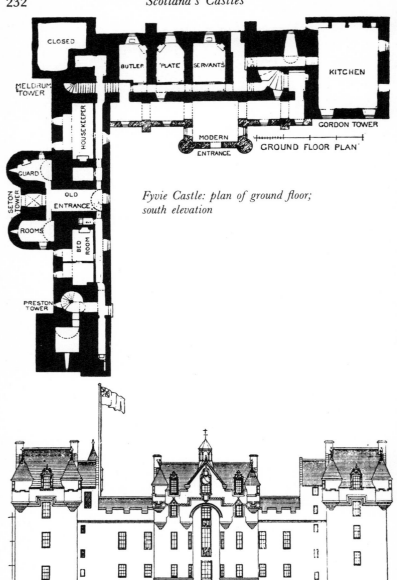

*Fyvie Castle: plan of ground floor;
south elevation*

him by her father, and died of grief as a result, the trumpeter blowing balefully in her direction from the house-top ever after. If this is true, of course, then the effigy is not Jacobean but Georgian, and could not have been copied at any other seventeenth-century castle, as has been suggested. Fyvie is L-shaped but of huge proportions, the Seton wing being nearly 150 feet long, the western one only about 10 feet less. At either extremity are the oldest and newest towers respectively, all being in the same style, which makes the building very rare indeed, presenting the appearance of having been built at the same time, though the first bit is mostly of the fifteenth century and the last of the nineteenth. In its homogeneity Fyvie hardly has an equal, almost every detail being in the Jacobean castellated style, and those parts that are not are sympathetic to it. It is perhaps worth adding that after a variety of occupants the present laird is descended from Sir Henry Preston who built the oldest tower.

The River Ythan winds placidly, southern English fashion, towards the sea just north of Aberdeen, past the gaunt ruins of Castle Gight and its notorious pool, in which the devil is said to hold court and sup with warlock Gordons, through the wooded policies of Georgian Haddo and on to its end in the sand dunes near Collieston and Old Slains. The latter is the modern seat of the Countess of Erroll, Chief of Clan Hay and High Constable of Scotland, who does not have to walk backwards when leaving the Queen's presence. The Castle of Old Slains was already reduced to rubble when she and her family decided to live on it, literally, by building a super-modern house on the site, and so perpetuate a long history and a long association with a particular property. To the south lie Donside and Deeside and that galaxy of Scottish *châteaux* that in their own way rival those of the valley of the Loire, at least in their extent and variety if not in their size and importance. Dominating the scene hereabouts is Bennachie, a small but distinctive mountain which has encouraged the National Trust for Scotland to produce a helpful pamphlet, with the title *Back o'Bennachie,* covering some of the better-known castles and gardens in the district, including the two most famous in Scotland: Crathes and

Craigievar. Before turning to these Jacobean masterpieces, however, perhaps we should take a final glance northwards to Fraserburgh, a fishing port in Buchan founded by Sir Alexander Fraser of Philorth in the late sixteenth century, where that laird's castle, on the rocks of Kinnaird's Head, has become a lighthouse, but without despoliation. The interior has been adapted to its new purpose, but externally Sir Alexander's tall tower remains intact, whitewashed but retaining its projecting bartisans, rounded at the four corners, rectangular in between, and supported by the usual elaborate corbelling. There are precedents for this as well, for when Sir Walter Scott was one of the light house commissioners he was able to have Scotland's oldest 'House o'Lights' on the May Isle, in the Firth of Forth, restored, crenellated, whitewashed and turned into a romantic folly beside the newer light then erected.

On the very edge of the sea, below Kinnairds lighthouse-cum-castle, is another old building called 'The Wine Tower', for what reason no one seems to know, except that being above a cave it may have smuggling associations. In fact, this is most unlikely, the tower is a generation older than the castle and possesses on its third floor a fine vaulted room with the royal arms of James V on one of the ceiling bosses; another bearing the symbols of Christ's crucifixion in the form of an angel displaying the nails, the scourge, the hammer, the wounded heart, hands and feet, emblems that may also incidentally be seen at Castle Fraser, and which post-date the Reformation by more than fifty years. No doubt the vaulted room in the 'Wine Tower' was a chapel, and may even have marked the site of some holy place. The only other explanation for its existence so far offered is that it was built as an occasional residence by Sir Alexander Fraser's father and replaced by the son when he founded Fraserburgh and built his own larger tower higher up.

As one passes over the watershed from the Ythan to the Don basin, Barra Castle, not to be confused with anything on the west coast, rises charmingly on a rise by the roadside just south of Old Meldrum, at the point where the prospect is pleasantest and most extensive, and Bennachie comes into

view. This is less of a castle than almost any other building
of its size and period in Aberdeenshire, having no original
turrets, only one small run of extremely utilitarian corbelling,
and being built neither as an obvious 'Z' or 'L' but on three
sides of a courtyard, more like a town house. The fact that
it was a Seton residence may explain some of this, but not
all, for the place is modest by comparison with other Seton
homes, and rough, if interesting, in its exposed granite surfaces. Barra does have three round towers with conical roofs,
there were probably four at one time, but they come right
down to the ground and are not for defensive purposes; the
kitchen is vaulted and elsewhere there is some good late
seventeenth-century panelling, pine, and painted as it should
be, with thick Queen Anne astragals in the windows, not the
reedy-looking things that so often replace them in modern
restorations. Barra has no evident history, but its site is
historical, being near where the Regent John Comyn, Earl of
Buchan, was defeated by Robert Bruce in 1308.

Two of the places in the National Trust for Scotland's *Back
o'Bennachie* pamphlet are close together and make a suitable
joint visit. The Great Garden at Pitmedden is one of the
wonders of the North-east having been entirely recreated
from the kitchen garden status it had descended to before
becoming the property of the Trust in 1952. In essence this
grand layout is modelled on the formal garden planted for
Charles I at Holyrood as depicted in a contemporary 'Bird's
Eye View', which Dr James Richardson, former Inspector of
Ancient Monuments in Scotland, studied before beginning
the work of restoration. This type of garden emanated from
Italy and was frequently quite small, with box hedges and
gravel paths and shrubs in tubs making a set pattern such as
one sees from the windows of the Palazzo Piccolomini at
Pienza, the creation of Pope Pius II in the fifteenth century.
The Pope, who actually came to Scotland in the reign of
James I, was a humanist and leader of the Renaissance, and
the little town of Pienza, near Siena, was built by him to
supplant the smaller village nearby in which he had been
born. Much larger gardens than his were later developed but
the idea of taking the salon out of doors rather than bringing

nature indoors, which many modern folk prefer, was typical of the Italian search for ever more refinement and sophistication. The French took up Italian ideas with enthusiasm and reproduced Renaissance gardens on a vast scale. Le Nôtre laid out whole parks with parterres and formal hedges, like Vaux-le-Vicomte and Versailles, and included full-grown trees in the overall pattern, pollarding and training them mercilessly, bringing in waterworks, pavilions, terraced vistas, and generally bending nature to conform to man's desire for order and symmetry.

Francis Bacon refers to the Renaissance preoccupation with formality in his essay "On Gardens", describing a Jacobean layout in detail and making the comment that the more civilized the age the more likely will a man make his garden first and build his house second. Sir William Bruce did this at Kinross, and it is to Bruce that Sir Alexander Seton of Pitmedden owed much of the inspiration for the Great Garden he made in 1675, he having previously spent much time as a lawyer in Edinburgh and being familiar with the Palace of Holyroodhouse which Bruce was building for the King. The influence of the royal architect is particularly noticeable in the end pavilions at Pitmedden, and in the form of the high terracing on the house side of the garden, which emulates his own 'Italian' terrace at Balcaskie, in Fife. Pitmedden Castle is no more, replaced by a modern house, but the architectural conception of its garden survives. One sees it best from the top of the terrace, looking down, and in early summer, when the different plants, not yet grown big, do not hide the box hedges and coloured chips of the paths between, so that the baroque patterns show up well. The whole experience is worth repeating at Edzell, in Kincardineshire, where the less ambitious and slightly older formal garden created by Lord Lindsay has likewise been restored to something approximating its original state, this time by the Ancient Monuments people. It represents a variation on a theme, Jacobean not Caroline, and with bath house and pavilion in keeping.

The walk from Pitmedden to Tolquhon can be very pleasant, and en route one will probably notice the tall white

*Pitmedden: the Great Garden*

tower of Udny which dominates the scene roundabout. This
is square and rather stark after the removal of the newer
house with which it was until recently associated, the
building now being reduced to a single, turreted edifice
nearly 100 feet high. Udny boasts five storeys and gives the
appearance of being older than it is, in fact, of being
developed from an ancient 'keep', with newer upper floors. In
reality it is a typical Aberdeenshire tower house of the
Jacobean period which instead of becoming L-shaped, Z-
shaped or any other complicated shape is rectangular and
plain, with all its decorative features: rich corbelling, fake
battlements and extinguisher roofed turrets on top.
Tolquhon is quite different: it is a genuine development from
a fifteenth-century tower, now ruined, which was converted
into a bakehouse when the later, less ruinous part was added
at the end of the sixteenth century. This was meant by its
builder, William Forbes, to be a fortified mansion and not a
castle; consequently, instead of soaring to the skies it is low
and ranged round a courtyard, possibly in imitation of the

royal palaces of Falkland and Holyrood, even to the extent of being entered through a similar twin-turreted gatehouse. Unhappily the turrets themselves have gone, and indeed none of Tolquhon is roofed any longer. Above the main door is a panel with an inscription dating the rebuilding to between 1581 and 1589, plus some jolly sculpture, including quaint figures peering down at one from the corbelling and perhaps imitating French work, certainly in the same spirit as the mock windows and related sculpture at Huntly. Tolquhon has a double courtyard, and when Billings visited it part was still roofed, but only the bare walls remain today, carefully preserved by the Department of the Environment.

The term 'Castles of Mar' is sometimes used to describe that group of well-known Aberdeenshire fortalices that includes Castle Fraser, Midmar, Craigievar, or Craig-mar, meaning Rock of Marr, Crathes and Drum, all of which, apart from the old 'keep' at Drum, date from the end of the sixteenth or first half of the seventeenth centuries. If one excludes Glamis, which is the grandest and most famous of Scottish castles in the vernacular, this quintet represents both the sum and diversity of the Scottish castellated style in its heyday, when defensive features had become largely ornamental and for a couple of generations local masons and architects displayed a degree of ingenuity and imagination which has never since been repeated and which seems more particular to this part of Scotland than any other. Douglas Simpson in the guide he produced for the National Trust when they took over Craigievar in 1963 used the charming expression "a mountain château" to describe this supreme example of its kind, which does, in truth, stand not far off 1000 feet above sea level, though still technically in the Lowlands. I have spoken several times of the almost chance arrival at perfection in such buildings, and certainly compared with its nearest rival, Crathes, Craigievar makes a more satisfactory immediate impression, being compact and slender where Crathes is spread out, though the latter's details are more varied and refined. It may be, of course, that Craigievar did not entirely arrive by chance, since it was not completed until the second year of the reign of Charles I,

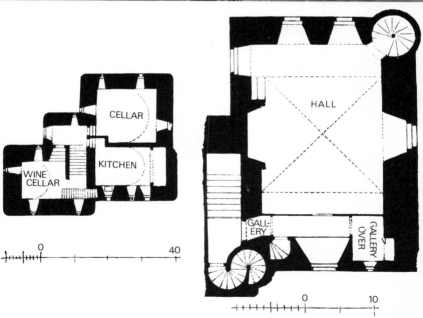

*Craigievar Castle: general view. Note tower of barmkin, left; plans*

which is very late for a building of this character, and 'Willy the Merchant', as this other William Forbes who commissioned it is normally referred to, may have laid down limits as to expenditure and size, which resulted in its narrow neatness. The castle is L-shaped but with a difference, the projection in the entrant angle does not contain the staircase, but only a lobby, and the stairs, which begin straight, wind up to left and right throughout the building, serpent-like.

As with most Aberdeenshire castles of the period, the base is plain and unadorned, the ornament, false gargoyles, cannon, elaborate corbelling, conically capped turrets, ogee-roofed cap houses, of which there are two, and balustraded finish to the tower at the entrant angle: all are gay and fanciful and were astonishingly created for a rich timber merchant, albeit the brother of the Bishop of Aberdeen. There have been few changes at Craigievar since its completion in 1626, though clearly the Georgian sash windows were not in evidence then, nor the slate roofs; there must have been shutter-board windows with fixed leaded lights above and opening wooden shutters below, and the roofs covered with split stone slabs. In the late Lord Sempill's visitor's book an interesting entry briefly describes conditions pertaining just over a century ago. The entry was made in 1903 by someone born in the early part of the nineteenth century and mentions the fact that Craigievar then still had its courtyard walls and several small round towers, of which one remains, and original outer entrance. The forecourt was paved where now it is grassed over or made into a pink granite chipped drive.

In 1842, when the writer in the Craigievar visitors book was six years old, we find that rushes taken from the banks of the burn near the castle were strewn freshly every day on the stone floors of the bedrooms, the same rushes being pithed to provide wicks for the crusie lamps. Craigievar has never had any electricity in it but, of course, in more recent times candles and more modern oil lamps replaced the traditional forms. The box-beds too, which lined the walls in 1842 and in one of which the boy slept with the gamekeeper, have practically all gone, a few kept as souvenirs on the

*Craigievar Castle: the Great Hall*

upper floor and one recess turned into a small bathroom. One can see where the beds were, however, in the pattern of the plaster ceilings which adorn every room in the castle. They almost all date from about 1627, when Joseph Fenton and his associates came up from Glamis and Muchalls, a small castellated house south of Aberdeen in Kincardineshire. Their principal contribution at Craigievar is the great vaulted ceiling in the Hall, which, using the same moulds as elsewhere but more imaginatively, creates an impression of baronial splendour and Renaissance *bravura* that places it in a class on its own. The subject matter is common enough, common to most countries in Europe in the sixteenth and seventeenth centuries, and comprises the heads of mythical and Biblical heroes, the co-called 'worthies', cherubs, floral features and armorial devices, while the heavy pendant bosses heighten the illusion of depth and solidarity which, in fact, does not exist, the whole conception being carried out entirely in plaster. Over the chimneypiece, itself an Italian-inspired object of some size, are the royal coat of arms of the Stuart kings as borne in Scotland 'supported' by two useless caryatids, useless because they actually support nothing. They are also single and not paired as at Glamis and Muchalls, one being male and one female at either end.

Many of the rooms at Craigievar are panelled in memel pine, a generic term for timber taken from Scots fir but grown elsewhere, which is left visible, unpainted. Most of it dates from the eighteenth century, but in the Hall the woodwork is Jacobean and includes a version of the 'screens', behind which in medieval times was the pantry and working area. It has been suggested that a tiny, cramped space above this was meant to be a minstrel's gallery, though Lord Sempill doubted it, and it was probably only a representation of such a feature, just as the plaster ceiling represents stone vaulting. There is also a curious story about the present kitchen, below the screen, having been a dungeon, and that between the floors earth was placed in order to deaden the sounds of misery and prevent the groans of prisoners reaching the womenfolk in the Hall. Since the earliest date of any part of Craigievar is 1610, and it was completed in

*Craigievar Castle. Representation of royal arms of Great Britain as correctly displayed in Scotland*

1626, one would have thought this most unlikely. There is only one door to Craigievar, but a picturesque assortment of stairs, including a secret one, really the laird's private escape route down from the top of the building to the hall, where it comes out behind a cunningly conceived corner cupboard. There is also a 'laird's lug' in the form of a tunnel in the thickness of the wall above a window in the hall into which a man could slip and eavesdrop if he wished. This was not unusual in the North-east and there is a similar tunnel at Crathes, and a more complicated arrangement at Castle Fraser, where a man could actually sit in comparative comfort to do his private spying. Lord Sempill, on whose demise the castle went to the National Trust for Scotland, was the eighth Baronet of Craigievar and nineteenth Lord, the Sempill family acquiring the property through marriage and themselves being of considerable antiquity, the gauntlets of the first Lord, who perished at Flodden, still being cherished.

Castle Fraser, unlike Craigievar, is neither compact nor narrow, and lacks the immediate attraction of its neighbour. It stands on lower ground in a less interesting setting, and although finished in 1618, and therefore slightly older, seems almost younger. Its chief feature is the great 'table', more like a tapestry in stone, of the royal achievement of James VI and I, which decorates the original façade, plus an enormous amount of largely irrelevant baronial ornament which, in the case of the gargoyles, mock their original purpose. The 'laird's lug' was discovered by James Skene of Rubislaw, a particular friend of Sir Walter Scott, whose notes made on a trip to France provoked the writing of *Quentin Durward* and set the author on the road to international fame. Skene explored Castle Fraser, and puzzling over the tiny hidy-hole between the vaulting of the hall and a room above, tested it, finding that when in it one could hear every word, even whispered, beneath. The 'lug' is formed in the thickness of the wall at one corner of the building and entered from behind a window shutter. Below is a tiny room, itself reached via a movable slab, so that once inside the only sounds one hears come from the hall. This is by far the most elaborate spying chamber of its kind in Scotland, and is said to have

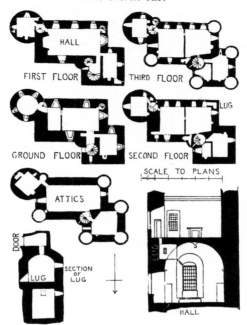

*Castle Fraser: plans and sections*

been copied by James I in the Tower of London, though
given up when he found it constricting and draughty.

Castle Fraser is Z-shaped, with a round tower at one
corner and a square, almost 'keep-like' one at the other. It
was built by John Bell, of a family of masons of whom
another, George Bell, had a generation earlier been responsible for Midmar Castle. The architectural links between the
two are close, Castle Fraser's baronial ordnance, if one can
use the term, being applied to a not dissimilar but plainer
framework derived from Midmar. It is instructive, for instance, to compare the finish to Midmar's big round tower
with that of Fraser, which is balustraded instead of
battlemented, and yet decorated with deep and quite extraneous corbelling. The most charming addition is actually
the cap-house, which is clearly of French inspiration, with its
double row of Renaissance arcades and pilasters, while
Midmar's is entirely without ornament. Though both castles

*Midmar Castle: view from the south; the sundial; pedimented bee-boles*

are similar in plan, Fraser does not give that feeling of soaring height that is the hallmark of a really good Scottish baronial design. Midmar does, but it lacks history, while Castle Fraser, built more than forty years later, just falls into the beginning of the Covenanting period, and consequently played a more active role. Its laird was raised to the peerage by Charles I, but took the Covenanting side when his castle was attacked and rendered defenceless by Montrose. Later Frasers returned to the royalist fold, going so far as to disclaim the title in order to demonstrate their contempt for the behaviour of Andrew Fraser of Muchall-in-Mar, the first Lord.

Neither Midmar nor Castle Fraser are normally open to the public, and Midmar, which was built in 1575, is not even marked in gothic writing on the Ordnance Survey map. Drum Castle, in the Dee Valley, is, and its 'keep', which dates from the days of Bruce, is still roofed and hale. It is only partly used and attached to a delightful manor house dating from 1619, and thus contemporaneous with Lord Fraser's pile. The two make excellent foils for each other, the martial-looking old tower standing beside the peaceful manor house. The 'keep' is probably the oldest and certainly the best-preserved tower of its kind north of the Border, and can be dated either to the last years of the thirteenth century or the first of the fourteenth, when Robert Bruce granted the royal forest of Drum to the family of Irvine, who came from south-west Scotland, the confirming charter being dated 1st February 1323. At that time the whole territorial shape of Lowland Scotland and parts of the Highlands changed when the former supporters of Edward I and the English faction were displaced by those who had sided with Bruce; it was then that the Setons and Gordons came up from the Borders, together with the Frasers, the Hays and other families already mentioned. With the Irvines arrived the Burnards, Saxon in a predominantly Norman company, and both, rather like the Roses at Kilravock and the Calders at Cawdor, have been in possession of neighbouring lands ever since, the Burnards obtaining their charter from King Robert I one month later than the Irvines.

*Drum Castle: The Bruce tower; from the south west*

The Burnards subsequently became known as the Burnetts of Leys, after Loch Ley on an island in the middle of which they first established themselves. The Irvines at once lived in a sturdy stone tower on the royal estate of Drum, the mason being in all probability the same who constructed the Brig o'Balgownie in Old Aberdeen; indeed it has been suggested that the timber centring from the pointed arch in the upper hall of Drum Castle was also used for centring that celebrated bridge over the Don. Be this as it may, the name of Richard Cementarius has been associated with both projects, and while the Brig o'Balgownie may have been restored and strengthened at various times it is probably substantially the same as built in the early part of the fourteenth century. Drum castle suffered only minor alterations in the course of its long history: the closing-up of a few windows, a new floor in the Laich hall, a stone forestair to reach the first floor in place of a removable wooden ladder, and the lowering of the roof pitch and replacement of stone slabs with slate. The walls are very thick, 12 feet at the base, 9 feet higher up, and within them one stair descends from the first floor to the barrel-vaulted basement, while another curls round inside the north-eastern corner to reach the upper hall, which was once divided by a timber floor into two storeys. This has pointed vaulting and was the lord's solar, or private quarter, with bedroom above; it has deeply set windows with stone seats and primitive lavatory, or *garderobe*. There was probably also an attic floor, but this has gone with the lowering of the roof. The battlements are not unlike those at Kilravock and Loch Leven Castles, of which only the latter may be contemporary, and both these have open bartisans which Drum has not; instead there is a slight heightening at the corners, which are rounded from foundation to parapet. There are large crenellations and simple, functional corbelling, with no unnecessary gargoyles or other decorative features, only one water spout per run of roof. The castle is private property and the Jacobean house alongside is inhabited, but the historic part is open to the public in summer and protected under an agreement with the National Trust.

Crathes, though also on the Dee, and not so very far from Aberdeen, is in Kincardineshire. It is by no means as ancient as Drum, not having been begun before 1553, and not finished until 1595. The Burnards, or Burnetts, did not leave the safety of their lake dwelling until the fifteenth century, and eventually, when they made Crathes their principal seat, they obtained a new charter. The lands round about were placed in Kincardineshire in the seventeenth century after the first baronet had built a dower house for the family at Muchalls, near Stonehaven, and acquired large estates south of the Dee. Following the local trend in politics and religion the Burnetts refused to recognize the Covenant and were forced to go into exile for a while, though later in the same century Bishop Burnett of Salisbury sided with William of Orange, and thus Crathes and its lairds were not so involved in the Jacobite rebellions as they might have been. This is not to say they were completely devoid of Stuart sympathies: they were episcopalians, and when that branch of the Scottish church was penalized for its adhesion to Charles Edward they stood their ground. They came through these experiences more or less unscathed, however, and in 1951 Sir

*Crathes Castle: the Jacobean roofline*

James Burnett of Leys, who with Lady Burnett had largely created the splendid garden at Crathes (extending it from an older formal one of 1702) presented the property to the National Trust for Scotland, the family residing in the Queen Anne wing.

Crathes, because of its rather squarish shape, does not dominate by its height in the same way as Craigievar, but as already indicated what it loses in slenderness and soaring effect it gains in detail, the skyline being full of variety, yet without crowding. In the centre of the south elevation is a projection, with a clock and suggestion of a bartisan crowning what is really a gable end; it starts rectangular, drops down to become semi-circular and ends half way up the building, supported on continuous corbelling which returns at the sides to make a frame. The corbelling, which is in horizontal bands only slightly broken by indented features, makes a sort of frieze until it breaks out again at eaves level to support conically capped corner turrets, the modest pitch of which contrast with steeper roofs at Kellie and Glamis, where the turrets are more romantic in feeling and clearly less authentic. Fake cannon sprout from the sides of the turrets, and also from the central bartisan above the clock. Turning the corner and glancing up above the door, which retains its iron yett, is a decorative version of a *bretèche,* resembling in outline a defensive feature which had it not been adapted to contain a dormer window would have been used for pouring boiling oil and other deterrents down on the heads of unwanted visitors, the corbelling being broken by a wide gap for the purpose. Further round on the same, eastern, side of the castle is a high-level houselet, gabled and taking the place of a semi-circular corner turret. This seems to derive from a simpler version at Midmar, but the corbelling here is much more complicated and varied, the mixture of horizontal and curved lines being particularly clever. There are also amusing gothic sprockets in each gablet.

The castle is best seen from the top garden whose 270-year-old yews, now more than 12 feet high, make a fine background, hide the Queen Anne wing, now rebuilt after a recent fire, and disguise Crathes' apparent squatness. Inside the difference between it and Craigievar is striking, and on the whole more to the advantage of Crathes, which, belonging to a generation before plaster ceilings had become the vogue, and the true medieval spirit had not yet been swamped by Renaissance ideas, is more naïvely fanciful. The chief glories inside are its painted ceilings, not its plaster-work, of which there is none in the rich Jacobean manner, and the principal ceiling is that in the Chamber of the Nine Nobles, where we are back with the heroes of the Bible and Antique lore. The Nine Nobles, or 'Worthies', appear in almost every Renaissance castle or palace throughout Europe from the Rhine to the Douro, the Loire to the Arno, in varying guises, either as carved roundels, for example in the François I courtyard at Falkland, as tapestries, like those ordered by James V for his palace at Stirling, wooden panels as at Craigston, plaster roundels as at Craigievar, Glamis and Muchalls, and painted on the joists between the beams as here. The nine personages are Hector, Alexander and Julius Caesar; representing the heroes of pagan antiquity; Joshua, David and Judas Maccabeus, from the New Testament; and Arthur, Charlemagne and Godfrey de Bouillon, whose praises were sung by the troubadours in the days of the Crusades. Another painted ceiling, but with a less stereo-typed subject can be seen in the Green Lady's Room, which is said to be haunted, while in the Chamber of the Nine Muses we return to a typical set piece of the period. The Muses, engagingly portrayed singing, reciting or playing, are joined by five Virtues, Wisdom, Justice, Faith, Hope and Charity, and explained in rhyming inscriptions.

As if this was not enough to make Crathes worth a considerable detour, the castle also boasts the only oak-panelled and ceiled Long Gallery in Scotland, the winter exercise room running the whole width of the building at the top and decorated with Royal and family carved bosses. The Long Gallery had uses other than recreational, the Burnetts having the right of 'pit and gallows' and administering justice on behalf of the king, hence the royal coat of arms on the ceiling is that of the King of Scots, not of Great Britain. There is

*Crathes Castle: detail of ceiling in room of Nine Muses*

*Crathes Castle: the oak-lined Long Gallery*

also a small chapel, or oratory, which must have been handy in the days of religious persecution, it being tucked away almost insignificantly in a corner of the gallery. This was a much more common practice in Scotland than in England or France, where a separate building in the grounds was more usual. There is a lot of original and interesting furniture at Crathes as well. I will not attempt to list it all, but the bed made for Alexander Burnett, who finished the castle, and Katherine Gordon, his wife, is there, also their wardrobe and chairs, the latter with tall narrow backs, one higher than the other and both resembling French *caquetoires,* or cackling chairs. Some lovely old high-back chairs of the late Stuart period can be seen, together with oak kists and a separate High Table for the laird and his lady, not to mention a number of portraits by the Aberdonian 'Van Dyck', George

Jamesone. To paraphrase Baedeker in his remarks about Urbino and Florence, and their relation to the Renaissance, one might say that a day at Crathes gives a better impression of the life and taste of a Scottish laird and his family in the Jacobean era than a week in the museums of Glasgow or Edinburgh.

By the time Alexander Burnett's son Thomas completed Muchalls in 1627, the English plasterers and their apprentices had arrived in the North, and what Crathes missed in that direction Muchalls, which MacGibbon and Ross call a house, not a castle, got in its superb drawing-room ceiling. This is flat, and low enough for every detail to be examined and fully appreciated, which one cannot do at Craigievar or Glamis, where the same figures, flowers and armorial devices exist, plus the splendid pedant keys that are such a feature of this type of ceiling. The royal achievement over the chimneypiece is perhaps the best of the lot and is coloured, as it should be; the virility of the lion and unicorn and bemused appearances of the intertwined male and female figures at each end have to be seen to be believed, the whole having a robust immediacy not so obvious when seen at a greater distance. Muchalls is L-shaped, but with a court-yard enclosing the remaining sides, as one suspects Barra

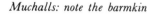

*Muchalls: note the barmkin*

may have had before the wings were built up. Here, however, the courtyard wall is unusual in being fortified, with open bartisans at the corners and shot-holes in triplicate on either side of the arched entrance. The battlemented top which would have linked the bartisans on this wall has been replaced with ornamental features, but what remains is mostly original. The tiny castle, or fortified manor, retains its old Angus slates, or split stone roofs, some handsome corbelling and two corner turrets, or studies, which are quaintly set back, but not oversailed, to meet the main roof behind. The lower floors are vaulted and groined, which possibly reflects the current revival of interest in gothic architecture which we have noted elsewhere. Muchalls was bought after the war by Mr & Mrs Maurice Simpson for the price of a suburban bungalow. They had never lived in a castle before, large or small, but rose to the challenge and are very proud of their home, which they adapted with a minimum of renovation and restoration. It stands on high ground set back from the sea, between Stonehaven and Aberdeen, amidst a few protecting but windswept-looking trees, and is open twice a week in summer.

On the southern outskirts of Stonehaven is what must be Scotland's most dramatic and exciting castle site, that of Dunnottar, which for some reason or another Slezer transposed from Wemyss, in Fife, which is also dramatically sited by the sea, but not so much so. Dunnottar, in any case, is not a single building but a complex of ruins ranged round, one might almost say scattered about, a rocky headland, with but a tiny low-level isthmus connecting it to the mainland. The principal fame of Dunnottar rests in its having sheltered the Honours of Scotland at the time of Cromwell, and the skill and heroism of the governor's lady and the minister's wife of Kinneff in getting the crown, sword and sceptre out of the castle and away to safety, hiding them under the pulpit in the kirk. These symbols of Scotland's independence and national identity thus escaped the clutches of the Lord Protector, and when the castle finally surrendered to General Lambert the small garrison marched out with colours flying, drums beating. The actual buildings are not of immense age, and are all ruinous or collapsed. Here was the seat of the Keiths, hereditary Earl Marischals of Scotland from the thirteenth century to the eighteenth, when the last to hold office supported the Jacobite Rebellion under the Earl of Mar. He, together with his brother, confidant of Frederick the Great and one of that monarch's foremost generals, lived abroad for the rest of their lives, leaving Dunnottar to the elements.

One can visit the castle for a fee, when the strength and weakness of its position can be assessed; strength as one meets it at the sea-girt entrance, which is guarded by a gun-looped tower, and narrow arched gatehouse, weakness because this very entrance is overlooked and exposed to cannon fire from the land and there is no adequate escape route, the cliffs falling sheer to the ocean. Curiously enough, or perhaps not so curiously in view of what I have just said, Dunnottar was not founded as a castle but a church, and when the first secular building arose on the site in the fifteenth century its Keith builder was excommunicated by the Bishop of St Andrews for sacrilege. He was subsequently relieved of this by the Pope himself, on condition he provided a new parish kirk in a more convenient place. The offending tower survives: it is L-shaped and stands near the edge of the cliff nearest the mainland. Beyond are various other crumbling remains, including a more modern court-yard block, chapel and priest's house; but it is the site that draws one, its history and the wildness of the surroundings with their bleakness and exposure to the salty winds. A soft summer's day is the best on which to visit Dunnottar if one does not want to be blown into the sea or frozen stiff.

A little inland are several interesting small castles one of which, Fiddes, is open on application, its owners having received a grant from public funds for its restoration. It is a very odd little building made somewhat odder by the new harling with which most of it, but not the rude outbuildings that might have benefited thereby, has been patterned. The effect is peculiar, especially the sight of a large stair tower, semicircular and battlemented, which has been partly harled and partly not, producing the most disturbing result. This

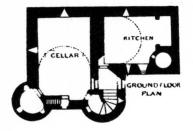

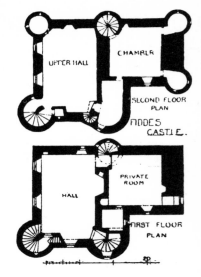

*Fiddes Castle: plans*

has been done according to the theory that ashlar masonry
should be left visible and random rubble covered up, which
is logical enough, if only the ashlar in question did not
disconcertingly stop half way along its course. Fiddes is
roughly L-shaped, with the wide main stair tower running
right round one corner of the 'L' into the entrant angle,
almost masking its true shape. The lower floors are barrel-
vaulted and there are at least three other staircases, one
straight up in the thickness of the wall from cellar to hall, the
laird's private way to his wine. The oldest part of the castle
dates from the sixteenth century and was probably begun by
Andrew Arbuthnot, who received a charter from the infant
Mary, Queen of Scots in 1553. The Arbuthnots are amongst
the best-known families in this part of the world. Arbuthnot
House, by the Bervie Water, is their present seat. Between
that pleasant manor house and the sea is Allardyce Castle,
ancestral home of yet another old east-coast family. Really a
fortified manor, like Muchalls, the castle has been enlarged
and altered since the early seventeenth century, when it was
built as a simple laird's tower. Today that tower still stands
up white and attractive near the river, like a small *château*. It

has no shot-holes, while Fiddes has them all over the place, and especially high up, and apart from a fantastically gay little cluster of turrets and what is known as label corbelling (that is: mainly horizontal corbelling, broken here and there with indentations and reminiscent of the drip hood of a mullioned window), it is simply a modest country house. It is not open to the public.

Further inland, in the How, or Hole of the Mearns, which is really part of Strathmore, lies Balbegno Castle, nestling snugly against the hillside in lovely wooded country at the foot of the Fettercairn Pass. This dates from 1569, or rather the original L-shaped tower does, being joined on the south by a seventeenth-century addition and on the north by a lower eighteenth-century one. There are two features particular to Balbegno that make it not quite unique but certainly notable. The first is the groined vaulting of the upper hall, which although medieval in conception does not predate the rest of the tower, but again represents Jacobean interest in gothic forms. One has seen this at Towie Barclay, where, however, the feeling is decidedly ecclesiastical, and especially since the hall there houses a little chapel and religious sculpture; here, however, despite the almost complete repetition of the size and style of Towie Barclay, the effect is quite different, the corbel carvings are grotesque, while the other decorations consist of armorial devices painted directly onto the stone vaulting. The other thing about Balbegno is its roofline, which consists in a very small space of a host of features, crowsteps, oversailed turrets, open bartisans, cap-house and corbelling to entertainingly fake figures at the gables, on the battlements, looking out of false windows, as at Huntly, and as at the Palais Jacques Coeur at Bourges.

We are getting down into Angus and the region around Brechin and Forfar, where nature has been kind and there are broader acres and richer woodlands than one finds further north, and indeed in some parts in the South. One is tempted to think Angus may be the bonniest part of Scotland, with the best climate and the happiest way of life, in the country districts that is, for unfortunately progress has ravaged the towns and conservation and preservation do not yet count for much. There are delightful little valleys running down from the Highlands, many with castles at salient points, one of the best being at Edzell, where besides the ruined 'keep' of the Lindsays of Glenesk there is a remarkable Renaissance garden which was created in the early seventeenth century by the then Lord Lindsay. He imported foreigners to run and work his estate, some of whom contributed to this splendid layout. It is enclosed within attractive red walls and includes a vaulted summer house, with turreted roof and the residue of a bathhouse, the vaulting being goined in the contemporary Gothic-Revival manner, and the garden wall made to express masonically the builder's heraldry. In the centre of the garden is a raised knot, or mound, surrounded by a formal pattern of lawns, topiary and rose beds, the latter outlined in low hedges cut to form family mottos. There were other gardens of this sort in Jacobean Scotland, but this is the only one that survives so well and includes its armorial wall, with a checkerboard of square openings making the fesse-chequey of the Lindsays, the dished holes being planted with blue and white lobelia in

*Edzell Castle: the doocot*

summer, which, with the red stonework, recreates the laird's colours. Above are his mullets, or stars, and in the intervening spaces are bee-boles, or holes for bee skeps, plus a series of decorative figures representing gods and goddesses, the sciences and virtues, these being the work of Lord Lindsay's imported craftsmen. Edzell is in the care of the Department of the Environment who look after the garden nicely, bringing the necessary flowers for the heraldic display from Holyrood every year. The castle was more extensive at one time, with a large barmkin or outer wall, hence the very handsome doocot with label coursing and oversailed turret that stands, seemingly alone, across the field from the present entrance.

The Glenesk from which the Lindsays of that Ilk took their barony refers to the River North Esk, of which there are several in Scotland as well as several South Esks, the main ones, however, being here in Angus. The local South Esk flows down into Strathmore near Kirriemuir, birthplace of J. M. Barrie, and on through Brechin to reach the sea at Montrose. It gives its name to Lord Southesk, whose collateral is Lord Northesk, both titles being granted by Charles I to brothers in the Carnegie family. The first Earl of Southesk was a noted cavalier whose daughter married the young Montrose, and at Kinnaird Castle, near Brechin, the present Earl's seat, they have five Jamesones on one wall, including the portrait painted of Montrose when still a student at Aberdeen University and aged seventeen. He was then betrothed to Magdalen Carnegie and obliged to stay with her at Kinnaird until an heir was born before being allowed to return to his studies and make the Grand Tour of the Continent. The castle as one sees it today has been twice rebuilt and enlarged, hiding and camouflaging in the process both an earlier laird's tower and a Georgian rebuilding, now faced in nineteenth-century Scotch Baronial designed by Sir David Bryce. On the estate is Farnell, a little fortalice, actually the *Palatium Nostrum,* or summer palace of the Bishops of Brechin, which Lord Southesk has restored with the help of a Government grant, the result not being to his liking. He is a keen archaeologist and was horrified when the

*Edzell Castle: view from
the Jacobean garden; the garden*

ancient masonry, some of it genuinely medieval, was covered up with pink 'toothpaste', for that is what it looks like, making a tower house and ecclesiastical adjunct of great character sadly bijou.

There are a number of peculiarly interesting things about Farnell, some of them due to its previous episcopal use, but not all, and some not easily explained. From the north one sees the least attractive side of the castle, where the join between the older part and the newer is clearly visible, the limits of the bishop's palace being marked by conspicuous crowsteps finished with gablets, as at Dornoch. The corbelled supports, and label, or drip hood, at the eastern end, show there was originally a covered timber stair to a door on the first floor, now blocked up, replaced by a new stair turret on the south elevation, with a rectangular top-piece corbelled out. This was erected by the late sixteenth century when the castle ceased to be episcopal and was adapted for secular use. More curious is a tiny, double-battlemented addition of one storey that sticks out from the bottom of the south-west corner of the building and which, had it been at the south-east end might have been attributable to some ecclesiastical purpose, but here defies explanation, unless, of course, it is yet another of those Jacobean recreations of gothic which were so popular hereabouts.

Amongst the loyalest supporters of the Stuarts, and a family which almost ruined itself in expressing that loyalty, were the Ogilvys of Inverquharity, now represented by Sir David Ogilvy who lives at Winton, and of Airlie, represented by the Earl of that name and his brother, the Hon. Angus Ogilvy, husband of Princess Alexandra. Three castles on the edge of the hills opposite Forfar recall their story, two once belonging to the Inverquharity branch, and one, Airlie Castle itself, associated with the main line. Airlie was burned and sacked by Argyll during the Civil War, when the family moved to Cortachy, which they had bought from Thomas Ogilvy of Inverquharity earlier; and from the mid-seventeenth century until the end of the eighteenth, when the attainder on the Earls was lifted and they returned to rebuild Airlie, Cortachy was their seat. In practice much of

*Kinnaird Castle, Brechin, redesigned by Bryce*

*Farnell, former summer palace of the bishops of Brechin*

the eighteenth century was spent abroad, in exile, the
Ogilvys raising a regiment to fight for Prince Charlie, and
Lord Ogilvy, having to flee to France after Culloden, raised
another regiment on the Continent. All that remained of the
fifteenth-century castle of Airlie by then were the broken-
down outer walls and gatehouse, which were rebuilt, and
behind arose the existing Georgian mansion. Cortachy was
likewise sacked, but by Cromwell, which was lucky for the
owners, since the Lord Protector had no personal axe to
grind and merely 'slighted' the castle, making it useless
militarily. Thus part of the original fortalice can still be
made out from the array of battlemented towers and turrets
that arose in the nineteenth century, when Cortachy became
baronial. Inverquharity remained uninhabited until it was
restored recently. The restoration is one of the most successful since the war and the restorers are to be congratulated
on the way they have dealt with an awkward problem. The
ancient 'keep' of the Ogilvys had survived almost intact from
the fifteenth century, with its battlements, crowsteps and
authentic late-medieval defences, while the Jacobean wing
that once made it L-shaped had largely fallen down or been
removed as building materials. The Grants who live at
Inverquharity wisely left the old tower as a show piece, tidied
it up, then rebuilt the Jacobean wing as a comfortable
four-storeyed house for themselves in keeping with what had
been there before. The result is most attractive, and the new
work not being harled, but honestly left to show itself as local
red sandstone, does not in the least clash with the smooth
reddy-grey ashlar of the 'keep' that rises beside it so evocatively and majestically.

None of these Ogilvy castles gets an entry in MacGibbon
and Ross or Billings' *Baronial and Ecclesiastical Antiquities of
Scotland,* perhaps understandably in view of their rough
histories, though the tower of Inverquharity was standing
intact and unharmed when both sets of authors were alive;
and it at least deserves its gothic figures on the Ordnance
Survey. Airlie, incidentally, is now open to the public, and
Cortachy on special days for Scotland's Gardens Scheme.
Glamis, of course, is another matter, and is regularly open

*Inverquharity: after restoration*

throughout the season. It is the most famous private castle not only in Angus but in Scotland, perhaps in Britain. H.M. The Queen Mother was not born there, but it was her childhood home and the Scottish seat of her parents, the Earl and Countess of Strathmore. Princess Margaret was born there. Glamis also features largely in *Macbeth* and its claim to be the scene of Duncan's murder is as strong as Cawdor's, in fact, since the Tutor of Glamis was one of those involved with the Earl of Gowrie in the kidnapping of the boy James VI and his taking to Ruthven Castle, it is more than probable that Shakespeare, anxious to please the king in later life, chose Glamis specially. In any event, Malcolm II of Scots died there, but in what kind of building, of stone or timber, is not known, though hardly in the room one is shown today.

Glamis, like Drum, was a royal hunting lodge, and may, therefore, have acquired a stone tower at an earlier date than most private castles; it is thought, for instance, that no personal fortress was built in stone before the middle of the fifteenth century, while the 'keep' at Drum undoubtedly belongs either to the end of the thirteenth century or the beginning of the fourteenth, and may have been erected at the instigation of Robert Bruce himself. Thus the L-shaped tower which still forms the nucleus of a greatly enlarged and face-lifted Glamis was probably in existence when it passed to Sir John Lyon, Chamberlain and Keeper of the Seal to Robert II, on his marriage to that King's daughter in the second half of the fourteenth century. The castle has pretty well everything: a ghostly lady who can be seen praying in the chapel in certain lights, and a ghastly legend the full facts about which we are not likely to discover since it is a close family secret. There have been hints of a monster or mongol son being kept locked up in a remote room which has no window; all very mysterious and a little on the lines of the terrible story of the son of the Duke of Queensbury, who, while his father was away voting for the Union of the Parliaments in 1707, got loose and found his way to the kitchen, where a boy was turning the spit for dinner. When the Duke returned it was the boy who was on the spit and

Glamis Castle, seat of the Earls of Strathmore

'Glamms House', as it appears in Theatrum Scotiae

his son turning it. Perhaps the Glamis secret is not as horrific as that, but from what one has heard the potentialities may have been there.

The first additions and improvements at Glamis were probably made in the fifteenth century, with more in the sixteenth and seventeenth, when the original L-shape became a 'Z'. James V, whose hatred of the Douglas family verged on the paranoiac, regained the castle for the crown by the simple expedient of arresting the widowed Lady, who was a Douglas, and having her burnt as witch in Edinburgh. She was entirely innocent. Her son, still a minor, was also arrested, but his execution was postponed until he should reach maturity, which fortunately for him he did not do until after the demise of the king, who with his Queen, Mary of Guise, occupied Glamis for the rest of his reign. The young Lord Glamis was subsequently released and created Earl of Kinghorne by James VI; and it was he and his descendant, Patrick Earl of Kinghorne, who largely made the castle as we see it today. With little to thank the earlier Stewarts for, except possibly a dash of royal blood, it is remarkable how devoted the Bowes Lyon family became to that house in the seventeenth and eighteenth centuries, but then in that part of the country most of the gentry were royalist and epis-copalian, the example of the Ogilvys being not untypical. James Francis Edward actually stayed at Glamis, and left in such a hurry he forgot his silver watch, which was found under his pillow, and his sword, both of which souvenirs are shown to visitors today. The chapel at Glamis is also a remarkable memorial to local and lairdly inclinations, and in it the old liturgy of the Scottish Episcopal Church in Jacobite times is still in use. The walls are decorated with painted panels commissioned from Jacob de Wet by the Earl of Strathmore, including one about which the guide is liable to give a curious account. The scene is Easter morning and Our Lord is shown dressed as a seventeenth-century gar-dener, wearing a hat, as Mary Magdalene kneels at His feet. Such realism was quite usual in those days, but local lore has produced an explanation which tells how de Wet painted Christ in contemporary guise, and wearing a hat, to annoy the Earl of Strathmore because he had not been paid. In fact, the boot was on the other shoe, for de Wet had broken his contract to do all the artist work himself and instead brought in inferior painters from Dundee, so it was the Earl who was cheated.

MacGibbon and Ross say that the drawing of Glamis that appears in Slezer's book is not what he saw but taken from an earlier sketch and represents the castle as it was restored by the Earl of Kinghorne in the reign of James VI and I. It is a most interesting view and at first glance seems to bear little relationship to Glamis as it is now, indeed it may be another of the Captain's wrong attributions. This suspicion is heightened by the fact that the present Lady Strathmore recently came across the original copper plate for an engraving of Glamis that was probably intended for a second edition by Slezer, but never actually used. It closely resembles the existing castle and is evidently based on what was proposed in his face-lift by the third Earl, who is shown pointing to it in a large portrait in the drawing-room. It has been suggested that the first engraving, labelled 'Glamms House', might depict Dalkeith Palace near Edinburgh, though that building was completely altered and refaced in the severest Palladian style during the lifetime of Captain Slezer and he most assuredly would have seen it in that form. It is all a little curious and made more so by closer inspection of the older print, on which the L-shaped nucleus of Glamis appears to be in its proper position, rising above drawbridge, battlements and advance towers. All of this was described by visitors to the castle at various times, and a few remnants still survive as follies in the park.

It took a long time to remove these extensive medieval defences, some of which were still visible in the eighteenth century, in fact Sir Walter Scott, in an essay on landscape gardening, waxed very wrath about their final disappearance. He hated the cult of the *cottage orné,* and the informal English landscape. "The huge tower of Glamis", he wrote, "once showed its lordly head above seven circles of defensive boundaries ... and a disciple of Kent had the cruelty to raze all those exterior defences and to bring his

*Glamis Castle: the Lyon
sundial; restoration
gateway*

mean and paltry gravel-walk to the very door from which, deluded by the name, we might have imagined Lady Macbeth issuing forth to receive King Duncan". The castle does, in truth, stand like a country house in the shires, isolated in a vast 'Capability Brown' park, lacking its formal parterres and advance works, horticultural and architectural, with only two of the lead statues of Stuart Kings, James VI and Charles I (the others were of Charles II and James VII and II), looking from their pedestals at the degraded prospect, or what Scott would have thought degraded.

The vision is picturesque and romantic enough for us of the twentieth century, who have never seen a real medieval castle, nor felt the sensation Scott did when staying at Glamis, when he conjured up the terrors of *Macbeth* as portrayed by John Kemble and Sarah Siddons. The forest of turrets and towers, wrought-iron railings, dormers, chimneys, battlements and proud armorial devices assail the eye as in a fantasy—not an authentic fantasy but one well within the concept of Scotland and Scottish baronial architecture as widely understood, and, ironically enough, made universally acceptable by the bard of Abbotsford, whose writings, like Shakespeare's, reached to the ends of the earth. There it stands, complete, and in its way the epitome of a Scottish castle; one must excuse the gothic touches, the over tall wimples crowning the corner turrets, and the stiff, regimented fenestration of the newer wings, but notice how even those windows are casemented and leaded, almost uniquely in Scotland, the iron bars protecting others, and the fine sweep of the semicircular stair tower which expresses so much better what is inside than the rectangular towers of Fyvie and Noltland. As for heraldry and external sculpture, there are two rows of coats of arms set in panels, one running across the elevation horizontally, another rising vertically, a little like Huntly, where the armorial features form part of the overall design of the stair tower. The later sculpture, plus a roundel bust in lead of the Earl of Strathmore, who was the architect of this transformation from medieval 'keep' to fanciful *château,* may have been the work of Dutch craftsmen previously engaged by Sir William Bruce at Holyrood and

Kinross. They were probably also responsible for the splendid multifaceted sundial which stands on the lawn in front of the house, supported by 'Lyons' holding individual gnomons, and some of the baroque gateways to the park, the best of which bears a remarkable likeness to the 'Fish Gate' at Kinross, with its quaint rustications and odd sculpture.

Glamis has a back door as well as a front, and as one walks up the drive one will even see a doocot, without which no self-respecting Scotch castle would be. The back door is set in ruder masonry, more like Glamis was before the Earl got busy on his frontispiece. There one will see crowsteps of the traditional kind, dormers and plainer corner turrets, smaller windows and simple, one-course corbelling. Inside too there are things recalling a more distant, less elegant past, the entrance door with its great iron yett behind, and straight stair leading down to the laich hall, which is the oldest part of Glamis, and served as the common hall. The wall space is made use of here to provide closets and a well, so necessary in time of siege, with tiny spirals leading up and down. The main stair is also spiral, with a central newel nearly 3 feet across and total width of more than 15 feet; it rises gently and is not supported by extraneous overhead arches like those at Fyvie and Noltland, which spoil the effect and reduce the headroom. On the first floor is the "Hall I did ever love" of the first Earl of Kinghorne, with its superb barrel-vaulted plaster ceiling and huge chimneypiece with double male and female caryatids. The pairs, each holding fertility symbols and naked to the waist are not identical, which makes them more interesting than others further north. At the far end of the Hall is a large family portrait showing the Earl of Strathmore and his sons with a prospect of Glamis as transformed by him in the background, including the parterres that were later removed. This is by De Wet and is in much the same style as the portrait on the Picture Staircase at Blair of the first Marquis of Atholl. Below, in a corner, with a picture front and back, is a panel by Clouet of the young Earl of Kinghorne, then still Lord Glamis, and his secretary, a lad named George Boswell, who were painted whilst on the Continent, the secretary holding

an inkwell and having a quill behind his ear, and sporting a
poem which ends:

> I shall do my devoir
> God grant me have sic skill
> As had my father befoir

The date is 1587. The chapel I have already described, and
visitors see The Queen Mother's rooms and King Malcolm's,
but perhaps the most unexpected feature is the external
Long Gallery, that is to say instead of a big long room at the
top of the castle, as at Crathes, the roof outside has been
made into a promenade, with elaborate wrought-iron thistles
keeping one from falling over the edge.

The Sidlaw Hills divide Strathmore from Dundee and the
Firth of Tay, where industrial activity takes the place of
agriculture, and historic monuments are less numerous, their
settings generally less attractive. Dundee city preserves in
Dudhope Park the castle that once belonged to Viscount
Claverhouse, 'Bonnie Dundee', but they do not know what to
do with it and although it is maintained and roofed, it has

*Claypotts, Dundee*

suffered rather a lot in the course of time and is not particularly interesting. Much more worthwhile is Claypotts, in
the eastern suburbs of the city and also associated with John
Grahame of Claverhouse. Claypotts is still roofed, and despite its quaint rather than picturesque appearance is the
perfect example of a Z-shaped tower house in which utilitarian purposes take precedence over ornament. It was built
for defence by firearms, and dates from the second half of the
sixteenth century, being provided with as many awkward
corners as possible, round and square ended, the lower parts
riddled with large shot-holes and devoid of windows, the
living quarters ranged high above in a series of little houses,
each with its own crowstepped gable, projecting from the
main wall. These do not entirely lack grace, one 'crow's-nest'
sporting a handsome dormer decorated with Renaissance
pilasters, crockets and fan-shaped tympanum, but except for
the skews, chimneystalks and where there is a short run of
sentry walk ending in an open bartisan, the masonry is rough
and somehow in keeping with the extraordinary plan of this
unbeautiful structure. The base is rectangular, with large

*Claypotts: plans*

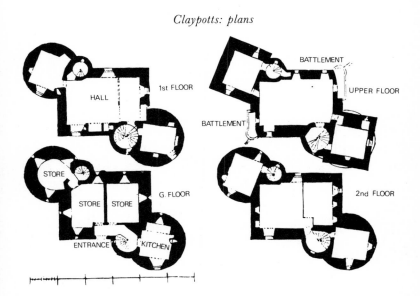

round towers at the diagonals, linked on either side by smaller round towers that rise directly from the ground to take spiral staircases to the little oblong 'cottages' on the fourth floor.

Claypotts is in the care of the Department of the Environment, so is Affleck, a little to the north-east. Nothing could be more different, and more refined, than this older fortress that was built not for defence by firearms but bows and arrows. Affleck is completely without fuss, so much so that seeing it standing in the garden of a large white Georgian farmhouse makes one think of it more as a folly than a genuine medieval fortalice. Affleck is that rare thing in Scotland, a complete fifteenth-century 'keep', roofed and inhabited as recently as the mid-eighteenth century, when despite its superior appointments, superior that is to sixteenth-century Claypotts, it eventually became too uncomfortable even for an impoverished bonnet laird. Still, it is in at least as good condition as Borthwick, which is still somebody's home in summer. The wish to live in tall tower houses dies hard, which is why so many of them are now being brought back into use. Affleck would certainly make an excellent essay in resuscitation, as a dwelling, structural restoration scarcely being necessary since it is in such first-rate condition, but it is not available. Where Claypotts is contrived both on plan and in effect, Affleck is straightforward to a degree, a plain rectangle made into a slight 'L' by the addition of a small stair tower which reaches to the battlements. The latter are plain and unindented, supported on a single run of corbels and rounded at the corners, where broken by small open bartisans. The roof is gable-ended and crowstepped, and the cap-house battlemented. Simplicity is the keynote, and there are few and small windows, some retaining their iron bars. The castle is built of rubble but unharled, with wrought stone finishes; it is four storeyed and has a double basement, barrel-vaulted at the top level. The other floors are of timber, and there are two special features one must mention; the very high standard of the workmanship throughout and the considerable sophistication of the planning. The oratory is considered unique in Scotland

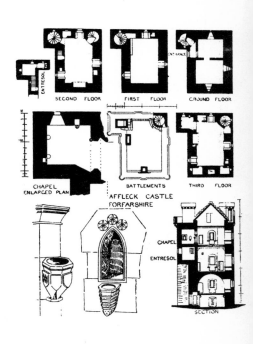

*Affleck Castle: interior of Hall; view showing battlements and bartisans; plans, section, and details*

and is perfectly preserved, retaining its liturgical features, such as holy water stoop, piscina, aumbry for sacred vessels and corbels to support candles, intact. It opens from the lord's withdrawing room, or solar, which has a late-medieval chimneypiece of good design, replete with deep lintel and fine gothic columns. Immediately below the chapel, at the top of the main stair on a sort of mezzanine floor, is a small closet and *garderobe,* from the tiny window of which all movement in the hall and on the stair could be observed in secrecy. This spy hole is clearly an early version of the much cruder 'laird's lug' of Jacobean times, but is geared to seeing rather than hearing. Affleck was the ancestral home of the Boswell's of Auchinleck, of whom Johnson's biographer is perhaps the best known; and when they moved to Ayrshire they took the original pronounciation as well as the name with them.

# V

# *Glasgow and the West*

A TRIP from Edinburgh to Glasgow is almost like a trip to another world, so different is the atmosphere of the two cities. To a Glaswegian a trip to Edinburgh is like going to the country, while for the Edinburger the reverse is like a trip to Manchester or Liverpool from, say, York. Nowadays the contrast between the capital and the industrial heart of Scotland is not so depressing as it used to be, especially since the advent of the Clean Air Act, and although the landscape between is littered with buildings, and the eastern and southern outskirts of Glasgow resemble something from a bad American dream, one can at least see across the maze of factories, concrete eyries and motorway junctions to the hills beyond. Indeed, one can actually see the spire of St Mungo's Cathedral and Sir Gilbert Scott's imitative repeat at the University. The site of Glasgow was once thought idyllic, visitors at the end of the seventeenth century and beginning of the eighteenth comparing it to Oxford, with its smooth flowing river, green parks, fine buildings and renowned medieval university and cathedral; and so it remained until the nineteenth century, when the Bishop's Castle was demolished to make room for the Royal Infirmary and the process of demolishing and rebuilding practically the whole city began. Glasgow's western and northern environs, despite the encroachment of both suburbs and industry, are still amongst the most varied and beautiful in Europe, with Loch Lomond and the Highlands within half an hour's run by car, and the Firth of Clyde equally accessible. Thousands may now prefer Spain, but the local 'costa' retains its devotees, and will return in favour with others once the Costa Brava becomes too expensive and overcrowded with rich Germans and Scandinavians seeking their places in the sun.

Shipbuilding has been for a hundred years or more im-

*Newark Castle, Port Glasgow: the old tower; the entrance*

portant to Glasgow, and all the way to Greenock, yards, still
working or closed, remind one of the fact. In the midst of
Port Glasgow is the surprising survival of one of the best-
preserved sixteenth-century castles in Scotland, roofed and
well cared for by the Department of the Environment.
Newark, as it is called, is in a curious position, amongst
warehouses and cranes down by the water, and until taken
over by the Ministry was in danger of destruction by vandals
as much as by time and the polluted atmosphere. Happily it
is now safe for posterity, though empty except for a caretaker. The plan is almost symmetrical, with two wings
projecting from a rectangular main building, the latter being
Jacobean in date and displaying good Renaissance details in
doorways, dormer finials and in a particularly handsome
chimneypiece in the hall. Newark Castle grew from an
original oblong 'keep', which is joined to the newer work,
having been refaced and re-capped; and there are features
that remind one of Kellie and Elcho in the linking of the
disparate parts, though on plan the result is more like Castle

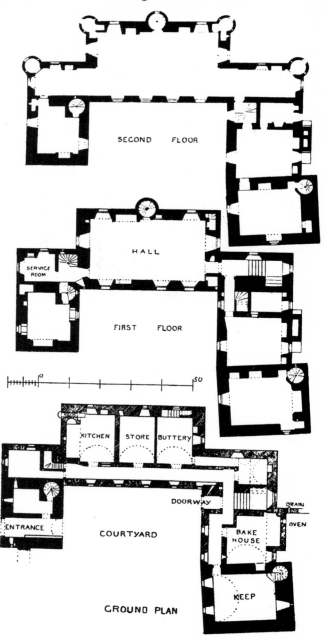

SECOND FLOOR

HALL

SERVICE
ROOM

FIRST FLOOR

0                    50

KITCHEN    STORE    BUTTERY

DOORWAY

ENTRANCE

COURTYARD

DRAIN

OVEN

BAKE
HOUSE

KEEP

GROUND PLAN

*Newark Castle: plans*

Stewart on account of its symmetry. There are a great many corner turrets with conically capped roofs and a stair tower that rises in the middle of the north wall, supported by corbelling from the second floor. Newark was a Maxwell house, the old tower having welcomed James IV when en route for the Western Highlands in 1495. He was the last Scots king to have the Gaelic and the first to visit the more remote parts of his kingdom in state.

Across the river from Newark, easily reached by the new Erskine Bridge, which replaces an ancient ferry, is Dumbarton Castle, with the scanty remnants of one of the oldest forts in Britain, looking down on the industrial wastes at the mouth of the River Leven as it reaches the Clyde from Loch Lomond. This is a British site, as opposed to a Scots or Pictish one, being the principal stronghold of the Strathclyde Britons from the sixth to the eleventh century. They were a people whose affinities were more with the Welsh and Cumbrians and Manxmen than with the inhabitants of Ireland or north and eastern Scotland. Nothing survives at Dumbarton from their era, and only scraps of masonry from later periods until one arrives in the seventeenth and eighteenth centuries, when the Rock of Dumbarton, having lost most of its strategic importance, was reduced to a coastal battery and guardian against possible Highland invasion in Jacobite times. Historically it was one of the four Scottish castles that remained fortified after the Union of the Parliaments in 1707, and thus, what one sees today was largely created by General Wade, and after him William Skinner, of Fort George fame. Wade's engineer, Captain John Romer, was responsible for the Governor's House and V-shaped battery in the form of a small ravelin in front. These are the two most conspicuous parts of Dumbarton Castle, where one can study at close quarters an excellent specimen of one of Romer's pepper-pot sentry boxes, which, with their domed tops and corbelled supports, recall the forts of the Spanish Main without being inappropriate in a Scottish setting. William Skinner's memorial at Dumbarton is a barrel-vaulted Georgian powder magazine of surprisingly refined classical proportions and detail.

*Dumbarton Castle, in the seventeenth century*

*Dumbarton: the Governor's House and ravelin*

In the days before Mr Benn and state-supported 'sit-ins' shipbuilding provided a good living both for men and employers in the west of Scotland, and beyond the city's purlieus rose the baronial piles and Florentine villas of wealthier owners. These are now mostly hotels, sports complexes or institutions, and stand on many a sightly point along the shores of the lochs and islets that make the Firth of Clyde so pleasant. Further afield, nearer to the true Highlands, some of them have survived as private houses—notably Ardkinglas on Loch Fyne, home of a recently retired Secretary of State for Scotland, which is reached over the pass known as 'Rest and be thankful', from the head of Loch Lomond. Here the Noble family built for themselves, with Sir Robert Lorimer as their architect, what might be thought the baronial pile to end all such, yet which the late John Noble assured me was extremely comfortable and convenient, and not at all subservient in plan to its romantic skyline of turrets, dormers and crowsteps. Needless to say, Ardkinglas could scarcely be built today, even for a retired Trade Union official with a life peerage and a sheaf of directorships, since the skills and materials are entirely lacking, and few architects are capable of designing anything like it. One wonders too if it would still be possible to organize a restoration at Dunderave, or Dunderawe, which lies just across the loch from Ardkinglas and was taken in hand by Lorimer for Miss Noble in the second decade of this century. It is probably the architect's most successful resuscitation, one in which his more virile style seems well suited to a western castle in a wild site, this former stronghold of the MacNaughtons with its sturdy simplicity.

Dunderave was built in 1596 by Iain, Chief of the Mac-Naughtons, who was also Sheriff of Argyll, and is an L-shaped structure with a largish round tower at one corner and conically capped corner turrets at two others. It was inhabited until the nineteenth century so cannot be said to have been a complete ruin when Sir Robert Lorimer began the work of restoration. Very sensibly he did not attempt to reconstruct the old tower of the MacNaughtons but replaced its turret roofs and dormers in traditional style and adapted

*Dunderave, a MacNaughton seat on Loch Fyne*

the interior to modern living, adding a small adjuct on the
loch side to make up for deficiencies in the original plan. As
at Balmanno he introduced some fine plasterwork ceilings
based on Jacobean models, and a certain amount of good
panelling, but it is the overall effect which attracts here, the
use of materials and methods of construction, showing a
proper appreciation of local practice. Lorimer's irregular
layout of the courtyard and its informal planting may
perhaps go against seventeenth-century ideas, but he introduced shut-holes under the windows of the annexe and
left the whole castle in its rough stone facing, as he found it.
Although dating from so late a period the entrance doorway,
and armorial plaque above, are decorated with Norman
dog-tooth borders, a feature which we have seen at
Amisfield, which is more or less contemporary; while alongside there survive some odd carvings with a decidedly Celtic
look about them, especially one which depicts a figure in

long flowing robes playing a reed pipe. A number of such pipers, plus the chief's harpers, went with Alexander Mac-Naughton and two hundred of his clan by sea to La Rochelle to aid King Charles I in that famous siege; and the Mac-Naughtons thenceforth lived in the south, at court, the same Alexander being knighted by the king and made a Gentleman of the Privy Chamber. He died in London, his successors having difficulty in resuscitating their Argyll property after his quasi-desertion of Dunderave. Yet they remained loyal to the Stuarts until they finally lost their ancestral lands by confiscation after Killiecrankie. Dunderave, which is the 'Castle Doom' of Neil Munro's novel, has over the entrance an inscription which reads: "Behald the end. Be nocht Vyser nor the Hiestes. I hoip in God'. Scottish version of the more common Renaissance device "Remember the End", which appears in a number of houses and had its apotheosis in the motto of Mary, Queen of Scots, "En ma fin est mon commencement".

The former seat of the MacNaughtons stands on a little point jutting out into Loch Fyne, and a few miles further south the bay of Inveraray comes into view, with the castle

*Inveraray Castle, built by Roger Morris for the third Duke of Argyll*

of the Dukes of Argyll showing through the trees. This only dates from the middle of the eighteenth century, the old castle having been abandoned when the present 'gothycke' building was erected after 1743. The new castle is actually on the site of the former village, it being removed *in toto*. The architect for the castle was an Englishman, Roger Morris, and his design was one of the very first executed according to Georgian Gothic-Revival precepts, in fact, it predates any building of comparable style and importance either in Scotland or England. The conception is entirely romantic and pseudo-medieval, with pointed windows, and arches to the bridges crossing the false fosse, or dry moat; and there are castellated round towers at each corner of the roughly square building. The internal courtyard was not left open but covered rather clumsily with a crenellated 'keep', to create a suitably baronial silhouette when seen from a distance, but most unsatisfactory from a structural point of view; and the effect was spoilt in the late nineteenth century when the ninth Duke, married to Princess Louise, daughter of Queen Victoria, made various additions and improvements. More room was found for bedrooms in the roof, with unsympathetic dormer windows, and the round corner towers were crowned with excessively tall wimples, which, far from giving the castle a more Scottish look, related it more to Grimm's *Fairy Tales*. Taymouth Castle, Perthshire seat of the Campbells of Glenorchy, was remodelled to some extent on Inveraray, but taking advantage of the experience gained to create the effect Morris probably intended, the central 'keep' was raised higher, and more successfully, and with less contrived support.

The Adam family acted as contractors at Inveraray, a role they were quite used to, as we have seen at Fort George, while inside the rooms were decorated by Robert Mylne, last in the long line of masons of that name the first of whom had been Abbot of Cambuskenneth and builder of the bridge over the Tay at Dunkeld. Robert Mylne was trained in Italy and later appointed Surveyor to St Paul's Cathedral. He designed Old Blackfriars Bridge; in fact, bridge design was a Mylne *forte*. His bridges over the Aray, with two spans, and the Shira, with one, at the entrance to Inveraray, are magnificent, the small bridge having an almost Venetian quality in its lightness and grace. Mylne's interiors are in the neo-classical taste but nearer to Sir William Chambers and the French mode than to Robert Adam, who was, by the time these rooms were completed and Boswell and Johnson had paid their call on the Duke, already the 'master' of his own style. Mylne also laid out the new village, really a small burgh and county town, with its courthouse and church, the latter divided down the centre, with one section for Gaelic-speaking worshippers the other for English, the division being marked externally by the addition of a slender *flèche*. Unhappily this was removed during the war at the instigation of the R.A.F. and so far has not been replaced, an argument going on as to who should pay. Had it been demolished by enemy action it would have been rebuilt long ago from war-damage compensation. Yet Inveraray itself, white-washed and couthie, is a little gayer than its castle, the stone of which goes quite black when damp and creates a most gloomy effect, one which seems to go with the history of the clan whose chief resides there. The scene is completed and presided over by the wooded hill of Duniquoich, whose conical form is topped by an early Gothic-Revival folly disguised as a watch tower. It is perhaps worth adding that until the death of the tenth Duke of Argyll, in 1949, not a stick nor a stone of Campbell property had ever been sold and that once, when some government department said they wanted some of his land, the Duke replied that if they or any of their minions put so much as one foot on it he would call out his lieges and disperse them. This apparently produced second thoughts, if not confusion, in London, but I fear it would not do so now.

A low pass to the north-west brings one to the upper reaches of Loch Awe, and the sight of Kilchurn Castle, rising in ruinous but evocative grandeur at the end of a marshy peninsula near where the River Orchy comes into the loch. This was a seat of the Campbells of Glenorchy, afterwards Earls and Marquises of Breadalbane, and the oldest tower of it was probably built in the second half of the fifteenth century by the wife of Sir Colin Campbell, first of Glenorchy, a Knight of Rhodes, while he was away in the Middle East. The bulk of the castle is much later, with an inscription over the only entrance bearing the initials of 'Slippery John', first Earl of Breadalbane, and his wife Mary, and the date 1693 to confirm it. The castle was then made into a courtyard structure and rather barrack-like, as MacGibbon and Ross rightly state. In fact, Hanoverian troops were stationed there during the Forty-five, leaving signs of their occupation in the kitchen quarters. Kilchurn, therefore, is more or less contemporary with Barcaldine, the coastal seat of the Campbells of Glenorchy, which was completed in 1696. It is now under the care of the Department of the Environment, but not at present open to the public, though to tell the truth it looks well enough at a distance; comfortably sited on a small rocky elevation above the reeds on the edge of the loch, with the mountains all round.

At the other end of Loch Awe, between its head and Kilmartin, is Carnasserie, which was the home of the first Protestant Bishop of the Isles, John Carswell, who translated the Reformed Liturgy into Gaelic, having it printed in 1567. The diocese had been carved out of the ancient Norse diocese of Sodor and Man shortly before the Reformation, and it did not survive for long, its cathedral at Iona being sacked and left to decay, reduced, until a recent restoration, to the burial place of the Dukes of Argyll. Nor is Carnasserie a true bishop's palace or a castle, being a bit of both, a fortified tower attached to a Jacobean manor house. The 'castle', though in the care of the Ministry, does not get gothic script on the Ordnance Survey. It was certainly more of a private residence than otherwise, and in that capacity it was besieged and captured in the Monmouth rebellion of 1685, when the Earl of Argyll blew it up. This is the region of the Crinan Canal, and there used to be a splendid combined ticket to take one back to Glasgow, partly by steamer through the Kyles of Bute, and partly by bus and train the rest of the way. Thus one came to Rothesay, on Bute, and one of the largest and finest of the medieval castles of western Scotland. It belonged to the Bute family, who put it in order

before presenting it to the nation; and standing in the
middle of the town Rothesay Castle is a favourite haunt of
visitors to the Clyde resorts.

Rothesay Castle was also reduced to ruins by the Earl of
Argyll in 1685, but now, with the moat cleaned out and
filled with water, and the castle approached by a new
drawbridge and guarded by a handsome gatehouse it makes
a grand sight. The most interesting thing about it is the plan
of the *enceinte*, which, notwithstanding the rectangular

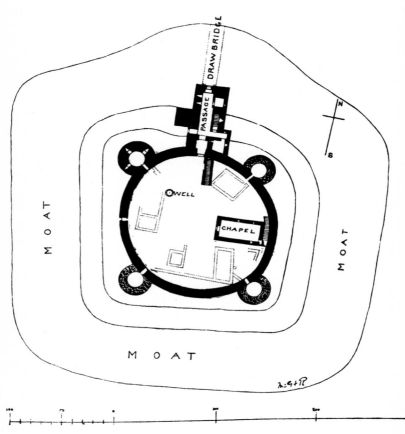

*Rothesay Castle: plan*

outline of the moat, is circular and supported by four round towers, one of which is in a much better state than the others. A timber fort of some kind probably once stood on this same grassy mound near the sea and is said to have been attacked by a Viking fleet in the thirteenth century, at the time of the Battle of Largs. A hundred years later it became a Stewart residence, and both Robert II and Robert III lived there, the eldest son of the latter being created Duke of Rothesay, which title is amongst those held by the Prince of Wales. The Stewarts came to Scotland via the west coast, as many other Norman and allied families did in the eleventh, twelfth and thirteenth centuries. The Bruces and Balliols arrived in Annandale and Galloway, respectively, from north Yorkshire and south Durham, while Sir William Wallace may have been a Welshman, his name being a corruption of Wallis, or Valais. He thus could have been descended from the ancient Britons, which is interesting as the Stewarts were Bretons emigrating to Scotland via Shropshire. They had been Dapifers, or Stewards, to the Counts of Dol, near Mont St Michel, an apprenticeship that stood them in good stead when they became Lord High Stewards of Scotland, in which capacity they served king and country with distinction for over two hundred years. They acquired royal blood by the marriage of Robert the Steward to Marjory Bruce, who brought with her the bad luck that haunted them ever after, giving birth to her son, the first Stewart monarch, following a fall from her horse, and herself dying in the process.

Robert II and Robert III lived most of their lives as rich and powerful nobles, not as kings, their favourite residences being Rothesay Castle, on Bute, and Dundonald, in Ayrshire, which Robert II made into a royal fortress by merging an old 'keep' and a younger gatehouse to form a single rectangular building, the fairly massive bulk of whose collapsed walls crowns a curiously isolated hill between Kilmarnock and the sea. The panorama from this is all embracing and reminiscent of a similar hill near Dol, in Brittany, which may or may not be a coincidence. Dundonald overlooked the Stewart domains in this part of Scotland, almost as far as Paisley, where the new king's ancestors had founded a Cluniac abbey. This marked the beginnings of Stewart piety, which showed itself later in a preference for ecclesiastical houses, such as Scone and Holyrood, and in a preoccupation with religion verging on superstition, which came with them to England and stayed with them when in exile on the Continent.

In an earlier chapter I have said something about the difficulties encountered by the first Stewarts in establishing superiority over the other nobles, and how these efforts were often made more difficult by the activities of their own, quasi-royal relations, of whom the Stewarts of Darnley were amongst the most important and troublesome. Their redoubt was near Glasgow, at Crookston, which Sir Alan Stewart bought in 1330 from the descendants of Robert Croc, a vassal of the High Steward. Sir Alan's grandson was that Sir John Stewart of Darnley who fought in the Hundred Years' War in France and became first constable of the Garde Ecossaise of the French kings. Charles VII also gave him the Lordship of Aubigny, which has descended via the Earls of Lennox and other successors to the present Duke of Richmond, Gordon and Lennox, who is also Duc d'Aubigny in the French peerage. Henry Stewart, Lord Darnley, the husband of Mary, Queen of Scots, was of the same branch and he and the Queen stayed at Crookston, which remained royal property until sold by the notorious Louise de la Kéroualle, mistress of Charles II, to the first Duke of Montrose, in 1702. Later in the same century, Crookston became the property of Sir William Maxwell, Bart, of Nether Pollok, whose twentieth-century representative, the late Sir John Stirling Maxwell, presented the castle to the National Trust for Scotland.

The Maxwells were amongst the smaller number of Saxons who settled in Scotland before and shortly after the Norman invasion, their principal seat being Caerlaverock in Dumfriesshire; but they gradually moved north, to the eastern borders and to the Glasgow region, building Newark Castle on the Clyde, and settling on the banks of the Cart, at Nether Pollok, as long ago as the thirteenth century. Sir John and his father were remarkably civilized and public-spirited men, Pollok House becoming the repository of one of the most valuable art collections in the country, and Sir John himself being a founder member of the National Trust for Scotland as well as one of the first Royal Commissioners for Ancient Monuments in the North. Before presenting Crookston Castle to the Trust (their first gift, incidentally) he repaired it and completed the one remaining corner tower. Crookston is very much a ruin, and is perhaps most significant for its having belonged to such distinguished lairds, and for its gifting to the National Trust setting a precedent that has happily been followed by others. Nevertheless there are interesting features worth a brief mention, the plan is unusual, for one thing, in that the rectangular tower of the Stewart of Darnley period had four square corner repeats, a little like Hermitage but on a much smaller scale. Of these only one rises any distance above ground level, and this contains a pit prison, or dungeon, with entry from above and tiny ventilating chute in the immensely thick wall. The little tower might be considered more an extension of the main building than a separate structure, the 12 to 15 feet walls constituting a veritable rabbit warren of passages and stairs, *garderobes* and small closets, the windows sunk deeply into them. More interesting still is the ground layout of this former quasi-royal seat, where the three necessities of a pre-stone castle of the early Middle Ages can still be made out: that is, ditch, mound and hedge, the latter surviving in a few ancient hawthorn bushes, once part of the outer defences of a timber castle.

Another problem the early Stewarts had to contend with was marital, for both Robert II and Robert III married commoners, Robert II twice, and twice had to obtain papal dispensation to regularize his affairs. His first partner, who bore him heirs out of wedlock, including the future Robert III, was Elizabeth Mure, daughter of Sir Adam Mure of Rowallan, an estate a few miles to the north-east of Kilmarnock. The castle at Rowallan is one of the most attractive in this area, being an early version of the courtyard plan and like Tolquhon, in Aberdeenshire, showing distinct affinities with Falkland, and in this case not without reason.

The twin-turreted gatehouse with conically capped roofs in imitation of royal examples is dated 1562, and bears the royal arms above its arched entrance, and below the arms of Mure, or Muir, with a moor's head, the family crest, carved on the keystone. Needless to say, the royal links were by then wearing a bit thin, but the laird was proud enough of what reflected glory remained to adorn his rebuilt *château* in this manner, and to conceive it on a more ambitious scale than the average. Thus Rowallan is probably unique amongst private houses of the period in being completely devoid of corner turrets, bartisans, false or genuine, and undefended except for a ring of not very convincing-looking shot-holes made in the form of cannon mouths that run round the base of the twin round towers at the entrance.

The castle is unoccupied and in a much less hale condition than when MacGibbon and Ross visited it in the late nineteenth century. Its contents, including some fine seventeenth-century panelling, have been removed and only two sides of the courtyard buildings are still roofed. They stand on a slight rise on the banks of the delightfully named Carmel River, in the park of a larger, twentieth-century

*Rowallan Castle with its twin-turreted entrance*

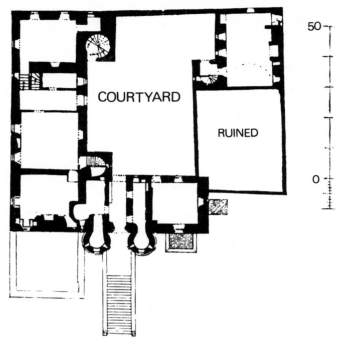

*Rowallan Castle: plans*

castle designed by Sir Robert Lorimer for the first Lord
Rowallan, but can be seen, externally at least, without
restriction, under the guardianship of Ancient Monuments.
The modern castle was never finished through lack of funds,
and is one of those elaborate essays in recreative baronial of
which Ardkinglas is the largest completed, and the grounds
are entered through an arched gatehouse which is rather
grim and unfortunately fails to achieve what was obviously
intended, namely to create an atmosphere of what one might
find within, as at Earlshall and Balmanno. Only here there
is nothing within, not for a quarter of a mile, only an avenue
of trees, leading at the end to a bridge, and the sight, on the
far side of the Carmel, of Rowallan's twin turrets and
straight forestair. Lacking the usual defensive ordnance, the
castle has a more reposeful appearance than many of its

contemporaries, its roofs are crowstepped and pierced by swept dormers, and the only remarkable decoration is provided by the Muir heraldry and a bold cable course that encircles the twin towers at first-floor level. There is also a gay seventeenth-century doorway made through the remnants of a barmkin, or outer defence wall, by Sir William Muir in 1661. His father, also Sir William, improved the castle quite a lot and was well known as a poet and lover of beauty, besides being, somewhat perversely, a supporter of the Covenanters, for whom he wrote a version of the psalms which was much too good for them.

The Muirs were not the only family in Ayrshire with royal connections, nor is Rowallan the only interesting castle in the neighbourhood of Kilmarnock, for within the boundaries of that town, in a deep wooded glen, lies Dean Castle, restored for the late Lord Howard de Walden by Dr James Richardson, working in a private capacity and not as Inspector of Ancient Monuments. Dean was the seat of the Boyds, who succeeded in marrying into real royalty, for the first Lady Boyd was none other than Princess Mary, sister of James III of Scots, and, therefore, the daughter of the Flemish Mary of Gueldres and granddaughter of Joan Beaufort, a Plantagenet. The Boyds also managed to get control of the King's person, seeking as others had done before to govern the country thereby. They overstepped themselves, however, and the Princess herself was imprisoned for a while in Dean Castle. Her husband had been made Earl of Arran, but when he died she remarried Sir James Hamilton, taking the Arran title with her and becoming the ancestress of the Dukes of Abercorn and of Châtelherault. There are a number of fetures about Dean which relate it both to Doune and Craigmillar, the latter in its defensive structure, the former in its internal appointments. The fact is, Dean Castle, most of which was built in the fifteenth century, is a castle of *enceinte* but with a separate 'keep' instead of a fortified gatehouse, as at Craigmillar; it is also a courtyard edifice with ancillary buildings attached to the *enceinte,* as at Doune, with which it may be considered contemporary.

*Dean Castle, Kilmarnock: the restored building from the motte; the motte from the castle*

Dean was inhabited until the first part of the eighteenth century, when the then Lord Kilmarnock, a Boyd still, came home to find it burned down; and not long afterwards he himself came to grief in the Jacobite Rebellion of 1745, when he was taken prisoner at Culloden and executed on Tower Hill. Since then, or at least until the beginning of this century, the castle remained a ruin. Dr Richardson was an incurable romantic as well as an expert on Scottish historic architecture and his restoration amounted almost to a reconstruction of what he thought might have been, including the novel re-erection of the wooden fighting plat-forms along the battlements, and the substitution of panelling and other woodwork, which he procured from derelict houses elsewhere. It is interesting to note also that the contractor for work was named Boyd. The castle is not really habitable despite its thorough restoration, because it is more of a medieval rehabilitation and a museum than a house, Lord Howard de Walden's magnificent collection of arms and armour being housed in the Hall, with another collection, of old musical instruments, in the upper hall, which has in one corner a small oratory or chapel. There is a laird's stair down from the hall to the vaulted basement, unusually also giving into the courtyard, and a window and corbels at a high level showing where the minstrel's gallery once was. The gatehouse is entirely modern. Not modern is the artificial grassmound, crowned with tall trees and standing a hundred yards or so away from the existing castle, on which a timber fortress was built, the whole making a fascinating study of medieval practice and planning.

The Boyds had another seat at Penkill, down the coast near Girvan, which provided a haven in the nineteenth century for Gabriel Dante Rossetti and his daughter, and a retreat for William Bell Scott, art teacher from Newcastle, who regularly travelled by train to the west of Scotland in the company of Christina Rossetti, who was probably in love with him—he certainly was with her, but neither declared themselves. Because of this connection, and the fact that Scott designed a new wing for the castle to contain the Boyd pictures and *objets d'art,* Penkill ranks more as a pre-

*Dean Castle: restored fighting platforms in the courtyard*

Raphaelite sanctuary than a lairdly Scottish seat or ancient tower house. The interior does indeed exude a Rossetti-ish aura, while William Bell Scott's deteriorating wall paintings still decorate the entrance hall and spiral staircase with scenes from the poems of James I of Scots, the so-called 'King's Quair'. Externally part of the Boyd tower house survives, restored in the seventeenth century by Thomas Boyd and his bride, Marion Muir of Rowallan, who brought him a decent fortune, and again in the Victorian era, when the big round tower with mock battlements preceded Scott's art gallery by a few years. I remember visiting Penkill with the Forty-five Association, when Miss Courtney Boyd, despite her attachment to the Jacobite legend, and vicarious descent from the Royal Stewarts, insisted on us singing every verse of the National Anthem, including "Confound their politics, frustrate their knavish tricks", which in the latest hymn books is omitted. This took place in the art gallery, surrounded by appropriate Victorian furniture and pictures, our hostess accompanying us at the piano.

On the same day we were taken to Killochan, which is in the same valley, almost within sight of Penkill, and was a seat of the Cathcart family. Its plan is much the same as that of Dunderave, that is, L-shaped with a single round tower at one corner, only the staircase to the first floor is a wide, scale-and-platt affair, which is rare at this period, 1586.

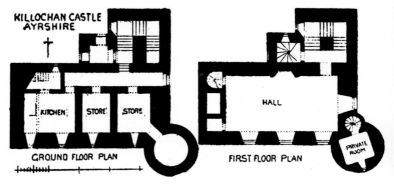

*Killochan Castle: plans*

Above it becomes a spiral, and there is another tiny turnpike stair in one corner of the round tower, which was the lord's private retreat off the hall. The roof line has been changed, but in general Killochan remains a Jacobean tower house of the South-west, with typical continuous run of plain corbelling on its unaltered side in place of the more elaborate, broken up forms found in Aberdeenshire and the North-east. The present occupiers have assembled a number of interesting folk objects, also some Napoleonic souvenirs, which include the Emperor's travelling kit, his Sèvres coffee service and pipe used on St Helena. These came through a family connection with the Kirkpatricks of Closeburn, of whom the Empress Eugénie was one. She had ancestors going back to the Pictish kings, and claimed thereby a more ancient royal strain than any in Europe. Be this as it may, it was a Kirkpatrick of Closeburn who assisted Bruce in the murder of the Red Comyn in the Kirk of the Greyfriars in Dumfries, and a Kirkpatrick who went to Spain in the eighteenth century as a wine merchant and was the grandfather of Eugenia de Montijo, who married Napoleon III in 1853. The old tower of the Kirkpatricks at Closeburn survives, modernized somewhat, not far from Thornhill, in upper Nithsdale, and is of sufficient antiquity for the Royal Commision on Ancient Monuments to mention its original iron yett.

At first glance Kelburn Castle, or the sixteenth-century part of it, for there are two distinct houses involved, gives something of the feel of Killochan, though it is theoretically Z-shaped, with two round towers at opposing corners and conically capped turrets at the others, creating a well-punctuated skyline. It does not sprout any gargoyles, however, nor any other martial or obviously baronial feature. Kelburn is the seat of the Earl of Glasgow and besides the old tower of the Boyles, of which family he is the head, the rest of the building consists of a most attractive, slightly Dutch-looking manor house dating from 1700. The castle is open by appointment, having benefited from a grant from public funds, when the visitor will also see a superb seventeenth- century sundial with an obelisk top and quite marvellous wrought-iron finial with thistle and armorial devices which are remarkable for their refinement of conception and execution. Kelburn Castle stands in a fine park, in part used as a golf course, opposite the Isle of Cumbrae, to which new site the cathedral of the Isles was transferred in the nineteenth century, when the sixth Earl of Glasgow, imbued by the ideals of the Oxford Movement, commissioned William Butterfield to design the beautiful buildings there, and where eventually he was buried. A little to the north, on the mainland, is Skelmorlie Castle, former seat of the Montgomeries of that Ilk and still in the ownership of the Earl of Eglinton, who is partly a Montgomerie, but mostly a Seton, and who lets the castle out to tenants. His more important residence used to be at Eglinton, in whose park the celebrated tournament of 1839 was held. This was a recreation of a medieval holiday, with jousting and fighting by hand, inspired by the works of Sir Walter Scott and the Romantic movement generally, and amongst those present was Prince Louis Napoleon, later Napoleon III, who composed some rather poor verses, whilst waiting for the rain to stop, in the hall of the castle.

Eglinton Castle, influenced in its design by Robert Adam's work at Culzean, was basically Tudor in conception, and after having been rendered uninhabitable by Commandos during the war was blown up in the 1950s. Skelmorlie, which suffered a fire shortly afterwards, has risen again from its ashes, the more severely damaged part only dating from the nineteenth century, thus making it possible to restore the older, fifteenth and sixteenth-century parts and make them more manageable. So Skelmorlie sits nicely again on its mound, set back a little from the road yet visible to the passer by and well cared for. The red sandstone castle is not open to the public but one can and should go to Largs, there to see the Montgomerie of Skelmorlie aisle, all that remains of the ancient kirk, and one of the marvels of Renaissance architecture in Scotland. It was built by Sir Robert Montgomerie in 1636, and consists of a charming little gable-ended house, with ogee-arched entrance and family armorials, with the magnificent memorial of its founder inside. The decor derives directly from Roman precedents and possibly reflects the Montgomerie family's Continental associations, they being soldiers of fortune for centuries. The aisle is in the care of the Department of the Environment, and on the outside may be seen a smaller but contemporary monument to the Boyles of Kelburn. It was, of course, at the Battle of Largs in 1263 that Alexander II, a species of Scottish Harold, only successful, defeated the Vikings and saved Scotland from invasion by sea, rewarding many of the local families, notably the Boyds, and Muirs, with lands in Ayrshire.

Across the water is Arran, whose rugged mountains rise dramatically from the sea, the highest, Goat Fell, reaching to nearly 3,000 feet. Below it, at Brodick, is one of Scotland's best-known castles, formerly a seat of the Dukes of Hamilton and now in the care of the National Trust. A quick glance at Brodick and one thinks of Ayton, in Berwickshire: both are built of red sandstone, both are 'baronial' and both largely the creations of the same nineteenth-century architect, James Gillespie Graham. At that time Brodick was the seat of the

*Skelmorlie Castle, Largs: the Renaissance wing*

*Brodick Castle, Isle of Arran: Princess Marie's drawing-room*

Marquis of Douglas and Clydesdale, elder son of the tenth
Duke of Hamilton, and his wife Princess Marie of Baden,
who was a de Beauharnais on her mother's side, and consequently related to Napoleon III. In fact she had been an
early 'flame' of Louis Napoleon, who, as Emperor, created
her husband Duc de Châtelherault, though in doing so he
overlooked the fact that there already existed a perfectly
legitimate holder of that title, also a Hamilton, the Duke of
Abercorn, who tested his right in the French courts and had
it upheld. The drawing-room at Brodick is very much a
Princess Marie of Baden room, indeed a Second Empire
room, with pouffes and fringed chairs familiar to the
Empress Eugénie, who often visited the castle before and
after the fall of the Empire in 1871. The Duke and Duchess
of Hamilton were actually given precedence at Court after
the Imperial family and visitors to Brodick will see a photograph of the Prince Imperial in the khaki uniform he wore
as a 'Soldier of the Queen', not to mention souvenirs of the
Eglinton Tournament in which his father had taken part.

Brodick has an older part, which Gillespie Graham
adapted so successfully that one scarcely notices the
difference between it and the new until one looks carefully,
the turreted, western end being the newest, the plain, un-
battlemented building to the east being the oldest and
probably dating from the fifteenth century. Linking the two
is an addition made by Cromwell to house his troops after
taking the castle in 1652, the second Duke of Hamilton
having died at Worcester and being buried near the high
altar in the cathedral there. Inside this portion is the Old
Library, with new battlements and crowsteps above, the
work of Gillespie Graham in 1844, in the style not of a
Jacobean tower house, which was the basis for most recreations of the nineteenth century, but in a more medieval
manner, with plain runs of corbelling to the west, and
rounded open bartisans instead of conically capped corner
turrets. The great glory of Brodick is partly its site, partly its
two gardens, a formal one dating from 1710 and another
wild one created by the late Duchess of Montrose, a
Hamilton by birth, and partly its contents, its rich fur-

nishings, some of which belonged to William Beckford of
Fonthill, whose daughter and heir, Susan Euphemia, married
the tenth Duke of Hamilton. His Grace not only inherited
the Beckford fortune but a taste for emulating his eccen-
tricities, which he displayed to the full in the recasting of
Hamilton Palace, in Lanarkshire, demolished earlier this
century on account of mine workings below, and in the
building of a splendid mausoleum for himself designed to
look like Hadrian's Tomb in Rome. This still stands, though
slowly sinking, and the Duke's antique sarcophagus from
Memphis has been removed with him to a public cemetery,
otherwise it might by now be floating in a mixture of coal
dust and sewage. The architect for this extraordinary
exhibition of *folie de grandeur* was that arch-baronialist, Sir
David Bryce, which only goes to show how versatile one had
to be in those days.

Of the fate of the Dukes of Hamilton one might say:
"How are the mighty fallen", at least in respect of their
property in Lanarkshire. The present Duke lives, as we have
seen, in modest state at Lennoxlove, near Haddington, and
when in Edinburgh, in his own apartments at the Palace of
Holyroodhouse where he is Hereditary Keeper. Châtelherault is commemorated in an odd layout of stables and
outbuildings and a formal French garden designed by
William Adam called the 'Dogg's Kennel'. It is extant but in
a decayed and precarious condition with no one quite sure
what the best thing to do would be. The state of the various
Hamilton titles too is a bit agley, with the Duke more of a
Douglas than a Hamilton, and Lord Home, head of the
Douglas family and living on the Douglas estates. To make
matters more complicated still, the Duke of Buccleuch is
both a Douglas and a Scott, and the only true Hamilton left
is the Duke of Abercorn, who is descended from the Earls of
Arran and the sixteenth-century Dukes of Châtelherault, and
lives in Northern Ireland. Because of these differences
between title, name and ownership of property, one going
with one but not necessarily with the other, Bothwell Castle,
on the Clyde and on the edge of the Hamilton estate,
belonged to Lord Home until presented to the Ancient

Monuments people to maintain. This tremendous ruin, made so by the Scots in order to prevent it falling into English hands, was built by William de Moravia, and is famous for its circular *donjon*, or 'keep', which was approached via its own ditch, or fosse, and private drawbridge. The ditch was cunningly used to drain off the lavatories and send the sewage through the outer walls down into the river. The lord lived on the upper floor of the *donjon*, which was cut in two in 1336, since when Bothwell had belonged to the Douglases who, in the Middle Ages, repaired part of the castle and lived in it. Today nothing is roofed and what we see are the remains of a great fortress, which was built before Edward I appeared on the scene with his 'belfry', a multi-storeyed wooden tower mounted on wheels from which English soldiers leapt onto the battlements to take the castle in less than a month. This huge machine was made in Glasgow and brought by road to Bothwell, followed by another timber structure on wheels, the field chapel of the 'Hammer of the Scots', who never undertook a siege without first placating Our Lady of Battles.

The Clyde valley in the vicinity of Hamilton and Bothwell is not beauteous, yet only a few miles further south, towards Lanark, the whole scene changes, when one arrives amongst greenhouses for early forcing and orchards which in spring clothe the steep hillsides with snowy blossom. In the midst of this mixture of whiteness and new greenery emerge two medieval specimens of note. Craignethan Castle, which is Scott's 'Tillietudlem', and Hallbar Tower, which is a brave little house, square and strong and seemingly strayed from the Borders where it would look absolutely in place. Hallbar is perfectly preserved, with its stone slab roof, simple but indented battlements and corbelling, a rectangular corner turret with stone pyramidical capping, waterspouts, crow-steps and the remains of projections to take either a timber fighting platform or a doocot. It is four storeys in height, with attic, the basement and third floor being vaulted, and the plain, sturdy walls are built in fine coursed masonry, pierced by the minimum of windows and entered, unusually for a tower of this sort, at ground level. The stair is straight

*Hallbar Tower: general view; plans*

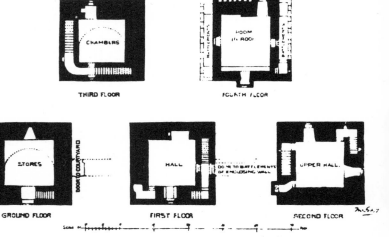

THIRD FLOOR

FOURTH FLOOR

GROUND FLOOR

FIRST FLOOR

SECOND FLOOR

up and down, without spirals, and climbs within the thickness of the walls right round the building, ending on the battlements. Besides the supposed 'doocot', there is also a little roofed lookout on one gable immediately over the door, supported on corbels to form a small *bretèche,* or place from which deterrent missiles or liquid could be dropped upon unwanted visitors. The tower dates from the end of the sixteenth century and in the seventeenth became the property of the Lockharts of Lee, whose legendary 'Lee Penny' is the Talisman of Sir Walter Scott's novel.

Craignethan lies on the opposite, or western banks of the Clyde, set back on a high terrace, from which it spies on the rest of the valley without being spied upon. It is a much larger affair altogether, and like Bothwell belonged to the Earl of Home until presented to the Department of the Environment. Its associations with Sir Walter Scott are well known, not only in respect of the name he gave it, but because he actually toyed with the idea of restoring part of it and living in the remaining habitable house near the entrance. Craignethan occupies a fairly extensive site, and is approached through two courtyards separated by a fosse, or dry moat. The first courtyard is vast and contains in one corner the seventeenth-century building which Scott thought of adapting instead of building Abbotsford, and this is still roofed. The rest of the castle is ruinous but well maintained, and since the Ministry took it over there has been a most interesting discovery in the form of a caponier, or tunnel, with low-level gun loops guarding the ditch, which could be raked with fire to the devastation of the unsuspecting besieger. This was the work of Sir James Hamilton of Fynnart, bastard son of the Earl of Arran and superintendent of royal palaces under James V. Fynnart had travelled on the Continent and was something of a gentleman-architect, being responsible in a major way for much of the Palace Block at Stirling and the Renaissance façade at Falkland. Cruel and bloodthirsty, he displayed many of the characteristics of the age, a mixture of refinement and ruthlessness not dissimilar to that shown by the king's own gifted bastard, Robert, Earl of Orkney. In common with most of his kind Sir James Hamilton came to grief in the end and was executed for treason, but not before he had rebuilt and strengthened his castle at Craignethan which he had been given by his father in 1529.

Once across the ditch and having avoided the caponier, the intruder would arrive at the inner and smaller courtyard and the entrance to the older, fifteenth-century tower, which is rectangular and divided down the long side, horizontally instead of vertically, with closets and apartments confined within the floor space and not in the thickness of the walls as is more usual. The arrangement at Hallbar is more typical, with basement for stores at the bottom, common hall above, the solar or lord's hall beyond and finally his bedroom. Here the tower is squatter and only has three storeys, the private quarters adjoining the hall, where there is also a large kitchen. Scott was shown Craignethan by the Douglas owner of the day, who offered it to him free for his lifetime, that was in 1799, but the future author of the Waverley novels was probably wise to refuse even though he said he had

*Craignethan Castle, Scott's 'Tillietudlem'*

fallen in love with it, for there was then as now "no roof (except on the seventeenth-century house), no windows and not much wall." Thus 'Tillietudlem' featured in *Old Mortality* instead and is today recalled in the name of the nearest railway station.

Still in Lanarkshire is Douglas, a mining village on the Douglas Water near where the one and only Duke of Douglas built, but never completed, an enormous copy of Inveraray in the late eighteenth century. It was to be four times the size of its model, but otherwise the same on plan and in general conception; the completed portion has since been demolished, possibly to the advantage of Lord Home, who lives in the vicinity in a less pretentious house. All that remains of Douglas Castle, not to be confused with Castle Douglas, which is a small town in the Stewartry of Kirkcudbright, is some armorial glass, which now illuminates the chancel of the episcopal kirk in the village, and a number of miniature cannon that stood decoratively on the battlements and which, the last time I saw them, were lying neglected behind St Bride's Church, the Douglas mausoleum. This is an Ancient Monument standing on the site of a Norman forerunner and houses medieval and later tombs which can be seen by visitors at all reasonable times. Included are altar tombs and memorials to most of the Douglas family, from the days of Bruce onwards, the place where they rest being the choir of a pre-Reformation parish church.

Just over the Dumfriesshire border from Douglas is Sanquhar, erstwhile seat of the first Duke of Queensberry, a Douglas, who returned to the castle, now ruined, after spending only one night at Drumlanrig, that great white elephant commissioned in the reign of Charles I and which was not finished until James VII and II went into exile in 1688. The Duke's grandfather, Sir William Douglas, afterwards first Earl of Queensberry, began Drumlanrig on the site of a much older castle in which he had entertained James VI and I, the original scheme being to recreate in the wilds of Dumfriesshire a copy of Heriot's Hospital, the finest Renaissance edifice in Edinburgh. This was built by William Aytoun, followed by William Wallace and the Mylnes, John and Robert. The Civil War prevented progress at Drumlanrig and it was not until 1679 that the new Duke of Queensberry decided to start up again, with the result we see today. The plan is undoubtedly a repeat of Heriot's Hospital in most particulars, being a courtyard building with square towers capped with pepperpot turrets at the corners, but there are curious survivals of the past, such as three iron yetts that continue to do service in the otherwise palatial *château*. The Duke seems to have taken advice from Sir William Bruce without actually engaging him, and using James Smith, Bruce's successor as Surveyor Royal in Scotland, as agent. He brought in craftsmen from Kinross and Holyrood to construct the castle for him.

The main entrance is at first-floor level, the door being reached via a handsome horseshoe staircase not unlike the one at the Queen's House, Greenwich, by Inigo Jones, hence Drumlanrig's posthumous connection with that architect, who died in 1651. Above the entrance is a cupola and clock surmounted by a ducal crown in imitation of the royal crown in the same position at Holyrood. The courtyard within is arcaded on one side, again in imitation of Holyrood, and also as it happens of Heriot's Hospital, only the delicate roseate hues of the masonry give Drumlanrig a less formal and more welcoming appearance. The colour of the stone is actually particular to this building, not being the same strong red as the town of Dumfries itself is built of, but more akin to the *gris-rouge* of Alsace, and coming from its own quarry. The façades are much plainer, even dull, and the castellated effect is more obvious, the balustrading that has replaced battlements ending in cable-coursed corbelling punctuated with fake gargoyles. On the south façade there is some excellent wrought-iron work, probably by the same smith who made the balcony on the garden side of Kinross, and outside stairs go up to the present dining-room, which is entered through a classical doorway in which the Doric order is used with a refinement not noticeable on the 'show front', This is probably the work of the reticent but knowledgeable James Smith.

Spiral staircases rise the full height of the castle within

Drumlanrig Castle: view from the west; looking down from a corner turret on to an entrance cupola, based on Bruce's at Holyrood, with the ducal instead of the royal crown

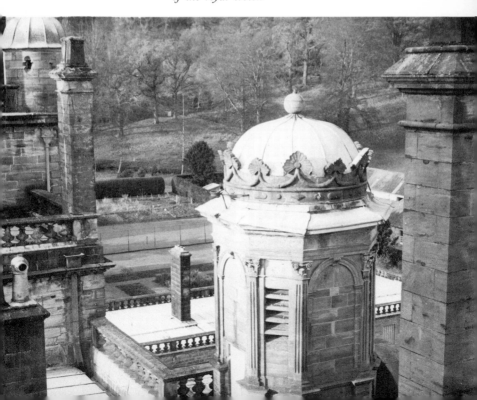

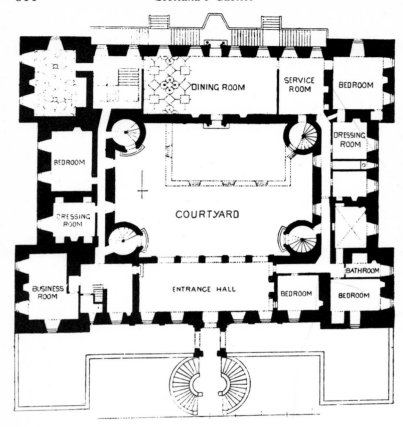

*Drumlanrig Castle: plan of first floor*

delightful ogee-capped towers, one in each corner of the
courtyard, but these are not the principal means of access to
the public rooms, which are reached via a ceremonial
scale-and-platt staircase dating from the late Stuart period
and matched by fine contemporary panelling. There are
chimneypieces and carving by Grinling Gibbon brought
from Whitehall Palace, now destroyed, by the Duchess of
Monmouth, who was also Duchess of Buccleuch in her own
right. MacGibbon and Ross also mention a picture gallery

on the top floor, but unfortunately this was broken up and partitioned into bedrooms to accommodate the almost perpetual houseparties that were a feature of the late Victorian and Edwardian eras. The dowager Duchess of Buccleuch has done a great deal to bring Drumlanrig back to its former state and is most anxious to get the gallery re-opened and used again for its proper purpose, especially since they have one of the richest private collections in Britain, including, beside the only important Leonardo not in a public gallery or museum, a superb assembly of miniatures which guests can look at in the dining-room whilst taking sherry.

The whole idea of Drumlanrig was and is idiosyncratic, though not quite the "poor mixture of the classic and the grotesque" the *Dictionary of National Biography* asserts. It was started out of time and finished out of time, and the excessive application of half-digested Renaissance motives to the huge baronial pile is in part at least explained by this fact, as well as by the newly ennobled Duke deciding to erect it miles from anywhere, amidst the hills and forests of what was once the Debatable Land. He was determined to emulate the greatest in the land and to employ the same craftsmen as the king, without, however, engaging the King's Architect to control their exuberances and relative ignorance of the laws of classical proportion. Happily, Mr Smith, not noted for his imaginative qualities but a confirmed disciple of Palladio, was called in at the end of the day to tidy things up, so that what we see now, if a bit wayward here and there, is not only a memorial to its begetter and the age in which he lived, but a theatrical *tour de force* of some note. One might add that early in the eighteenth century Sir John Clerk of Penicuik, second Baronet, who did the Grand Tour in his teens and in later life was the friend of Lord Burlington, designed a baroque cascade for Drumlanrig which was made, with water pouring down the hillside opposite the windows of the south front, and a grotto presided over by a giant Neptune. This was in the days of the second Duke, whose Duchess was related to Lord Burlington. She and her husband lie in a marble tomb designed by Van

Nost in the family burial chapel at Durisdeer, a few miles to
the north-east, while in the same churchyard will be found
the gravestone of William Lukup, mason at the castle, and
his children. The cascade went when the woods around were
cut down by the last of the Queensberry dukes, who offended
Scott so much and whose patrimony eventually came to the
Buccleuchs. The scar on the hillside can still be discerned.

About one and a half miles to the north-west of the little
town of Castle Douglas is Threave Castle, built on an island
in the River Dee, and once the redoubt of Archibald, called
'The Grim', illegitimate son of Sir James Douglas, the 'Good
Sir James', who was entrusted by Bruce with the task of
taking his heart to Jerusalem in part expiation for his murder
of the Red Comyn. Sir James was killed in Spain, fighting
the Moors, and the hero of Bannockburn's heart returned to
Scotland with William St Clair, Earl of Orkney, who had it
buried in Melrose Abbey. Archibald was called 'grim' by his
English opponents, but the local people had cause to con-
sider him grim since his castle was 'never without its tassle',
or corpse hanging from a gibbet on the battlements. The
Lord of Threave is one of those with an altar tomb in the
Church of St Bride, and although born on the wrong side of
the blanket succeeded to the Earldom of Douglas and
Lordship of Galloway. His successors, notwithstanding the
fact that one of them married Princess Margaret, sister of
James I of Scots, and became Duke of Touraine in France,
suffered from the intense emnity of the Stewarts. James II of
the Fiery Face besieged Threave Castle with one of his
favourite cannon, not perhaps the one that blew up in his
face and killed him at the siege of Roxburgh, but possibly
'Mons Meg', which exploded two hundred years later, whilst
firing a salute to the departing James, Duke of York, brother
of Charles II, when he went south to become James VII and
II. The weapon is traditionally said to have been cast by the
local blacksmith, McKim from Castle Douglas, and named
after his wife Meg, who hooped the cannon into shape
herself. In any event, it certainly reduced Threave Castle,
which henceforth became royal property.

In the reign of Charles I the keeper of Threave was the

Earl of Nithsdale, who withstood a three-month siege by the Covenanters before being dislodged, as he was from his own castle at Caerlaverock, and since then Threave has been a complete ruin and more interesting for its silhouette than for its crumbling parts which are more of an archaeological nature than anything else. The tower built by Archibald the Grim in the early fifteenth century still rises darkly to a height of seventy feet from its low marshy island, with the remains of some outer walls with round towers at the corners which were built after Flodden, when everyone feared that Scotland would be invaded by the English. It is an evocative setting, flat near the castle, with the rolling Galloway Hills

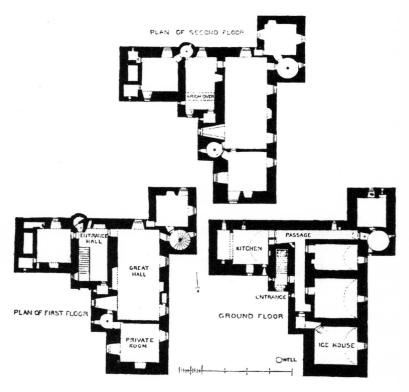

*Maclellan's House: plans*

in the background, and reached by ferry, the price being included in the Department of the Environment's entry fee. The Dee flows into the sea at Kirkcudbright, where the bulky skeleton of Maclellan's House, also known as 'the castle', stands in the middle of the burgh, not suggestive of a grisly past like Threave but of the transient glories of civic power. It was built by Sir Thomas Maclellan of Bombie, who was provost of Kirkcudbright in the second half of the sixteenth century and who, in 1569, acquired the lands and buildings formerly pertaining to the convent of the Greyfriars. He built his house from the stones, in the manner of a laird's tower on the L plan, but with an extra projection at one corner, and a multiplicity of staircases, rather in the manner of Elcho and Kellie. One can reach the upstairs rooms independently, though oddly enough there is no direct communication between the basement and the hall, a long passage having been inserted to link them via the main stair in the entrant angle. This seems to be peculiar to Maclellan's House; while off the first-floor landing is a small room with a tiny opening into the back of the big ingleneuk chimneypiece, obviously for spying on activities in the hall.

The building was crowstepped, with conically capped corner turrets and fairly massive chimneystalks, little of which has survived though there is some good corbelling and other decorative details, such as fake cannon, and a falsely blocked up window in the bottom panels of which appear the arms of the builder and his wife, Dame Grisel Maxwell, a Latin inscription and the date 1582. Not all the conventional buildings were demolished by the good provost, and what he left of the chapel has since become the local Pisky kirk, with Sir Thomas Maclellan's gaudy Jacobean memorial inside. It was erected in 1597 by his son and is in the form of an altar tomb, though not one, with the recumbent figures of the provost and his lady under an arched canopy, and suitable inscription. A descendant, William Maclellan of Bombie, lived at Barscobe Castle, higher up the Dee from Castle Douglas, not far from Balmaclellan. This is interesting because although graced with the name castle, and marked as such on the map, it completely lacks any defensive features whatsover, and although L-shaped has neither turret nor tower, nor even crowsteps. It is, in fact, a basic laird's house without extraneous features, decorative or defensive, merely the initials of the owner and the date, 1643, on the tympanum of a dormer, and the arms and initials of himself and his wife over the entrance. Barscobe remained in the possession of the Maclellans of Bombie until the end of the eighteenth century, but it is not ruinous and when last seen had been purchased with a view to adaptation by Sir Hugh Wontner, Lord Mayor of London in 1974, as a Scottish *maison secondaire*.

Dame Mary Maclellan was a Gordon of Lochinvar, whose castle of Kenmure stands at the head of Loch Ken, not far from Barscobe, and which has been bought by a descendant for restoration. Built as an L-shaped tower in the sixteenth century by Sir John Gordon, it sheltered Mary, Queen of Scots after her defeat at Langside, and was burnt down towards the end of the same century. It was rebuilt soon afterwards when Sir John's grandson, another Sir John, was created first Viscount Kenmure by Charles I. Loyalty to the Stuart cause was the Gordons of Lochinvar's undoing, and in 1715 William, sixth Viscount, was amongst those beheaded on Tower Hill for taking part in the Jacobite Rebellion. The castle subsequently suffered both change and decay, and when bought for rehabilitation had been gutted internally, leaving nothing but the walls. These Gordons were members of the same clan who migrated northwards earlier to occupy lands vacated by the enemies of Robert Bruce in the North-east of Scotland. The Galloway branch contented itself with more modest properties in their southern habitat. One, Alexander Gordon, was Bishop of Galloway at the Reformation, and took advantage of his new-won right to marry, while another, John Gordon, last Bishop of Galloway in the established kirk, was removed from his diocese in 1690, when he also lost his revenues as Dean of the Chapel Royal at Stirling, which went to the Crown.

The monogram of Sir John Gordon of Lochinvar appears over the entrance to Rusco Castle in the neighbouring valley of the Fleet, a little to the north of Gatehouse, beneath the

*Rusco, a Galloway tower of defence*

royal coat of arms and the date 1574. This typical Border
tower was almost certainly in existence before that time, and
has hardly been altered since the end of the fifteenth century.
It is not marked in gothic writing on the Ordnance Survey,
though it is fortified and looks quite martial. Its battlements
are crenellated and supported by a double row of billet
corbelling, each billet chequered to make an interesting and
varied pattern. There is a cap-house, and chimneystalks at
two gable ends, which, however, are not crowstepped. The
plan is rectangular, with the walls of the vaulted basement
thick enough to provide sleeping spaces for herdsmen within,
and there is the usual private stair up to the hall, as well as
a larger spiral to the second floor and the roof. A sort of
label, or drip hood, such as one sees over mullioned windows
in the Cotswolds, has been inserted above some of the
openings, a most unusual feature north of the Border, as is
the French basket-handle arch over the entrance, at ground
level. Rusco has also been bought by a would-be restorer,
and since it was inhabited until the first part of this century

and its walls are sound and complete should be most attractive when finished.

Practically at the extreme south-western extremity of Scotland, on the outskirts of Stranraer, is the tiny castle of Craigcaffie, which ultimate example of a laird's tower of defence displays practically all the attributes one would expect in any other part of the country, so homogenous is the Scottish vernacular. The small, oblong building is rather primitive in its planning, the walls are not thick enough to take either stairs or closets which thus bulge out into the room in a somewhat untidy manner. There is a well in the middle of the ground floor, which is barrel-vaulted, and above are two more floors and an attic, each with a separate chimneystalk, making three in all, two at the gables and one clumsily coming up at eaves level on the main elevation. Over the door are the arms of the Neilson family who built Craigcaffie in 1570, and higher is a small *bretèche,* as at Hallbar, to defend the entrance. The castle's most notable feature is its two single runs of crenellated sentry walk ending in small rounded, open bartisans. They are supported on plain, continuous corbelling, as at Killochan and elsewhere in the South-west.

There is a curious statement in the revised editions of MacGibbon and Ross, and repeated in other works, that Robert Bruce granted a charter to John, son of Neil, Earl of Carrick, of the lands of Craigcaffie, curious because Bruce himself was Earl of Carrick, inheriting the earldom from his mother, who was Countess of Carrick in her own right. One can only suppose that the Neilsons, who claimed descent from the Earls of Carrick, claimed it from an earlier period, as their neighbours the Kennedys also do. Carrick is the name given to a district roughly corresponding to southern Ayrshire, and the earldom is one of the many now held by the Prince of Wales, further confirmation of Bruce's entitlement to it. The Kennedys had one of their principal seats quite near Stranraer, on the isthmus between Luce Bay and Loch Ryan, at Lochinch, where Castle Kennedy survives as a folly ruin, the focal point of a vast park and garden laid out in the nineteenth century by Lord Stair in replacement

of the formal, French garden previously made by his ancestor, the second Earl of Stair, Field Marshal and Ambassador
Extraordinary in the reign of Queen Anne. The ruined castle
stands on the site of a fortalice built by John Kennedy, fifth
Earl of Cassillis, in 1607, and the property was given up later
to the first Earl of Stair, the notorious instigator of the
Massacre of Glencoe, the so-called 'Curse of Scotland'. His
son was no less of an anti-Jacobite, but his time in France at
the court of the ageing Louis XIV converted him into a
Francophile, so that when he returned home he planned the
park at Lochinch in imitation of what he had seen at Versailles, using the old castle of the Kennedys as the centrepiece
for his main vista, which it still is.

Cassillis House is further north, near Maybole, and is a
reconstruction of an older castle and the present seat of the
Marquis of Ailsa, the Kennedys being raised to the
Marquisite in the early nineteenth century, when the twelfth
Earl of Cassillis was a close friend of William IV. It is not
open to the public and not especially authentic in its present
form, but as one enters Maybole from the east the first thing
that strikes the eye is 'Maybole Castle', erstwhile town house
of the Kennedys and now the Cassillis Estate Office. The
conically capped corner turrets that rise up before one are
not, perhaps, very old, but a backward glance at the west
elevation will reveal something much more interesting and
rare in the form of an oriel window in the English style at a
high level in the gable of the old tower. This was almost
certainly put there by the same fifth Earl who built the now
ruined but extremely decorative Castle Kennedy, and is
replete with internal shutters in the 'study' it lights. Maybole
was the chief town of Carrick and besides the Kennedy
mansion there were others belonging to notables such as the
abbots of nearby Crossraguel Abbey, whose last abbot was
roasted alive by the fourth Earl of Cassillis in order to obtain
from him the abbatial lands, secularized at the Reformation.
This fearsome event took place at Dunure Castle, on the
coast, and the abbot, really commendator and not a lord
spiritual, was liberally basted with oil to prevent actual
burning of the skin. On failing to append his signature to the

document of transfer the treatment was repeated, this time successfully for the Kennedy earl. Despite being taken to law by the mutilated Abbot, he was allowed to keep his ill-gotten gains with the proviso that he gave his victim a lump sum of money and a pension for life.

The Kennedys, or at any rate the earlier ones, seem to have been a pretty vicious lot, getting as much as they gave, as well, feuding with each other and their neighbours, though Sir John Kennedy of Dunure managed to survive as the second of four husbands of Princess Mary, daughter of Robert III, while his brother James was the celebrated Bishop of St Andrews and founder of St Salvator's College. The first Earl of Cassillis died at Flodden, and his successor was found murdered on the beach near Culzean, after quarrelling with Sir Hugh Campbell. Happily, when the Culzean branch of the family became principals, cultural pursuits seem to have taken precedence in the Kennedy history, and in due course, Dunure was vacated for Culzean, a few miles down the Ayrshire coast. This was a much less exposed site, in fact the gardens there were already famous in the seventeenth century, when the local Pisky Minister, 'outed in 1690', described their 'excellent terraces and walls loaden with peaches, apricots, cherries, and other fruit'. The seventh Earl of Cassillis had decided to modernize the original castle at Culzean in the reign of Charles II, when the King's architect, Sir William Bruce, was consulted. It is not known if Bruce actually designed a new mansion for his noble client since there is nothing to show for it if he did, the entire castle having been rebuilt a century later for the tenth Earl by Robert Adam. On the other hand, it would not be entirely out of place if he had done something since he was already engaged in the vicinity for the Earl of Eglinton, reconstructing Cromwell's fort at Ayr as a seventeenth-century industrial estate with factories and housing; and the Reverend William Abercrummie does call Culzean 'The Mansion House' in his 1693 description.

The tenth Earl of Cassillis made the Grand Tour and was himself an amateur architect and connoisseur of art, and is even said to have worked with his own hands in the

*Culzean Castle, seen through Adam's mock ruin*

rebuilding of Culzean to Robert Adam's plans. They proceeded in stages, the first consisting of adapting the existing building to more modern use and adding to it on two sides wings in mock castellated style. The result is the façade one sees today facing the terraced gardens, in which all the fenestration is neo-classical while the battlements and many other purely decorative features are baronial. It is in some ways the least interesting side of the castle, perhaps because it is the best known, but also because it does not exhibit all Adam's skill at recreating the romantic Italian ideas he and the tenth Earl of Cassillis obviously admired; and it was when the next stage came, and the oval staircase and round drawing-room were added, that the full effect was achieved. This second part of Culzean was built right over the sea on a high cliff, with immense views across to Arran, Ailsa Craig, and the distant Western Isles, its only drawback being that externally it is best seen from a boat, though of course, in Georgian times, it was the view from the windows that counted, not the view towards them. Culzean seen from the sea, or from a slight distance to the north, closely resembles one of Robert Adam's Italian sketches, and is probably his most dramatic realization in the style he brought back from the Roman Campagna.

The finished castle scarcely shows a single Scottish vernacular feature, but in the days following the defeat of Prince Charlie at Culloden, and more particularly through the influence of Louise de Stolberg, the Prince's unsatisfactory wife, and her red-headed poet lover, Vittorio Alfieri, a Scottish cult developed, when Scottish scenery, in which wildness of form was matched with vegetational profusion, provided the masters of romantic revival with ready-made sites for experiment. What we have at Culzean, therefore, is a pseudo-Italian castle in a Caledonian setting in which the principal elements are still classical while the silhouette and certain details are mildly medieval. Internally, the castle is wholly in the accepted, more elegant, Adam style, the oval staircase being his *chef d'oeuvre* in that form, deriving from the Grand Staircase at Caprarola, by Vignola, and ultimately from Bramante's at the Vatican. Adam also designed much of the furniture and fittings, but although he sent to London for the finer pieces, it is worth noting that the Italian marble chimneypieces were made in Leith and the plasterwork executed by local craftsmen from Maybole, whence too the specially woven carpet for the oval drawing-room is said to come.

Both Robert Adam and the tenth Earl died in the same year, 1792, when Culzean was not quite finished, but nearly so, some of the park being laid out by Alexander Nasmyth, two of whose romantic paintings can be seen in the castle. He was a friend of the local boy made good, or at any rate famous, Robert Burns, and ostensibly an engineer by trade who took up painting and landscape gardening successfully. The castle is preceded by a wide forecourt enclosed to the north by a handsome castellated stable block, and approached through a gateway which Adam did not design but which bears on it a version of the Kennedy crest, where a dolphin is ridden by a cherub who is aiming a barbed dart at its head, no doubt the sculptor's way of expressing the

*Culzean Castle. Adam's oval staircase*

family motto 'Avis la Fin', which itself is just another way of saying 'Remember the End', as at Dunderave. Beyond is a small ravine, occupied by the somewhat exotic gardens described by the Reverend William Abercrummie of Maybole so enthusiastically, where, besides the fruit he mentioned, will be found palm trees and other rare plants, plus gothic gazebos and an orangery in which large, edible oranges grow. On the far side of this is a typical mock ruin, very cleverly conceived by Robert Adam and complete with shot-holes in the Scottish manner, a much more convincing disguise than most. More interesting still, and not yet fully appreciated by everyone, is the Home Farm, which Adam also designed, in the form of an arcaded square with arched and turreted entrances across the angles, making it octagonal, the effect being slightly ecclesiastical with large plain crosses surmounting four chapel-like buildings that protrude from the centre of each arm. The Home Farm is much more in the English Gothic-Revival manner than anything else at Culzean and shows how the architect, having begun in his own Italian castellated style gradually moved nearer towards a revived British medievalism, such as occurred at Strawberry Hill, and which, at Inveraray, preceded Culzean by more than thirty years. That is, before Adam had visited Italy and had met Charles Louis Clérisseau, the inventor of the neo-classical mode, undertaken with him 'digs' of Roman archaeological remains, or studied the castles of the Roman Campagna and made his celebrated sketches from which his Italian castellated buildings evolved.

Culzean was finished in 1879, with a sympathetic annexe designed by Messrs Wardrop and Reid, Edinburgh architects, using the same attractive pink stone. This addition follows the later, more romantic aspect of Adam's work, being on the cliff side, and still provides private accommodation, the rest of the castle and grounds having been presented to the National Trust for Scotland by the Marquis of Ailsa in 1945. In 1952 a top flat, over the round drawing room, was set aside for the use of President Eisenhower in recognition of his services as Supreme Commander of the Allied Forces during the Second World War, and in 1970 it

*Culzean Castle: the Home Farm*

was opened to the public on 8th May, the twenty-fifth
anniversary of VE Day. In 1973 Scotland's first Country
Park was established at Culzean, with the coastline to the
north, as far as Dunure Castle and doocot, protected under
a separate agreement.

# List of Castles Open to the Public

## In the care of the Department of the Environment (Secretary of State for Scotland)

*Aberdeenshire*
Glenbucket. Sixteenth century. Z plan, former Gordon seat.
Huntly. Ruins of Renaissance *château* of the Gordons of Huntly.
Kildrummie. Thirteenth-century castle of *enceinte*; dismantled 1715.
Tolquhon. Roofless Jacobean seat of Forbes family.

*Angus*
Affleck. Well-preserved fifteenth-century tower.
Claypotts. Perfect example of Z plan, late sixteenth century.
Edzell. Ruined seat of Lindsays of Glenesk in Renaissance garden.

*Argyll*
Carnasserie. Bishop of Isles Castle. Blown up 1687.
Castle Sween. Possibly earliest stone fortress in Scotland. Norman influence. Destroyed 1647.

*Ayrshire*
Loch Doon Castle. Medieval ruin re-erected on new site to facilitate hydro-electric scheme.
Rowallan. Sixteenth-century manor house near modern castle.

*Banffshire*
Balvenie. Largest and best-preserved ruin of fifteenth-sixteenth-century castle in North.

*Berwickshire*
Greenknowe Tower, Gordon. L plan, ruin.

*Berwick-upon-Tweed*
'Italian' fortifications, finest in Britain.

*Bute*
Rothesay. Substantial remains of thirteenth-century moated castle with circular *enceinte*.

*Clackmannanshire*
Castle Campbell, or 'The Gloom'. Second half fifteenth-century with fine loggia.

*Dumfriesshire*
Caerlaverock. Moated thirteenth-century castle with Renaissance courtyard. Dismantled by Covenanters.

*Dunbartonshire*
Dumbarton. Historic site crowned with mostly eighteenth-century buildings.

*East Lothian*
Dirleton. Norman castle besieged by and destroyed by Cromwellians.

Hailes. Rare example in Scotland of medieval fortified manor house, dismantled 1650.

Tantallon. Famous ruin of Douglas stronghold on sea coast.

*Fife*
Aberdour. Fourteenth-century castle. Sixteenth-century manor and 'doocot'.

Ravenscraig. Fifteenth-century castle built for defence by firearms. Recently opened to public.

St Andrews. Ruins of episcopal castle with Renaissance details and bottle dungeon.

Scotstarvit Tower. Seventeenth-century laird's tower, roofed.

*Inverness-shire*
Fort George. Eighteenth-century bastion against Jacobites, part work of William Adam and sons.

Castle Urquhart. Largely sixteenth-century ruin on historic site above Loch Ness.

*Kinross-shire*
Burleigh Castle. Ruined tower and well preserved gatehouse of former Balfour seat.

Loch Leven. Fifteenth-century tower and later *enceinte* on island on Loch Leven. Queen Mary's prison in 1567.

*Stewartry of Kirkcudbright*
Cardoness. Fifteenth-century seat of the McCullochs of Galloway.

Maclellan's Castle. Castellated town house of Provost of Kirkcudbright. Ruined since mid-eighteenth century.

Orchardton Tower. Unique round tower house near farm.

Threave. Ruined redoubt of Black Douglases on island site.

*Lanarkshire*
Bothwell. Principal English base of Edward I, part dismantled by Scots in 1336. Circular 'keep'.

Craignethan. Scott's 'Tillietudlem', former Hamilton fortress.

Crookston. Remains of Stewart of Darnley seat.

*Midlothian*
Craigmillar. Fourteenth-century with later additions, associated with Mary, Queen of Scots.

Crichton. Fourteenth and fifteenth century, with 'Italian' court-yard.

Edinburgh. Royal Castle (Crown Property) originally built of timber. Norman Chapel. Birthplace of first King of Great Britain.

*Moray*

Duffus. Ruined motte-and-bailey castle built by De Moravia or Murray family.

*Orkney*

Kirkwall. Earl's Palace. Unfinished Renaissance residence of Stewart Earls of Orkney.

Noltland. Isle of Westray. Incomplete Z plan castle dating from second half of sixteenth century.

*Perthshire*

Elcho. Roofed but empty former seat of the Earls of Wemyss.

Ruthven, or Huntingtower. Unoccupied but intact, painted ceilings, associated with Gowrie Conspiracy.

*Renfrewshire*

Newark. Well-preserved sixteenth- and seventeenth-century castle of the Maxwells at Port Glasgow.

*Roxburghshire*

Hermitage. Norman castle several times altered, associated with Mary, Queen of Scots and Bothwell.

Smailholm Tower. Sixteenth-century 'pele' in romantic border setting.

*Shetland*

Scalloway. Ruined redoubt in Shetland of Patrick Stewart, Earl of Orkney.

*Stirlingshire*

Stirling. Royal castle with fine Renaissance work and chapel built by James VI.

*West Lothian*

Blackness. Fifteenth-century Forth-side fortress modernized by military and since restored. Shaped like ship.

**Note:** The above list was complete in the summer of 1975 in respect of properties actually open to the public. Others are still under repair or can only be seen from the exterior, for further information please apply to: Ministry of Public Buildings and Works (Stationery Section), Argyle House, 3 Lady Lawson Street, Edinburgh EH3 9SP.

**Castles restored or renovated with public funds and open by appointment**

*Aberdeenshire*

Balfluig. Sixteenth-century L-shaped tower. Apply, Mark Tennant Esq, 8 New Square, London WC2.

Barra. Fortified manor on outskirts of Old Meldrum: Apply, Major F. C. Q. Irvine.

Craig of Auchindoir. L-shaped castle on estate near Lumsden. Apply, Mrs C. G. M. Barlas of Craig.

Craigston. Jacobean seat of Urquharts of Craigston, near Turriff. Bruce Urquhart Esq.

*Angus*

Airlie. Rebuilt after Jacobite rebellion. Earl of Airlie.

*Argyll*

Barcaldine. Seventeenth-century castle near Loch Creran. Apply, Thomson & Baxter W.S., Thistle Court, Edinburgh 2.

Duntrune. Rebuilt castle on ancient site on Loch Crinan. Col. G. I. Malcolm of Poltalloch.

*Ayrshire*

Cessnock. Sixteenth-century tower enlarged in seventeenth. Interesting ceilings. The Baron de Fresnes.

Kelburn. L-shaped base with Renaissance addition. Seat of Rear-Admiral The Earl of Glasgow.

*East Lothian*

Lennoxlove. Haddington seat of the Duke of Hamilton, to whom apply in writing.

*Fife*

Balgonie. Recently restored tower of medieval castle. Apply, D. H. Maxwell Esq, 116 Hanover Street, Edinburgh 2.

*Kincardineshire*

Fiddes. Sixteenth-century fortalice near Stonehaven. J. H. Johnson, Esq.

*Kinross-shire*

Tulliebole. Laird's tower with minstrel's gallery. The Lord Moncreiff.

*Midlothian*

Cakemuir. Isolated 'pele' tower with unusual sentry's walk. M. M. Scott, Esq.

*Moray*

Brodie. Nucleus of ancient tower enlarged by Wm. Burn. Fine Jacobean plasterwork. Apply, Brodie of Brodie.

*Nairnshire*
Kilravock. Fifteenth-century tower with seventeenth-century manor attached. Miss Rose of Kilravock.

*Perthshire*
Ardblair. Castellated house with Jacobite relics. Laurence P. K. Blair Oliphant, Esq.

*Stirlingshire*
Castle Cary. Tower house enlarged in seventeenth century. Hugo B. Millar, Esq.

## In the care of the National Trust for Scotland

*Aberdeenshire*
Craigievar. Seventeenth-century Scots castle *par excellence*. Completed 1626, never radically altered.

*Ayrshire*
Culzean. Robert Adam's masterpiece in 'Italian Castellated'.

*Bute*
Brodick. Fourteenth-century castle baronialized in 1844. Former seat of Dukes of Hamilton.

*Fife*
Kellie. Sixteenth- and seventeenth-century castle in pure vernacular style.

*Kincardineshire*
Crathes. Shares with Craigievar pride of place amongst Aberdeenshire Jacobean castles. Famous garden.

## Privately owned castles open to the public

*Aberdeenshire*
Braemar. Ancient seat of the Earls of Mar 'regimentalised' in eighteenth century. Captain Farquharson of Invercauld.

Delgatie. Sixteenth-century seat of the Hays. Painted ceilings. Captain Hay of Hayfield.

Drum. Early stone tower attached to seventeenth-century mansion. Mrs Forbes Irvine.

Druminnor. Restored fifteenth-century tower, formerly Forbes seat. Miss Joan Wright.

Towie Barclay. Recently restored Scottish seat of the Barclays. Marc Ellington, Esq.

*Angus*

Glamis. Historic home of the Earls of Strathmore. Rebuilt seventeenth century. Earl of Strathmore and Kinghorne.

Guthrie. Begun 1468 for Sir David Guthrie and added to. Guthrie of Guthrie.

Kellie. Seventeenth century rebuilding near Arbroath. J. Kerr Boyle, Esq.

*Argyll*

Duart. Restored seat of Macleans of Duart. Lord Maclean K.G., C.V.O., K.B.E.

Inveraray. Home of the Dukes of Argyll. 'Gothycke' castle designed by Roger Morris in 1745. His Grace the Duke of Argyll.

*Dumfriesshire*

Drumlanrig. Last traditional Scottish castle to be built, completed 1690. His Grace the Duke of Buccleuch.

*East Lothian*

Luffness. Small sixteenth-century castle on ancient site. Col. & Mrs Hope of Luffness.

*Inverness-shire*

Dunvegan. Seat of Chief of Clan MacLeod. Castellated mansion on ancient foundations. MacLeod of MacLeod.

Kisimul. Island fortress of the MacNeils of Barra recently restored. MacNeil of Barra.

*Kincardineshire*

Dunnottar. Ruined, sea-girt fortalice of the Earls Marischal of Scotland. Dunnotter Trust.

Muchalls. Jacobean dower house of Crathes with fine plasterwork. Mr & Mrs Maurice Simpson.

*Midlothian*

Lauriston, on outskirts of Edinburgh. Former home of John Law, founder of Banque Nationale de France in the eighteenth century. Edinburgh Corporation.

*Peeblesshire*

Neidpath. Border castle on dramatic site, suffered siege under Cromwell. Earl of Wemyss & March Discretionary Trustees.

Traquair. Celebrated royal hunting lodge turned manor house. P. Maxwell Stuart, Esq.

*Perthshire*

Blair. Twice-reconstructed seat of the Dukes of Atholl with finely furnished rooms. His Grace the Duke of Atholl.

Doune. Fourteenth century castle of *enceinte* partially restored in nineteenth century. Earl of Moray.

Drummond. Gardens and museum in 'keep' only. Earl of Ancaster.

*Ross and Cromarty*

Eilean Donan. Rebuilt Highland fortress of the Mackenzies. Last besieged 1719. J. D. H. MacRae, Esq.

*Sutherland*

Dunrobin. Ancestral seat of Earls and Dukes of Sutherland, several times enlarged. Countess of Sutherland.

**Note:** The above details were correct in 1975 and were taken from *Scottish Castles & Historic Houses* published by the Scottish Tourist Board for that year, and *Historic Houses, Castles & Gardens in Great Britain and Ireland 1975*. A number of other interesting castles open on specific days under 'Scotland's Gardens Scheme', including; Branxholm, Border seat of the Scotts of Buccleuch; Cawdor, associated with *Macbeth*; Cortachy, restored dower house of the Earls of Airlie; Craignish, Argyll castle with sixteenth-century 'keep'; Earlshall, Fife manor house on Z plan; Floors, seat of Duke of Roxburghe, partly designed by Vanbrugh; Kilcoy, restored Mackenzie castle on the Black Isle; Killochan, Ayrshire castle with Napoleonic connections; Megginch, restored sixteenth-century Perthshire castle; Castle of Mey, H.M. The Queen Mother's Caithness home (gardens only); and Oxenfoord, an Adam castellated mansion now a girls' school. For details apply; The General Organizer, Scotland's Gardens Scheme, 26 Castle Terrace, Edinburgh WHI 2El.

# Index

# Index

[Page numbers in italics indicate illustrations]